The Learning Guide to Excel for Windows 95

The Learning Guide
to Excel for
Windows® 95

Gini Courter

SYBEX®

San Francisco ▪ Paris ▪ Düsseldorf ▪ Soest

Series Concept: Julie Simmons
Associate Publisher: Amy Romanoff
Acquisitions Manager: Kristine Plachy
Developmental Editor: Sherry Schmitt
Editor: James A. Compton
Technical Editor: Betsy Walker
Educational Consultant: Shari V. Cohen
Production Coordinator: Kim Askew-Qasem
Technical Illustrator: Dan Schiff
Book Designer: Seventeenth Street Studios
Page Layout and Composition: Seventeenth Street Studios
Indexer: Ted Laux
Proofreader: Mu'frida Bell
Cover Designer: Ziegler Design
Cover Photographer: Travel Pix

The cover photograph appears courtesy of FPG International.
Screen reproductions produced with Collage Complete.
Collage Complete is a trademark of Inner Media Inc.
SYBEX is a registered trademark of SYBEX Inc.

TRADEMARKS: SYBEX has attempted throughout this book to distinguish proprietary trademarks from descriptive terms by following the capitalization style used by the manufacturer.

Every effort has been made to supply complete and accurate information. However, SYBEX assumes no responsibility for its use, nor for any infringement of the intellectual property rights of third parties which would result from such use.

Library of Congress Card Number: 96-67064

ISBN: 0-7821-1825-9

Manufactured in the United States of America

10 9 8 7 6 5 4 3 2 1

I spent most of my formative years afraid of and confused by mathematics. This book is dedicated to three people whose patience and teaching skills made numbers spring to life for me: Carol Egloff, my 6th grade math teacher; Adolph Wildfang, an outstanding middle school science teacher; and Tom Lougheed, who continues to teach managerial accounting in an outrageously inspired fashion at Mott Community College.

Acknowledgments

I want to give special thanks to Jim Compton, the editor for this book and *The Learning Guide to Word*, who kept things moving. Jim's flexibility has helped me keep the book on track and somewhat on time. Shari Cohen, educational consultant, provided invaluable information about the book outline and structure.

Betsy Walker, technical editor, went through each step and instruction given in the text. Her assistance was priceless, and very clearly contributed to the overall quality of this book.

In the middle of writing the *Learning Guide to Excel*, I had a chance to meet with Jim Compton; Bruce Spatz, Sybex Editorial Director; Kristine Plachy, Acquisitions Manager; and Julie Shell, Sales Administrator. The discussion at that meeting changed the vision and shape for this book in many positive ways. Thanks again to everyone at Sybex for your encouragement and support.

Contents at a Glance

Table of Contents

Guide to Quick Steps

Introduction

Microsoft Excel for Windows 95 is an extraordinary spreadsheet program. Excel can help you create and manage budgets and lists, analyze data and business problems, and create charts to illustrate numeric information. The possibilities are limited only by your imagination and your commitment to learning the many features available in Excel. By working through the twenty sessions in this book and completing the various exercises and projects, you will become an accomplished Excel user with skills and knowledge that you can also apply to other Windows applications.

ABOUT THIS BOOK

This book is divided into five major sections. In Part I, "Creating Basic Worksheets," you will learn how to create, edit, and format an Excel worksheet. Part II, "Advanced Worksheet Techniques," focuses on print settings, using Excel's special fill tools to quickly create worksheets, and using functions with numeric data. In Part III, "Creating Charts and Managing Data," you'll learn how to represent numbers graphically and manage and analyze lists of information. Part IV, "Customization, Functions, and Macros" shows you how to change the Excel interface to reflect the way you use Excel, provides experience with a group of advanced functions, and then introduces macro programming. In Part V, "Business Applications in Excel," you'll use some of Excel's more powerful business analysis tools to solve business problems.

At the beginning of each session, you will find a vocabulary list that identifies possibly unfamiliar words introduced in the session. Accompanying the list are the objectives for what you will learn in the session.

Each session includes descriptions of Word's major features with explanations of how to use these features. Throughout the session, you will find several step-by-step exercises that will guide you through the topics being discussed. The exercises look like this:

EXERCISE 3.4	TO TOTAL COLUMNS WITH THE POINT METHOD
	1. In Payroll, enter the label Total in A13.
	2. **Move the cell pointer to the cell where you want the answer to appear** (B13).
	CONTINUES ON NEXT PAGE

3. **Click the AutoSum button.**

4. **Select the range of numbers to be added** (the employee hours: cells B5: B11).

5. **Press Enter.**

The steps highlighted in **boldface** type are the general steps to follow anytime you want to complete the task indicated. (See the Guide to Quick Steps, following the Table of Contents, when you need to look up one of these procedures.) Instructions that are not in boldface are specific to the practice exercise. Read the entire step first and then follow the instructions.

At the end of each session, you will find a summary followed by a series of focus questions about concepts covered in the session. You will also find reinforcement exercises you can complete for more hands-on practice to help you integrate the new material you learned in the session with what you have already mastered. Many of the reinforcement exercises build from session to session. If you're not going to do them all, it's better to complete exercises with the same number. For example, always complete Reinforcement Exercises 1 and 4 rather than doing 1 and 2 in some sessions and 2 and 3 in others.

Following Sessions 10 and 20 are projects that provide you with the opportunity to apply your skills. These projects cover major topics from multiple sessions. (Many of the projects and the exercises in this book are modeled after Excel worksheets created in various businesses that I have consulted with.) Projects A and C let you use Excel to work with information from your home or business—real information that you are familiar with. Use your imagination and creativity to make the projects useful to you.

At the back of the book is a Glossary of terms included in the text; all the terms that appear in the Vocabulary lists are defined here.

STYLE CONVENTIONS

When you are making choices from a menu, the ➤ symbol lets you know that your first selection leads to a second menu. For example, an instruction to choose File ➤ Save means that Save will appear only after you have chosen File.

I hope you enjoy using *The Learning Guide to Excel for Windows 95* and that you can easily transfer the skills learned from the book to other work in

Excel. You can contact me at the address below if you have any comments or suggestions about the book:

Gini Courter
c/o Sybex, Inc.
2021 Challenger Drive
Alameda, CA 94501
E-Mail:72557.1546@compuserve.com

PART I

Creating Basic Worksheets

Vocabulary

- application window
- applications (apps)
- close
- data
- desktop
- hardware
- icons
- launch
- maximize
- microcomputer (PC)
- Microsoft Excel for Windows 95 (Excel)
- minimize
- mouse
- operating system
- Shut Down
- size
- sizing tool
- software (programs)
- spreadsheet
- Start menu
- Taskbar
- Windows 95

Getting to Know Windows 95 and Microsoft Excel

ICROSOFT EXCEL IS A power-ful spreadsheet program designed to run under Windows 95. Using Excel, you can analyze and manipulate numbers. This session introduces terminology that will be helpful while you are learning Excel. At the end of this session you will be able to:

- Define the difference between hardware and software
- Explain the relationship between Windows and Excel
- Launch Excel for Windows 95
- Minimize and maximize the Excel window
- Exit Excel
- Shut down Windows and turn off the computer

3

SECTION 1.1: COMPUTERS, WINDOWS 95, AND MICROSOFT EXCEL

Until the 1970s, computers were so large and expensive that the idea of using them in homes and small businesses was a dream reserved for science fiction. Only the largest businesses, research centers, and governmental units used computers. In the past two decades, advances in technology have made computers more powerful, more compact and more affordable. The **microcomputer (PC)** sitting on your desk may be more powerful than any computer available in the 1950s—at about a hundredth of the size and cost. The low cost of computers has made computing available for household and small business use.

A computer is a system for converting **data** (words and numbers) into useful information. Computer systems include both hardware and software. **Hardware** refers to the physical parts of the computer: the components you can see and feel. There are some basic pieces of hardware included in computer systems: the screen (or monitor), keyboard, memory (RAM), disk drive, mouse, and the computer itself, the microprocessor. Your PC may also include other hardware: a printer, a fax/modem, a CD-ROM drive, or a sound card.

Software refers to computer programs. There are two basic kinds of software: system software and applications. System software includes **operating systems**, groups of programs that manage the computer's hardware. An operating system allows you to enter information with a keyboard or mouse; print to a printer; or copy a file to or from a disk. **Windows 95** is a graphically oriented operating system designed to help you harness the power of today's faster, more powerful microcomputers.

Once you have an operating system like Windows 95 running on your computer, you can use application programs. **Applications** (also called "apps") like Microsoft Excel are used to complete specific tasks. While application software is relatively new in a historical sense, the tasks you perform with it have been around for a long time. Database programs such as Access are used to maintain lists that were maintained manually on index cards or in file folders before the use of computers. Computerized drafting programs like AutoCAD have replaced the pencils and templates used to create blueprints and schematics. Word processors such as Word are used to construct documents that were formerly created with typewriters.

Spreadsheet programs including Microsoft Excel were originally created to analyze and manipulate financial information like budgets and payrolls. The first spreadsheets were simple applications used largely in place of a calculator for basic mathematical operations. Today's spreadsheets have many capabilities and are used in a variety of work situations as well as in home businesses. Using Excel, you can analyze virtually any numerical information and present that information in many formats, including charts as shown in Figure 1.1.

Figure 1.1
An Excel worksheet
and chart

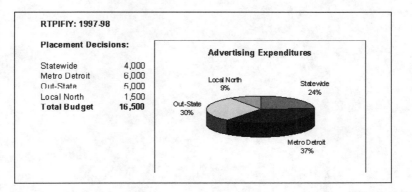

Excel is one of the most powerful programs designed for use on PCs. Yet it is also highly **intuitive**—it works in ways that are easy to comprehend and master. With very little work you will be able to create slick, accurate presentations of numerical information—even if you're not completely comfortable working with numbers.

Before you can begin working with Excel you must turn on your computer system. The Windows 95 operating system starts automatically when you start your computer.

EXERCISE 1.1   **TO START WINDOWS 95**

- **Turn on your computer. Windows 95 will load automatically.**

SECTION 1.2: STARTING MICROSOFT EXCEL FOR WINDOWS 95

The screen shown in Figure 1.2 is the Windows 95 **desktop**, the control center for Windows 95. There are a number of **icons** (small pictures representing hardware or software) on the desktop. At the bottom of the screen is an area called the **Taskbar**. The current time is displayed at the right end of the Taskbar. On the left end is the Start button.

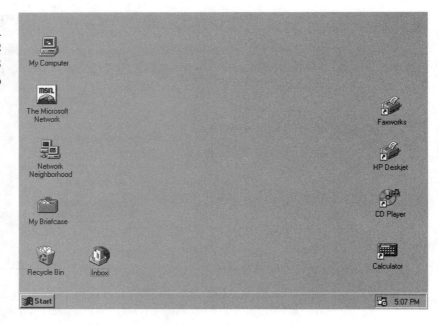

Figure 1.2
The Windows 95
desktop

To work with Windows 95 and the applications developed for it, you need to use both a keyboard and a mouse. A **mouse** is an input device that allows you to make selections or start actions by moving the pointer to an item on your screen and pressing one of the mouse buttons (usually the left or primary button). This is referred to as "pointing and clicking." Pointing at the middle of the Start button and clicking once on the left mouse button opens the **Start menu**, shown in Figure 1.3.

Figure 1.3
Opening the
Start menu

The Start menu includes Windows 95 programs like Help and Shut Down. It also provides access to various menus, including the Programs menu.

(A menu selection that leads to another menu has an arrow pointing right.) Moving the mouse pointer to the right into the Programs menu and then down to Microsoft Office opens the Microsoft Office folder, as shown in Figure 1.4. Here you'll find Microsoft Excel. If there is no Microsoft Office folder, Excel will be included on the Programs menu. Clicking on the Microsoft Excel program icon launches Excel for Windows 95.

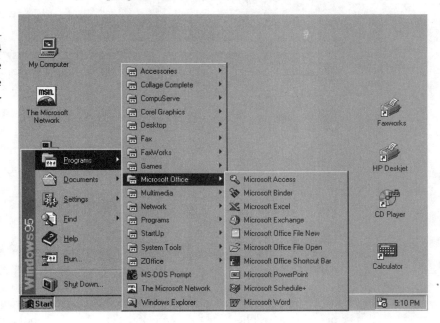

Figure 1.4
Opening the
Microsoft Office
folder

| EXERCISE 1.2 | TO LAUNCH MICROSOFT EXCEL FOR WINDOWS 95 |

1. **Move your mouse pointer to the Start button and click once to open the Start menu.**

2. **Move your pointer to Programs to open the Programs menu.** (You don't need to click.)

3. **Slide your pointer into the list of programs; then up or down the list to the Microsoft Office folder.**

4. **Slide your pointer into the list of Microsoft Office programs, and then down the list to Microsoft Excel.**

5. **Click once on Microsoft Excel to launch the application.**

Launching a program copies it from disk into the memory of your computer so you can use it. Windows 95 adds a button for the program to the Taskbar and opens an **application window** to contain the program, as shown in Figure 1.5.

Figure 1.5
The Excel for
Windows 95
application
window

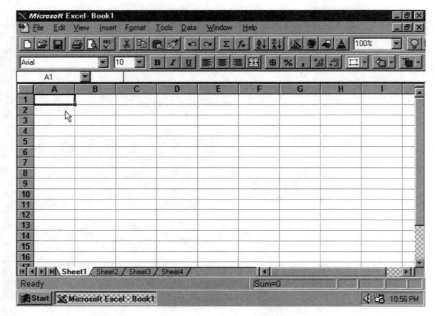

At the top of the Excel application window is a title bar that includes the name of the application, the name of the current workbook, and three buttons:

You'll learn about workbooks in Session 2. The current workbook is called Book 1. This is a temporary name assigned by Excel; you'll change it the first time you save the workbook.

SECTION 1.3: WORKING WITH WINDOWS

The three buttons at the right end of the title bar are used to minimize, size, and close the application window.

Note: There is a set of identical buttons directly below the Excel title bar buttons. These buttons control the workbook window, not the application window. Ignore them for now.

On the left is the Minimize button. **Minimizing** an application reduces it to a Taskbar icon, putting the application "on hold." A minimized application is still running, but is inactive. Clicking on Excel's Taskbar icon will restore the application window to its former size, making it available to use again.

EXERCISE 1.3	TO MINIMIZE THE EXCEL APPLICATION WINDOW

1. **Click on the Minimize button on the title bar.** This reduces Excel to a button on the Taskbar.

2. **Click on the Excel icon on the Taskbar to restore the Excel application window to its former size.**

 Unless a user has changed the settings, the Excel application window fills the screen when Excel is launched. The middle button, known as the Restore button, lets you keep Excel active without filling the entire screen. Clicking this button changes the Excel application window to an intermediate size, as shown in Figure 1.6.

Figure 1.6
The Excel application window after clicking Restore

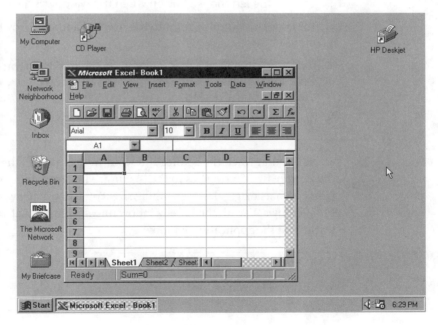

EXERCISE 1.4	**SIZING THE EXCEL APPLICATION WINDOW**
	■ Click the Restore button on the right side of the title bar.

 After clicking a window's Restore button, you can make it larger or smaller (size it), and move it to a new location within the display. To change the size of the application window, you use the **sizing tool** in the lower-right corner of the window. Point to the sizing tool; then hold down the left mouse button while dragging the mouse pointer (and the corner of the window) to a new location. The window can be moved as easily as it can be resized. Dragging the title bar to a new location moves the entire window.

EXERCISE 1.5	**SIZING AND MOVING THE EXCEL APPLICATION WINDOW**
	1. Point to the sizing tool in the lower-right corner of the Excel window.
	2. Hold down the left mouse button and drag the pointer to the left to make the window smaller or to the right to make it larger.
	3. Release the left mouse button when the window is a size you like it.
	4. To move the window, point to the title bar and hold down the left mouse button.
	5. Drag the window to a new location on the desktop. (You'll probably still want to be able to see the entire window, so don't move it too close to the edges of the desktop.)
	6. Release the left mouse button.

 Notice that when the application window does not fill the entire desktop, the Restore button changes to the **Maximize button**, which returns the Excel window to its original, screen-filling size. You will usually want to use Excel for Windows 95 with the Excel window maximized, so that you can see all the features in the application window.

EXERCISE 1.6	**MAXIMIZING THE EXCEL WINDOW**
	■ Click the Maximize button.

SECTION 1.4: ENDING THE EXCEL SESSION

 The Close button appears in all application window title bars. Clicking the Close button ends your Excel session, returning you to the desktop. It is important to close Excel properly when you are finished using the program. If you create or change a document during your work session, Excel will make certain you have saved the latest version of it before closing the application window. If you have not, you will be prompted to save it. Also, there are a number of temporary files created by Excel. Closing the application deletes those files so they don't take up space on your disk or create problems in the future when you are saving files.

EXERCISE 1.7   **TO CLOSE MICROSOFT EXCEL**

- **Click the Close button in the Microsoft Excel title bar.** (If you pressed any keys or entered text while the document window was open, you will be asked if you want to save changes to Book 1. Click No.)

It is equally important that you shut down Windows before turning off your computer. The **Shut Down** option on the Start menu prepares your computer to be turned off, deleting temporary files that were created by Windows 95 and severing any network connections created when you started the computer.

EXERCISE 1.8   **TO SHUT DOWN WINDOWS 95 AND TURN OFF YOUR COMPUTER**

1. **Click on the Start button.**

2. **Click on Shut Down.**

3. **The option button in front of** Shut down the computer? **should be selected. If it is not, click on it once.**

4. **Click on Yes.**

5. **When Windows prompts you to do so, you can safely turn off your computer.**

What You Have Learned

You know how Microsoft Windows 95 and Excel for Windows 95 relate to each other. You are able to launch Excel from the Start menu. You know how to minimize, size, and maximize application windows. Finally, you know how to exit Excel and safely shut down your computer.

Focus Questions

1. Name three pieces of hardware that are part of your computer system.

2. What are the two basic types of software?

3. What is an application?

4. What kinds of information is manipulated using Microsoft Excel?

5. What is the purpose of the Start menu?

6. List the steps for launching Excel.

7. What happens to an application when you minimize it?

8. How do you move a window to a new location?

9. Why is it important to close an application before shutting off your computer?

Reinforcement Exercises

Exercise 1 Using the Start menu, locate an application other than Microsoft Excel. How can you tell that it is an application? List the steps it took you to get to the application's icon.

Exercise 2 Launch Microsoft Excel from the Start menu. Practice minimizing, sizing, and maximizing the application window. Resize the window and move it so that just the title bar is visible at the bottom of the desktop. Maximize the application before you close it.

Entering Data in an Excel Workbook

N THIS SESSION you will begin entering data in a worksheet. You will learn several methods for editing existing data before saving your workbook. *Beginning with this session, you will need a formatted floppy disk so you can save your Excel workbooks.* At the end of this session you will be able to:

- Identify features of the Excel application window
- Move the cell pointer within a worksheet
- Enter labels and numbers
- Edit worksheet data
- Move between worksheets in an Excel workbook
- Use toolbars and the menu bar
- Name worksheets
- Save and close workbooks
- Open a new workbook

13

SECTION 2.1: PARTS OF THE EXCEL APPLICATION WINDOW

Let's start working with Excel by examining the Excel application window. Excel contains features common to Windows programs, as well as features unique to Excel. If you have used other Windows applications you may be somewhat familiar with the title bar, menu bar, toolbars, and document window used by Excel. If this is your first Windows application, learning about the standard window features and tools used in Excel will give you a head start on learning other Windows programs.

In Session 1 you used the button cluster on the title bar to size the Excel application window. The **menu bar**, directly below the title bar, contains a series of menus used while working in Excel. Clicking any item on the menu bar presents a drop-down menu of choices. The File menu (see Figure 2.1) includes options like Save and Exit. Selecting a menu choice that has an arrow (like Print Area) will open yet another menu. Menu selections like New and Open that are followed by ellipses (. . .) will open a dialog box to ask you for more information.

Figure 2.1

The File menu

Some menu choices are available only under certain conditions. For example, you cannot paste text or numbers until you have cut or copied them. Menu selections that are unavailable are "dimmed out."

A **toolbar** is a group of buttons you can click to run frequently used commands. Excel includes a number of toolbars, and you can create more of your own. The Standard and Formatting toolbars are opened automatically when you start Excel. Most of the buttons on the Standard toolbar offer selections from the File and Edit menus. The Formatting toolbar is equivalent to the Format menu. While the buttons aren't labeled, you can easily find out the name of a button. If you point directly to one of the buttons with the mouse, a **tool tip** with the name of the button will appear. The **name box** and **formula bar** are directly below the toolbars. At the bottom of the screen is the **status bar**.

EXERCISE 2.1	BROWSING THE MENU BAR AND TOOLBARS

1. Choose a command (File) from the menu bar and examine the menu choices.

2. Choose Edit from the menu bar. Some of the Edit selections aren't available now, so they are dimmed.

3. Click anywhere in the workbook window to turn off the menu.)

4. Point to the first button on the Standard toolbar. A tool tip will appear and provide the name of the button. Examine each of the buttons on the Standard toolbar.

The document window is directly below the toolbars (see Figure 2.2). The term *document* is the generic term for work created in any application. Since you will be creating workbooks in Excel, the document window is called the **workbook window**. Two **scroll bars** appear at the bottom and on the right side of the workbook window. **Sheet tabs** (labeled "Sheet1," "Sheet2," and so forth) are to the left of the horizontal scroll bar.

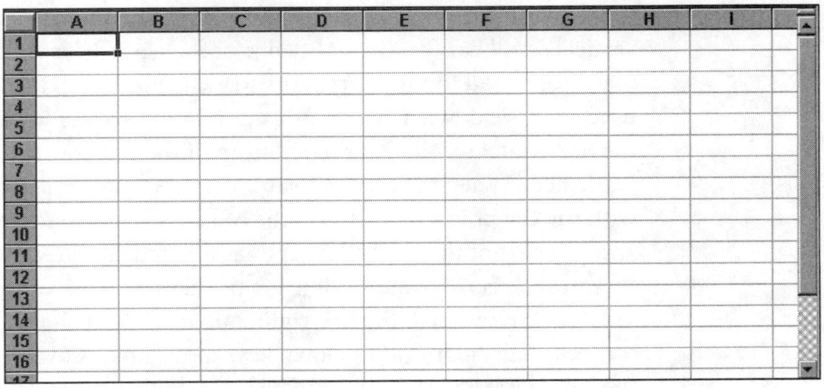

Figure 2.2
The workbook window

An Excel **workbook** is a group of worksheets. When you start Excel, a new workbook is opened with Sheet1 displayed. The blank worksheet shown in

Figure 2.2 includes vertical **columns** labeled with letters and horizontal **rows** labeled with numbers. Each worksheet is generously proportioned: 256 columns and 16,384 rows. The first 26 columns are labeled A through Z. Columns 27–52 are labeled AA–AZ, and column 53 is labeled BA.

The intersection of a column and a row is called a **cell**. Each cell occupies a unique space within the worksheet; the cell can be referred to by the **cell address**: the column letter and row number. For example, the cell in the upper-left corner of the worksheet is at the intersection of column A and row 1: cell A1. Cell addresses are always referred to first by column, then by row: A1, B25, IV16384.

SECTION 2.2: MOVING AROUND IN A WORKSHEET

As you move your mouse pointer into the worksheet window, the pointer changes shape to a hollow cross called a **cell pointer.** (When you move the mouse back to the menu bar or toolbars, the pointer changes back to an arrow.) In a new worksheet, cell A1 is the active cell. There is a border around A1, and "A1" is displayed in the name box. If you typed your name, it would appear in A1.

Before entering information in a cell other than A1, you must activate the cell by clicking on it with the cell pointer. There are three basic ways to move to a different cell: using the mouse, the keyboard, or the name box.

You can click on a cell with the mouse, to make it the active cell. If the cell you want to move to isn't visible in the worksheet window, use the scroll bars to move to the right or down in the worksheet, and then click on the cell. The vertical scroll bar (on the right edge of the worksheet window) has an arrow at the top (used to move up in the worksheet) and an arrow at the bottom, used to move down. Click on the up or down arrows to scroll the screen. Use the horizontal scroll bar at the bottom of the window to move left or right in a worksheet. When the cell you want to activate appears in the window, click with the cell pointer to activate the cell. Scrolling alone simply lets you view another part of the worksheet; it does not activate a cell.

You can also activate a cell using the keys on your keyboard. The arrow keys move one cell to the left, right, up, or down. The Enter key moves down one cell. The PgUp and PgDown keys move up or down a screen. To move to the last row (16384) of the worksheet, hold the Control key (labeled Ctrl on some keyboards), press the End key, and then press the down arrow. To move to the last column (IV), hold Ctrl, press End, and then press the right arrow.

To move to a cell using the name box, click in the name box, type the address of the cell you want to move to, and press Enter.

Whether you primarily use the mouse, arrow keys, or name box to move around in the worksheet, there is one keystroke combination you will want to know. To move back to cell A1 (where you started), hold Ctrl and press the Home key. Cell A1 is also called the home cell. (Pressing Home by itself returns you to column A.)

EXERCISE 2.2	MOVING IN THE WORKSHEET

Using the mouse, move to each of these cells:

- B25
- J7
- A200
- BZ218
- A1

Now, move to each of the listed cells using the keyboard. When you are back at the home cell, move to each of the listed cells using the name box.

SECTION 2.3: ENTERING TEXT AND NUMBERS IN EXCEL

There are two types of data you will want to put in a worksheet: numbers and text. Numbers are values you will want to add, subtract, multiply, divide, or compare. In the Time Sheet worksheet (see Figure 2.3), hours worked each day are numbers—and so are the dates. Excel treats dates as numbers so you can subtract one date from another to see how many days have passed, or add days to a date to determine, for example, the date when a library book will be overdue.

Figure 2.3

The *Time Sheet* worksheet

	A	B	C	D
1	Unicorn Software Time Sheet			
2	Week ending June 29			
3				
4	Name	23-Jun	24-Jun	25-Jun
5	Azimi	0	5	5
6	Beckley	6	6	0
7	Chiu	2	2	5
8	Jones	4	0	5
9	Collins	0	3	3
10	Barzona	8	0	8
11	Retzloff	4	4	0

Text is used to label the worksheet. The worksheet heading (Unicorn Software Time Sheet, Week ending June 29), the column heading for Name, and the employee last names are text. Text labels are used to explain the significance of the numbers; they are never used in calculations.

To enter data in Excel, you first move to the cell, then type in the information. As soon as you begin entering characters from the keyboard, a vertical line called an insertion point appears in the cell. The **insertion point** (also called a cursor) marks the spot where the next character you type will appear. The text or numbers you are entering appear in two places: in the active cell and in the formula bar above the worksheet window. Three buttons also appear on the formula bar:

Clicking the Cancel ✕ button clears the data you are entering without entering it in the active cell. (You can also accomplish this by pressing the Esc key.) Clicking the Enter √ button enters the data you have typed in the active cell without moving to another cell. (The third button is the Function button; you'll use this button to enter formulas in later sessions.)

You don't need to click any buttons on the formula bar to enter data. When you are finished typing and move to another cell, your data will be automatically entered.

Excel for Windows 95 has an **AutoComplete** feature, which keeps track of text entered in a column. When you start another entry beginning with the same letters in the column, the entry is automatically completed for you. If you type "Expense" in A5, entering "Ex" in A6 will cue Excel to finish the text entry. Once Excel has completed your entry, pressing Enter or moving to another cell places the completed text in the cell. If you instead wanted to enter "Excalibur" in A7, just keep typing. As soon as you type a "c" instead of the expected "p" in Expense, the AutoComplete text disappears. AutoComplete resets each time you leave a row empty.

EXERCISE 2.3	ENTERING DATA IN THE WORKSHEET

Create the *Unicorn Software Time Sheet* by entering the data shown in Figure 2.3 in the appropriate cells. If you make a mistake, don't worry about correcting it right now.

SECTION 2.4: EDITING DATA IN EXCEL

You can edit data in either of two ways. Entering new information in a cell replaces the old contents with the new data you type. If, for example, you typed "Joned" in A8 instead of "Jones," you can click once on A8, type "Jones" correctly, and then move to another cell. If you simply want to change the "d" to an "s," you can double-click on A8. The insertion point will reappear in the cell. Pressing the Backspace key deletes the character to the left of the insertion point. Pressing the Delete key (Del) deletes the character to the right of the insertion point.

You can move the insertion point within a cell using the arrow keys or the mouse. Pressing the ← or → key moves the insertion point one character to the left or right. To use the mouse, double-click on the cell, and move the mouse pointer over it. The pointer will change shape to an **I-beam**. Move the I-beam where you would like the insertion point to be; then click once to move the insertion point.

To delete all the data in a cell, click once to make the cell active; then press the Delete key (Del).

EXERCISE 2.4   **EDITING DATA IN A WORKSHEET**

1. Edit and correct any mistakes in your worksheet.

2. Collins worked 4 hours in place of Retzloff on June 23. Change both employees' entries for that date.

3. Change the title to *Unicorn Software Employee Time Sheet*.

SECTION 2.5: NAMING THE WORKSHEET

The Unicorn Software Time Sheet uses only one worksheet in the current Excel workbook. The **sheet tabs** at the bottom of the worksheet window are used to move between sheets in the workbook, and can be used to name each sheet. Clicking once on any sheet tab moves the selected sheet to the front, into the worksheet window. Double-clicking a tab opens the Rename Sheet dialog box, shown in Figure 2.4.

Figure 2.4

The Rename Sheet
dialog box

A **dialog box** is provided whenever Excel requires more information to complete a task. Dialog boxes include controls where you can type information or make choices. The Rename Sheet dialog box includes a text box displaying the current name of the sheet. The name Sheet1 is selected; when you start typing another name, Sheet1 will be replaced with the text you enter.

EXERCISE 2.5	TO NAME A WORKSHEET

1. Double-click the tab for the sheet you want to rename: Sheet1.

2. Type the new name (Time Sheet) **in the Rename Sheet dialog box.**

3. Press Enter.

The former Sheet1 is now named Time Sheet:

\ **Time Sheet** / Sheet2 / Sheet3 / Sheet4 /

Naming a worksheet makes the workbook easier to use, but it does not save the worksheet. If the computer were turned off right now, the Time Sheet would be lost. To keep work permanently, you need to save the workbook that contains Time Sheet in a more permanent location.

SECTION 2.6: SAVING YOUR WORKSHEET

Although you haven't finished the Time Sheet worksheet, you can save the portion you have completed in a file on disk. If you are the only person using your computer, you might usually save Excel work to the hard drive—a storage device installed in the computer case. You could, however, choose to save your work on a floppy disk, which provides removable storage. Work you save on a floppy disk can be moved to another computer. And after saving a file, you can take your floppy with you, preventing other users from changing or deleting your file. You will save files to a floppy disk while using *The Learning Guide to Microsoft Excel.*

The Save command can be accessed from the menu bar or the toolbar. To begin saving with the menu bar, choose File ➢ Save:

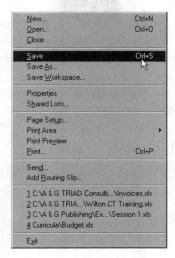

 To save using the toolbar, click the Save button on the Standard toolbar: Whether you use the menu bar or the toolbar button, the Save As dialog box (see Figure 2.5) will be opened.

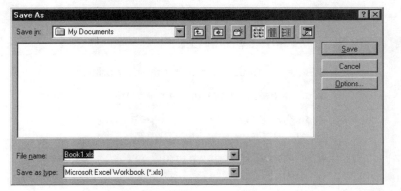

Figure 2.5

The Save As dialog box

Use the dialog box to specify a **file name** and location for the worksheet. The file name can be up to 256 characters long, which means you can enter a fairly descriptive name (and easily identify the file later). Each file on a drive or in a folder must have a unique name. The **default** file name (the name provided by Excel, which you can overwrite) is Book1.xls. The last three letters, *xls*, are a file **extension**. A file's extension is supplied automatically and associates the file with the application used to create it.

The Unicorn Software Time Sheet is only one sheet (Sheet1) in an Excel workbook. A **workbook** consists of one or more worksheets saved together in a file. You will be creating other worksheets in the workbook for payroll and inventory. All the worksheets will concern Unicorn Software. Rather than name the file Time Sheet (which only describes a single worksheet), we'll name it Unicorn Software to reflect the contents of the entire workbook file.

After you have specified a file name, Excel needs to know where to save the file. When Excel was installed, a default file location was specified: a folder on the hard drive. To save the file in another location, click the *Save In* control's drop-down arrow to select from a list of drives and folders available on the computer, as shown in Figure 2.6.

Figure 2.6
The Save In drop-down list

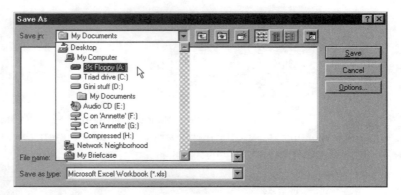

EXERCISE 2.6   **TO SAVE THE WORKBOOK**

1. Insert your floppy disk in the appropriate drive.

2. Click the Save button on the Standard toolbar.

3. In the File Name control, type a name. For this exercise, name the workbook file *Unicorn Software.*

4. Click the drop-down arrow on the Save In control.

5. Choose the drive from the list. Choose 3½ Floppy. (A:)

6. Click the Save button to save the file on your floppy disk.

The light on the floppy drive will come on, and the message *Saving Unicorn Software.xls* will appear on the status bar. The pointer will change to an hourglass shape, telling you to wait for Excel to finish the current task. When the file has been successfully saved, the file name (including the extension) appears in the title bar.

After you've saved a workbook once, you can quickly save any changes to the workbook by choosing Save again. Excel will resave the file in the same location using the same file name.

Before ending this session, you need to make some additions to the Time Sheet and construct a worksheet for Unicorn Software's payroll.

EXERCISE 2.7   **ADDING DATA TO THE TIME SHEET**

In columns E through H, add the column headings and hours for June 26, 27, 28, and 29 as shown here:

	A	E	F	G	H
1	Unicorn Software Time Sheet				
2	Week ending June 29				
3					
4	Name	26-Jun	27-Jun	28-Jun	29-Jun
5	Azimi	6	4	8	0
6	Beckley	0	6	4	4
7	Chiu	5	5	6	0
8	Jones	0	0	6	6
9	Collins	6	4	9	0
10	Barzona	0	6	4	4
11	Retzloff	0	8	6	4

EXERCISE 2.8   **CONSTRUCTING THE PAYROLL WORKSHEET**

1. Rename Sheet2 *to Payroll*.

2. Enter the text and numbers shown below on the *Payroll* worksheet.

3. Proof the *Payroll* worksheet and correct any errors before proceeding.

4. Click the Save button on the Standard toolbar or choose File ➤ Save to save the revised *Unicorn Software* workbook.

	A	B	C	D
1	Unicorn Software Payroll			
2	Week ending June 22			
3				
4	Name	Hours	Rate	Gross Pay
5	Azimi	28	8.75	
6	Beckley	18	8	
7	Chiu	36	10	
8	Jones	29	9.5	
9	Collins	32	10	
10	Barzona	35	9	
11	Retzloff	32	7.75	

SECTION 2.7: CLOSING A WORKBOOK AND GETTING A NEW WORKBOOK

When you are done using a workbook, you can close the workbook. The workbook will be removed from the screen. Choose File ➤ Close. If changes have been made since you saved the workbook (or if it has not yet been saved), Excel will prompt you to save the changes.

Workbooks allow you to group related worksheets together. You should, however, use separate workbooks for separate kinds of worksheets. Personal worksheets may share a workbook; budgets for different departments may each be kept in separate workbooks. To begin work with another workbook, choose File ➤ New or click the New button (the first button on the Standard toolbar) to open a new, blank workbook. If you open a new workbook using the menu bar, a New dialog box will open so you can select the type of new file. (Just click OK to select a workbook.) When you use the toolbar, a new workbook is automatically selected.

EXERCISE 2.9	TO CLOSE A WORKBOOK AND OPEN A NEW ONE
	1. **Choose File ➤ Close from the menu bar** to close the Unicorn Software workbook.
	2. **Choose File ➤ New or click the New button** to open a new workbook.

At the end of the session, remember to close Excel and Shut Down Windows 95 before turning off your computer. (And don't forget to take your floppy disk with you.)

What You Have Learned

You should now be comfortable with the parts of the Excel application window, worksheet window, and worksheet. You can move the cell pointer within the worksheet using the mouse, keyboard or name box. Text or numbers are entered in the active cell using the keyboard. Double-clicking a cell reactivates the cell for editing.

Worksheets can be renamed. Groups of worksheets are called workbooks. Workbooks can be saved to floppy or hard disk.

Focus Questions

1. What do the menu bar and toolbars have in common?

2. What is a column? a row? a cell?

3. What is the difference between a worksheet and workbook?

4. List the steps required to save a file for the first time.

5. How do you return to the home cell?

6. List the steps to close a workbook.

7. List the steps needed to open a new workbook.

Reinforcement Exercises

Exercise 1   If Excel is open, close the application. Launch Excel from the Start menu. Create the worksheet shown in Figure 2.7. Enter all the data shown, even if it appears to be wider than the column. You will be adjusting columns in a later session. Name the sheet *T-shirts*. Save the workbook on your floppy disk as *Wildlife Federation*.

Figure 2.7

The *Wildlife Federation T-shirt* worksheet

	A	B	C
1	WILDLIFE FEDERATION T-SHIRTS		
2	Stock on Hand, April 30		
3			
4	Item	Quantity	Cost
5	Anteater LS	116	14.95
6	Buzzard LS	16	14.95
7	Crab LS	27	14.95
8	Crab SS	57	9.95
9	Iguana LS	33	14.95
10	Snow Tiger SS	82	9.95
11	Wildebeest SS	35	9.95

Exercise 2   In a new workbook, create the worksheet shown in Figure 2.8. Enter all the data shown, even if it appears to be too wide for the column. You will be adjusting columns in a later session. Name the sheet *Budget*. Save the workbook containing *Budget* on your floppy disk as *Personal Worksheets*.

Figure 2.8

The *Budget* worksheet

	A	B	C	D	E
1	Week:	1	2	3	4
2					
3	Income				
4	Hardware	340	327.5	351.16	325.98
5	Other	0	50	0	0
6					
7	Expenses				
8	Rent	0	350	0	0
9	Phone	47.65	0	0	0
10	Groceries	32.65	23.1	12.05	42.74
11	Car Payment	0	0	298.34	0
12	Insurance	122	0	0	0
13	Gas/Car	23	18	26	39
14	Books	92	0	0	0
15	Entertainment	50	45	50	45
16	Misc.	65	32.56	15.9	42.89

Working with Numbers

XCEL IS DESIGNED SO that you can easily manipulate numbers. AutoSum lets you easily calculate totals for columns or rows. Formulas can be entered for addition, subtraction, multiplication, and division. At the end of this session you will be able to:

- Open an existing worksheet
- Select a range of cells
- View the AutoCalculated sum for a range of cells
- Total rows and columns
- Create formulas for simple mathematical calculations
- Fast print a worksheet

■ Vocabulary

- AutoCalculate
- AutoSum
- circular reference
- column header
- context button
- context menu
- open
- Order of Operations
- point method
- range
- row header
- select

27

SECTION 3.1: OPENING A WORKSHEET

To work with an existing worksheet document, you must first **open** it—copy it from disk to the computer's memory. You can open a document using either the menu bar or the toolbar. Selecting File from the menu bar provides a list of file commands, as you saw back in Figure 2.1.

Near the bottom of the list are the last four files opened or saved in Excel. If you are the only person who uses your computer, the files listed will be the last four files you accessed. (On a computer you share, some or all files listed may belong to other users.). If the file you want to open is listed, choose it.

Even if a familiar file name appears on the list, it may not be your file. Another user could have saved a workbook with the same name. If you open a file that is not yours, close the file and follow the instructions below to open files from your floppy disk.

If the file you want is *not* listed, choose File ➤ Open from the menu bar or click the Open button on the Standard toolbar. The Open dialog box will appear, as shown in Figure 3.1.

Figure 3.1
The Open
dialog box

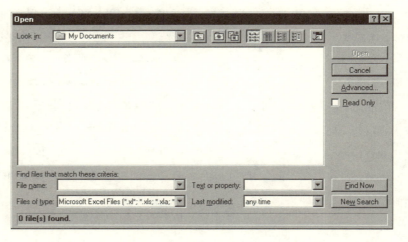

The dialog box displays the default file location that was established when Excel was installed on the computer. In Figure 3.1, the default location is a folder on the computer's hard drive called My Documents. The default location on your computer may be the A drive, the My Documents folder, or a different drive. In Session 2, you saved your workbooks on a floppy disk, so you need to direct Excel to the 3½" floppy drive if it is not the default location, as shown in Figure 3.2. You'll see a list of available files on the floppy.

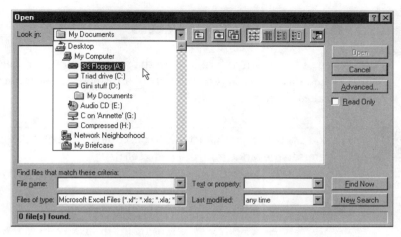

Figure 3.2
Opening a file
from floppy disk

To open a workbook file, either double-click on its name or click once and then click the Open button.

EXERCISE 3.1 | **TO OPEN A WORKBOOK USING THE MENU**

1. Launch Microsoft Excel if you have not already done so.

2. Insert your floppy in the diskette drive.

3. Click File on the menu bar.

4. Look at the list of files toward the bottom of the file menu to see if the file you wish to open (*Unicorn Software,* one of the files you created in the last session) is listed. If it is, point to the file name and click to open the workbook.

5. If the file is not listed on the File menu, click on Open to see the Open dialog box.

6. If the 3½" floppy drive is not the default drive, you will need to direct Excel to look at the files on the floppy. Click the drop-down arrow next to the Look In text box and select *3½ Floppy [?:].*

7. Click on the file (*Unicorn Software*) in the list that appears.

8. Double-click the filename or click Open to open the document.

Unicorn Software is opened. The workbook on your screen is a copy of the file you saved in the last session.

SECTION 3.2: SELECTING A RANGE OF CELLS

In order to sum or format a group of cells, you must be able to **select** (identify) the cells you wish to add or format. One or more selected cells is called a **range**.

TIP

You use the colon character (:) to describe a range of cells. For example, A5:B10 refers to the range from cell A5 to cell B10.

■ Selecting Cells

You can select a range of cells using the mouse. Point to the first cell you want to include in the selection, press and hold the mouse button, and drag to the last cell in the selection. Release the mouse button, and the cells will be selected.

To select a range of cells using the keyboard, move the pointer to the first cell to be included in the range. Hold the Shift key, and move to the last cell in the range using the arrow keys. In Figure 3.3, cells A5 through B8 are selected.

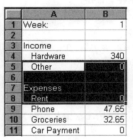

Figure 3.3

Selecting cells

There is a dark rectangle around the selected cells. Although A5 isn't shaded like the other cells, it is part of the selection. The active cell is always selected. The active cell here is cell A5—the first cell you selected.

If the selected cells contain numbers, Excel's **AutoCalculate** feature displays the sum of the values in the selected cells in the status bar. You can, therefore, quickly determine the total for a group of cells.

■ Selecting Columns and Rows

You can select all the cells in a column by clicking the column header. To select all the cells in a row, click the row header. To select the entire worksheet, click the Select All button in the upper-left corner of the worksheet to the left of column A's header. To select multiple adjacent columns or rows, first select one, then drag across the other columns or rows. To deselect a group of cells, click once to select any other cell in the worksheet.

■ Selecting Noncontiguous Areas

You can also select ranges of cells, columns, or rows that are **noncontiguous**—not next to each other. Begin by selecting one group of cells, then press and hold the Ctrl key while you select any other cells you want to add to the selection. For example, to select columns B, D, and F, you would select column B, hold the Ctrl key, and select columns D and F.

EXERCISE 3.2	SELECTING AREAS OF THE WORKSHEET
	Practice selecting, in turn, each of the following areas of the Time Sheet worksheet:
	Column C
	cell range A1:B10
	J15:M24
	columns A, C, and E
	row 14
	rows 1 and 2 and column A
	A4:A11 and E4:E11

SECTION 3.3: USING AUTOSUM TO TOTAL ROWS AND COLUMNS

The **AutoSum** button allows you to total numbers easily in a couple of different ways. You can quickly create totals for a block of numbers like the hours worked per day in the Time Sheet worksheet. To create column totals (the total number of hours worked in a day by all employees), select all the hours worked (B5:H11) and include row 12, the empty row directly below the hours worked. Click the AutoSum button on the Standard toolbar, and all seven columns will be totaled.

If you wanted row totals, you would select the range of cells containing the hours worked and the blank column to the right of the hours worked. To calculate both row *and* column totals, select the numerical data and both a blank row below and a blank column to the right of the numbers, as shown in Figure 3.4.

Figure 3.4

Using AutoSum
to calculate
totals

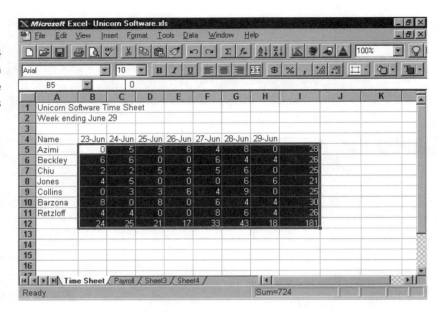

TIP

You can separate the totals from the numbers. Select the data, and two empty columns and/or rows. The row or column next to the numerical data will be left empty.

EXERCISE 3.3   **CREATING ROW AND COLUMN TOTALS**

1. Click the sheet tab to make *Time Sheet* the active worksheet.

2. Select cells B5:I12.

3. Click the AutoSum button.

4. Add the heading *Total* in cell I4, and *Totals* in A12.

Selecting your numbers and then clicking AutoSum works fine under most circumstances, when you want your totals placed directly below or to the right of your data. Figure 3.5 illustrates another way of using AutoSum. Here, a single total is needed below and to the right of the data (in C8).

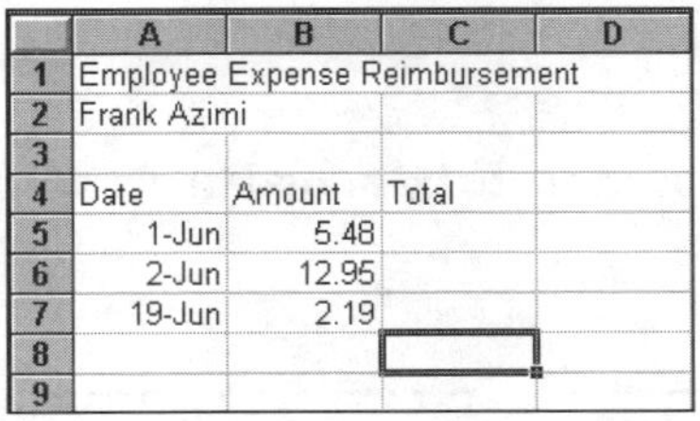

Figure 3.5

The *Reimbursement*
worksheet

Figure 3.5

The *Reimbursement*
worksheet

	A	B	C	D
1	Employee Expense Reimbursement			
2	Frank Azimi			
3				
4	Date	Amount	Total	
5	1-Jun	5.48		
6	2-Jun	12.95		
7	19-Jun	2.19		
8				
9				

With the **point method,** you can still use AutoSum to calculate this total. Move the cell pointer to the cell where you want the total to appear. Click the AutoSum button, and =*SUM()* appears in the cell. Now, use the cell pointer to point out (select) the numbers to be included in the total, as shown in Figure 3.6. A flashing marquee appears around the selected cells, and the cell range is entered in the active cell. Release the mouse button to finish the selection, and press Enter to calculate the total.

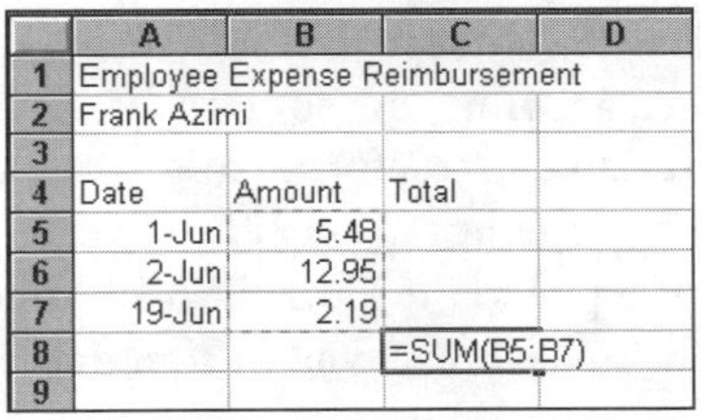

Figure 3.6

Calculating a total

	A	B	C	D
1	Employee Expense Reimbursement			
2	Frank Azimi			
3				
4	Date	Amount	Total	
5	1-Jun	5.48		
6	2-Jun	12.95		
7	19-Jun	2.19		
8			=SUM(B5:B7)	
9				

You can use this method to create row and column totals at any time. If you invoke AutoSum when there are numbers nearby, Excel will select a group of numbers to total.

How does AutoSum choose cells to include in a total when only a single cell is selected? When you click the AutoSum button, Excel searches for numbers within the row or column. If J22 is the selected cell, Excel will search upward in column J and to the left in row 22 for a group of numbers to sum. If there are numbers in row 22, Excel assumes you may want to add them. The cells Excel proposes to sum (inside the flashing marquee) will start with the first cell to the left of the current cell that contains a number and will include every cell that contains a number until Excel encounters text or an empty cell. If there are no numbers in either the row or the column, you must select cells to add.

It's very easy to accept Excel's "guess" about the cells to be totaled; you simply press Enter. Remember, though, that only you know what numbers should be added. Always check to be certain that the cells Excel has selected actually contain the numbers that belong in the total you are calculating. If not, use the point method to select the cells to be included. As you begin selecting cells, the Excel's selection will be cleared from the formula bar.

EXERCISE 3.4	TO TOTAL COLUMNS WITH THE POINT METHOD

In *Payroll,* enter the label Total in A13.

1. Move the cell pointer to the cell where you want the answer to appear (B13).

CONTINUES ON NEXT PAGE

> **2. Click the AutoSum button.**
>
> **3. Select the range of numbers to be added** (the employee hours: cells B5:B11).
>
> **4. Press Enter.**

SECTION 3.4: BASIC ARITHMETIC IN EXCEL

AutoSum only works for addition. There is no AutoMultiply or AutoSubtract button. You create formulas to subtract, multiply, or divide in Excel.

In the Payroll worksheet, a formula is required to calculate Gross Pay for each employee. Before you can create a formula, you must know what numbers are needed as well as the operation(s) needed to calculate the answer. For any employee, Gross Pay is equal to the Hours Worked multiplied by the Hourly Rate. This relationship, expressed as an equation, is:

Gross Pay = Hours Worked × Hourly Rate

■ Operators and Order of Operations

The following symbols are used for arithmetic in Excel (and other applications):

Operation	Symbol	Example
Addition	+	regular hours + overtime hours
Subtraction	−	sales price − discount
Multiplication	*	quantity purchased * price each
Division	/	divisional bonus / divisional employees
Exponentiation	^	3^2 (3^2)

You also need to be familiar with the **Order of Operations:**

- Formulas will be evaluated (calculated) from left to right.

- Operations in parentheses will be done before any other operation.

- In a formula with more than one operation, multiplication and division will be done first before any addition or subtraction.

The Order of Operations indicates that these two formulas are different:

A: 4*5+10/2

B: 4*(5+10)/2

Both formulas will be evaluated from left to right. In formula A, 4*5 will be evaluated first. Since all multiplication and division are done before any addition and subtraction, 10/2 will be evaluated next. The value of the partially evaluated formula (after one pass through from left to right) is 4*5 plus 10/2, or 20 + 5. The fully evaluated answer is, therefore, 25. In formula B, the parentheses force Excel to add 5 and 10 before doing any other operations. The partially evaluated formula is 4*15/2. Fully evaluated, the formula's value is 30.

The Order of Operations and the use of parentheses come into play more often than you might think. There is, for example, a difference between a sales discount calculated before a shipping charge is applied:

Price * Discount + Shipping

a discount on shipping only:

Price + Shipping * Discount

and a discount on both the product *and* the shipping cost:

(Price + Shipping) * Discount.

Once you understand the order of operations, you can include parentheses or not to make Excel evaluate your formulas in the order you desire.

■ Creating a Formula

Entering a formula once you've defined it is a simple process. In the *Payroll* worksheet, first move the cell pointer to D5, where the gross pay for the first employee, Azimi, should appear. Second, press the equal sign (=) key. Third, click once on the hours worked. The formula bar will display =B5.

Now, press the operator for multiplication, the asterisk (*). Click on the second number to be multiplied, the hourly rate for Azimi in C5. The formula bar will display =B5*C5. The formula is complete, so you can press Enter to calculate Azimi's gross pay.

You can also create the formula by selecting D5 and then typing =B5*C5, but entering formulas from the keyboard is a bad habit to acquire. Typing formulas involves looking at each cell, and then figuring out what row and column the cell is located in so you can type the cell address. Keyboarding formulas is both slower and more prone to error than the point method.

A **circular reference** occurs when a formula includes the address of the cell that contains the formula. For example, if the formula =SUM(B5:B10) was in cell B10, this would be a circular reference. Excel cannot properly evaluate a formula that includes a circular reference. A dialog box will open that says "Cannot resolve circular references." After you click OK to close the dialog box, create the formula again, making sure that you don't include a reference to the formula's cell.

In later sessions you will be creating more complex worksheets where formulas use the results of other formulas. More complex worksheets can create more complex circular references. For example, if the formula in B10 is =SUM(B5:B9) and the formula in B5 is =B10*2, this is also a circular reference—B10 relies on B5, and B5 relies on B10. Understanding how circular references occur will help you avoid them when creating formulas.

EXERCISE 3.5   **TO CREATE FORMULAS**

1. **In the worksheet** *(Payroll)*, **move the cell pointer to the cell where you want the result of the formula to appear** (D5).

2. **Press the = key.**

3. **Click once on the first number to be included in the formula:** Azimi's hours (B5).

4. **Press the operator.** Since you are going to multiply, choose the multiply key (*).

5. **Click on the second number to be included:** Azimi's rate (C5). Verify that =B5*C5 appears in the formula bar.

6. **If there are more than two numbers in the formula, repeat steps 4 and 5 until the complete formula appears in the formula bar.**

7. **Press Enter to complete the formula.**

8. Repeat the steps above to calculate Gross Pay for the remaining employees.

9. Use AutoSum to create a total for the Gross Pay column in D12.

10. Retzloff received a raise that should have been reflected in this pay period. Change Retzloff's rate to 8.00 per hour.

11. Change Jones' hours to 32 for the week.

Notice that the Gross Pay for Jones and Retzloff and the totals for hours and Gross Pay changed automatically when the values in the cells included in the formulas changed. If Azimi worked 10 hours at $10 per hour, it would be tempting to simply enter the value *100* for Gross Pay. But that value wouldn't change if Azimi's hours or pay rate changed. You would have to change the Gross Pay figure, also, or your worksheet would be incorrect. It is easy to change a number and forget to change values that rely on the number. For that reason, no matter how easy it is to calculate a result in your head, you should *never* enter a value for a total or the result of a formula in place of the formula on a worksheet.

SECTION 3.5: PRINTING A WORKSHEET QUICKLY

Printing is covered in depth in Session 7, but you can quickly print a copy of the selected worksheet by clicking the Print button on the Standard toolbar. Your printout will be sent to the default printer connected to your computer. Before printing a worksheet, you should click the Save button (or choose File ➢ Save) to save the updated file to your floppy disk. If you share a printer with other users, you should also enter your name in an empty cell of the worksheet, so that you'll know which printout is yours.

It's always a good idea to save a file just before printing.

TIP

EXERCISE 3.6	TO PRINT A WORKSHEET QUICKLY

1. **Make sure the sheet you want to print** *(Payroll)* **is active.**
2. **Click the Print button to print the worksheet.**

Don't forget to exit Excel and shut down Windows 95 before turning off your computer at the end of the session, and remember to take your floppy disk with you.

What You Have Learned

Before you can work with an existing workbook, you must open the workbook using the menu bar or toolbar. You can easily total rows and columns of numbers by selecting the range of numbers and clicking the AutoSum button. Formulas are used for subtraction, multiplication, and division. They are also used when you need to add numbers that aren't contiguous. You click the Print button on the Standard toolbar to print one copy of the selected worksheet.

Focus Questions

1. What is a range?

2. How do you select noncontiguous ranges of cells?

3. In what order are mathematical operations performed?

4. List the steps needed to create a formula.

Reinforcement Exercises

Exercise 1   Open the *Wildlife Federation T-shirts* worksheet. Enter formulas to calculate the value of each type of shirts, the total value of all shirts in stock, and the quantity of shirts in stock. Save *Wildlife Federation*. Print the *T-shirts* worksheet.

Exercise 2   Open *Personal Worksheets*. Change the column headings (1, 2, 3, and 4) to 4-Jun, 11-Jun, 18-Jun, and 25-Jun. Save and print the *Budget* worksheet.

Exercise 3   In the *Wildlife Federation* workbook, create the *Order Response* worksheet shown in Figure 3.7. In the Days column, create formulas to calculate the number of days needed to process each order (subtract the date an order was placed from the date it was shipped). Print the worksheet, and save *Wildlife-Federation*.

Figure 3.7

The *Order Response* worksheet

	A	B	C	D
1	Wildlife Federation			
2	Order Responsiveness Survey			
3				
4	Order	Placed	Shipped	Days
5	960001	2-Jan-96	5-Jan-96	3
6	960002	2-Jan-96	6-Jan-96	4
7	960003	2-Jan-96	5-Jan-96	3
8	960004	2-Jan-96	10-Jan-96	8
9	960005	2-Jan-96	5-Jan-96	3
10	960006	2-Jan-96	7-Jan-96	5
11	960007	3-Jan-96	8-Jan-96	5
12	960008	3-Jan-96	9-Jan-96	6
13	960009	3-Jan-96	9-Jan-96	6
14	960010	4-Jan-96	12-Jan-96	8
15				

Formatting Numbers in Excel

EXCEL LETS YOU PRESENT numbers in a variety of formats. Formatting is used to identify numbers as currency or percentages, and to make numbers easier to read by aligning decimal points in a column. You can format using the Formatting toolbar or a pop-up menu. At the end of this session you will be able to:

- Format numeric data
- Choose date or time formats
- Use pop-up menus
- Undo changes made to a worksheet

Vocabulary

- context button
- context menu
- format
- pop-up menu
- trailing zero
- undo

SECTION 4.1: FORMATTING NUMBERS

When you format a number, you change its appearance, not its numeric value. Formatting makes a worksheet easier to read. In the Payroll worksheet, the hours worked line up because they all have the same number of digits (see Figure 4.1). The values in the Rate column, however, have zero, one, or two digits after the decimal.

Figure 4.1

The *Payroll* worksheet

	A	B	C	D
1	Unicorn Software Payroll			
2	Week ending June 22			
3				
4	Name	Hours	Rate	Gross Pay
5	Azimi	28	8.75	245
6	Beckley	18	8	144
7	Chiu	36	10	360
8	Jones	29	9.5	275.5
9	Collins	32	10	320
10	Barzona	35	9	315
11	Retzloff	32	7.75	248
12				
13	Total	210		1907.5

The default format for numbers, General, doesn't display zeros that don't affect the actual value of the number. For example, 10.5 has the same numeric value as 10.50, so the extra or **trailing zero** is not displayed.

The Payroll worksheet will be easier to read and better looking if all the pay rates have the same number of decimal places and all the decimals line up. You might also prefer to add dollar signs to the values for Gross Pay and Rate, since the values in both columns are currency. These two changes, shown in Figure 4.2, are examples of formatting.

Figure 4.2

The *Payroll* worksheet with formatting changes

	A	B	C	D
1	Unicorn Software Payroll			
2	Week ending June 22			
3				
4	Name	Hours	Rate	Gross Pay
5	Azimi	28	$ 8.75	$ 245.00
6	Beckley	18	$ 8.00	$ 144.00
7	Chiu	36	$ 10.00	$ 360.00
8	Jones	29	$ 9.50	$ 275.50
9	Collins	32	$ 10.00	$ 320.00
10	Barzona	35	$ 9.00	$ 315.00
11	Retzloff	32	$ 7.75	$ 248.00
12				
13		210		$ 1,907.50

Simple formatting can be applied using the Formatting toolbar:

If the Formatting toolbar is not visible, choose View ➢ Toolbars to open the Toolbars dialog box, shown in Figure 4.3. Click the check box for Formatting; then click the OK button to display the Formatting toolbar.

Figure 4.3
The Toolbars
dialog box

To format a group of cells, first select the cells you want to format, and then click a button on the Formatting toolbar to apply the format. The Currency button adds dollar signs, a comma to the right of the thousands place, and two digits following the decimal, as in the Gross Pay figures in Figure 4.2.

The Percent button expresses the value as a percentage (the formatted number has been multiplied by 100 and followed by a percent sign). If you format the number 1 as a percent, it will appear as 100%. The number 0.87 will appear as 87%. The Comma format adds a comma to numbers with four or more digits before the decimal.

The next two buttons are used to increase and decrease the number of digits following the decimal. If decreasing the number of digits eliminates a nonzero digit, the number will be rounded. For example, if the number 9.75 is displayed with only one decimal place, it will be rounded to 9.8. If you display 9.75 with no digits following the decimal, Excel will round it to 10.

Remember, formatting affects only the display of a cell, not the cell's contents. To view the contents of a cell, click on the cell and look at the formula bar. The number in the cell appears in the formula bar exactly as entered regardless of the format that has been applied. Also, make sure you have *finished* entering the data in a cell before you try to add formatting.

EXERCISE 4.1   **TO FORMAT CELLS USING THE FORMATTING TOOLBAR**

If the Formatting toolbar is not visible, choose View ➢ Toolbars to open the Toolbars dialog box. Click Formatting and choose OK. Open the *Unicorn Software* workbook, and select the *Payroll* worksheet.

1. Select the cells to be formatted. In the *Payroll* worksheet, select column C.

2. Click a button on the Formatting toolbar to apply a format to the selected cells. Click the Currency button.

3. Click on any cell to turn off the selection.

4. For more practice, select column D.

5. Click the Comma button on the Formatting toolbar.

6. Click the Increase Decimal button once. Note the results.

7. Click the Decrease Decimal button to restore two decimal places.

■ Using the Format Cells Dialog Box

Three basic formats are available on the toolbar: Currency, Percent, and Comma. You can access additional formats from the Format menu. Selecting Format ➢ Cells opens the Format Cells dialog box, shown in Figure 4.4.

Figure 4.4
The Format Cells
dialog box

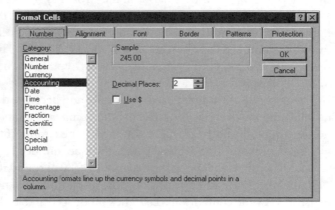

The Format Cells dialog box has separate pages for Number, Alignment, Font, Border, Patterns, and Protection. To move to the Number page (see

Figure 4.4), click the tab at the top of the page. The Number page has controls for categories of formats, decimal places, thousands separator, and treatment of negative numbers. (You'll be working with the other pages of this dialog box in later sessions.) The table below describes some of the Categories used for integer and decimal numbers.

Category	Description	Example
General	The default format.	1008.7
Number	Like General, but you can set decimal places and use a thousands separator.	1008.70
Currency	Values are preceded with a dollar sign immediately before the first digit. Zero values are displayed.	$ 1,008.70
Accounting	Values are lined up on the decimal point. If dollar signs are displayed, they will be spaced to line up. Zero values are shown as dashes.	$ 1,008.70
Percentage	Values are expressed as percentages, followed by percent sign.	100870%
Scientific	Values are displayed in scientific notation.	1.01E+03

Date and Time Formats Date formats are used for dates and times. If you select the Date category, you can also select a format from the following list:

The last two date formats include standard time (AM/PM) and international time, also known as military time. The Time category contains a similar list, and is used for times alone. To include both the time and date in a single cell, use a date format that includes time.

Fractions Formats The Fraction category allows you to choose from formats based on either the number of digits to display in the divisor (1, 2, or 3) or the fractional unit (halves, quarters, tenths, etc.).

Special and Text Formats These both convert a number to text.

The Special category includes four specific types of numbers that aren't really values: Zip Code, Zip Code + 4, Phone Number, and Social Security Number. You wouldn't want to add or multiply any of these numbers—they are informational labels just like a last name. (In some spreadsheet programs, this type of number is called a *numeric label*.)

The Text format changes the number to text without applying a Special format. There is a specific use for the Text format. While the regular formats allow you to determine the number of trailing zeros, all of them strip off any leading zeros. If you enter 00100, Excel records the value as 100. It isn't unusual, however, for employee numbers, item numbers, book numbers (ISBN), and the like to begin with a zero. Formatting the cell for text *before* entering the number will retain leading zeros. You can also enter numbers as text manually. Simply type an apostrophe (') before the number, and Excel will treat the number as text.

CAUTION

Unlike the other formatting categories, Special and Text *change the underlying value of the number.* If you format a number with Special or Text, you will no longer be able to use the number in mathematical operations unless you first reformat the cells with a numeric format.

Custom allows you to select from or make an addition to a list of formats for numbers, dates, and times.

SECTION 4.2: USING CONTEXT-SENSITIVE MENUS

You can also access the Format Cells dialog box from a pop-up menu. After you have selected a cell or range of cells, pressing the right mouse button (also called the **context button**) opens a **pop-up menu** (also called a **context menu**):

The choices available on the pop-up menu vary based on the mouse location and actions you have taken recently—the context. Select from the pop-up menu as you would select from the menu bar. To turn off the pop-up menu without making a choice, click anywhere in the workbook window.

| EXERCISE 4.2 | **TO FORMAT USING THE FORMAT CELLS DIALOG BOX** |

Activate the *Time Sheet* worksheet.

1. **Select the cells to be formatted** (row 4).

2. **Choose Format ➢ Cells, or click the context button and choose Format Cells.**

3. **Click the Number tab.**

4. **From the Category list, choose the appropriate formatting category** (Date).

5. **From the Type list, choose a format type.** Here, choose the format that spells out the first three letters of the month: (4-Mar-94).

6. **Click the OK button to apply the format and close the dialog box.**

    If you change your mind about a formatting change, you can remove it. The **Undo** button on the Standard toolbar allows you to retract the last action you performed, whether the action was formatting a cell, deleting a column, or typing over the text in a cell. To undo the undo, click the Redo button on the Standard toolbar.

| EXERCISE 4.3 | **TO UNDO/REDO A FORMATTING CHANGE** |

1. **Click the Undo button to undo the last formatting change** (the date format in *Time Sheet*).

2. **Click the Redo button to reapply the formatting.**

What You Have Learned

Formatting changes the appearance of numbers to improve the readability of a worksheet. Basic formats like Currency and Comma can be applied from the Formatting toolbar. Other formats are accessed in the Format Cells dialog box by choosing Format ➢ Cells or right clicking to open a context menu. If you don't like a formatting change you have applied, you can choose Undo immediately to undo the change.

Focus Questions

1. Why should you format numbers in a worksheet?

2. What kinds of numeric formatting can be applied from the Formatting toolbar?

3. What are trailing zeros?

4. How can you remove the most recently applied formatting?

5. What is the context button?

6. How do you access pop-up menus?

Reinforcement Exercises

Exercise 1   Open the *Wildlife Federation T-shirts* worksheet. Format the Cost column for currency. Format totals appropriately. Print and save the worksheet.

Exercise 2   Open *Personal Worksheets*. In the *Budget* worksheet, format all numeric columns as Comma. Format the date column headings using the 4-Jun type format. Print the *Budget* worksheet and save the workbook.

Exercise 3   In the *Order Response* worksheet in *the Wildlife Federation* workbook, format the dates in the Placed and Shipped columns using the format type 1/2/97. Reformat the dates using the original format: 2-Jan-97.

Exercise 4   In the *Wildlife Federation* workbook, create a worksheet for *Clearance*, as shown in Figure 4.7. Format the columns as shown. Use formulas to calculate the Savings to be included in the Clearance catalog. (Savings is equal to $1-$ Clearance/Price). Save the workbook, and print the *Clearance* worksheet.

Changing Worksheet Layout

YOU CAN CHANGE the layout of your worksheets. Text and numbers can be aligned to the right, left, or center within a cell. Titles can be centered across more than one column. You can adjust the width of columns. Rows and columns can be added to separate sections of the worksheet. One or more cells can be moved or copied to another location within the worksheet. This session concludes with some general rules on constructing your own worksheets. At the end of this session you will be able to:

- Adjust column widths
- Align text in a cell
- Center text across selected columns
- Insert and delete rows and columns
- Move text using cut and paste
- Copy text using copy and paste
- Lay out a worksheet to present data

■ Vocabulary

- align
- clipboard
- column width
- copy
- cut
- delete
- insert
- move
- paste

47

SECTION 5.1: ALIGNING TEXT

Text and numbers can be **aligned** (lined up) using the toolbar in four different alignments: left, center, or right within cells, or across selected columns. By default, Excel left-aligns text (including numbers formatted as text) and right-aligns numbers. Aligning across columns centers the cell contents across the selected cells. Figure 5.1 shows a column heading in each of the four alignments.

Figure 5.1

Examples of aligned text

	A	B	C
1	Alignment		
2	left	Hours	
3	center	Hours	
4	right	Hours	
5	across B and C	Hours	

Use the Formatting toolbar to align text and numbers in cells. Begin by selecting the cell or cells you wish to align. Then click the Left, Center, or Right alignment button on the Formatting toolbar:

Worksheet titles are often centered across the top of the worksheet. To center across a selection, select the cell containing the title and the cells directly to the right above the worksheet data. As you can see in Figure 5.2, you can align more than one title at a time. Click the Center Across Columns button on the Formatting toolbar.

Figure 5.2

Preparing to center across columns

	A	B	C	D	E	F	G	H	I
1	Unicorn Software Time Sheet								
2	Week ending June 29								
3									
4	Name	23-Jun	24-Jun	25-Jun	26-Jun	27-Jun	28-Jun	29-Jun	
5	Azimi	0	5	5	6	4	8	0	28
6	Beckley	6	6	0	0	6	4	4	26
7	Chiu	2	2	5	5	5	6	0	25
8	Jones	4	5	0	0	0	6	6	21
9	Collins	0	3	3	6	4	9	0	25
10	Barzona	8	0	8	0	6	4	4	30
11	Retzloff	4	4	0	0	8	6	4	26
12		24	25	21	17	33	43	18	181

The default settings reflect some standard rules for aligning text and numbers. Columns of text like the employee last names in the Payroll worksheet should generally be left-aligned. We are used to reading from left to right.

While you can center or right-align employee names, it makes the worksheet harder to read.

Generally, columns of numbers should be left in the default (right) alignment unless the numbers are of the same length. In Figure 5.3, both the section numbers and seat prices are centered. The section numbers are still easy to read, as they all have two digits. The seat prices, however, are difficult to compare when centered—the decimal points don't line up. The more the numbers differ in length, the greater the problem. (You could, of course, format all the seat prices with two digits after the decimal and take care of part of the problem caused by center-aligning the numbers.)

Section	Seat Price
10	10
11	12.25
12	13
13	16
14	12.75
15	12.75

Figure 5.3

Examples of aligned numbers

Column titles or headings should have the same alignment as the contents of the column, so that the heading will appear directly over the contents. If the column is filled with numbers, the heading should be right-aligned. Columns of text should have headings with the same alignment as the text: if the text is centered, center the headings.

There are more alignment options that aren't accessible with toolbar buttons. All alignment options can be accessed by choosing Format ➤ Cells (or choosing Format Cells from the pop-up menu) and clicking the Alignment tab on the Format Cells dialog box, shown in Figure 5.4. In addition to Left, Right, Center, and Center Across Selection (columns), the horizontal alignment selections include General, Fill, and Justify.

Figure 5.4

The Alignment page of the Format Cells dialog box

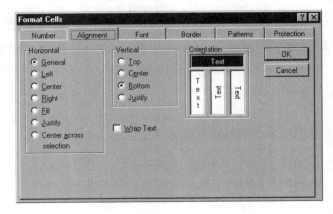

General is the default alignment: left for text, right for numbers. Fill "fills" the cell with the current contents by repeating it. If, for example, "-" is the contents of the cell and you choose Fill for the alignment, "- - - - - -" will appear in the cell. This can be used to draw a horizontal line through the cell by filling it with equal or minus signs.

In a justified cell, Excel adds space between words in the text so that the entire cell is filled with characters or spaces, providing a smooth right edge (like a newspaper column). If the text exceeds the width of the column, the text is wrapped and the row height increased, as shown in Figure 5.5.

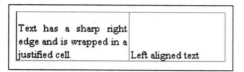

Figure 5.5

A justified cell entry

Justifying automatically wraps text, but you can wrap text in any alignment by clicking the Wrap Text check box in the Alignment dialog box.

Text and numbers rest on the bottom of the cell by default. The other vertical alignments can be selected to float the contents nearer the top or middle of the cell. Vertical justification adds space between the lines in a wrapped cell.

Use the Orientation control to turn text sideways. While you can change the orientation of worksheet text, this control is more often used when attaching text to an Excel chart.

EXERCISE 5.1   **ALIGNING CELL CONTENTS**

Launch Excel if it is not already running. Open the *Unicorn Software* workbook.

1. **Select the cells you want to center a title across, beginning with the cell that contains the title.** In the *Payroll* worksheet, select cells A1:D2.

2. **Click the Center Across Columns button to center the titles.**

3. Select and right-align the headings for columns B, C, and D.

SECTION 5.2: ADJUSTING COLUMN WIDTHS

By default, Excel columns are slightly more than eight characters wide. If the data in a worksheet is wider than the column, you need to adjust the **column width** so it is wide enough to contain the data. Narrow data, on the other hand, can seem "lost" in the default column width. You can either adjust column width manually or use "Make Fit" to fit the column width to the existing data.

To adjust the width of a column, begin by pointing to the border at the right side of the column header. Your pointer will change shape to a double-pointed arrow. Press and hold the mouse button, and the current column width will be displayed in the Name box. Drag the edge of the column header to the desired width; then release the button. As you drag the column header's border to narrow or widen the column, the new width is displayed in the name box.

If you double-click on the column header border instead of dragging the border, Excel will size the column slightly larger than the widest entry in the column. This feature is called "Make Fit."

You can select several columns and size them all at the same time. By dragging the header border of any selected column, all columns will be sized to the same width. Double-clicking the header border of any of the selected columns will size each column individually, to fit the data in the column.

EXERCISE 5.2 | **TO ADJUST COLUMN WIDTHS**

1. **Select the column(s) you want to adjust.** In the *Payroll* worksheet, select columns B, C, and D.

2. **Position your mouse pointer at the right edge of one of the selected columns' headers.** The pointer will change shape to a double-headed arrow.

3. **Double-click to have Excel adjust the widths of the selected column to fit the contents of the column.**

4. **Click anywhere in the worksheet to turn off the selection.**

5. Drag the right border of column A's header to make the column slightly wider.

SECTION 5.3: INSERTING AND DELETING ROWS AND COLUMNS

It's never too late to add or remove rows or columns in an Excel worksheet. To **insert** (add) a column between the current columns A and B, begin by clicking the column header for column B to select the column. From the menu bar, choose Insert ➢ Columns to insert a single column and shift the contents of column B to the right. You can insert multiple columns simultaneously by selecting more than one column before inserting. For example, to insert two columns, begin by selecting columns B and C. Rows are inserted in the same way.

Deleting (removing) rows and columns is much like inserting. Begin by selecting one or more rows or columns. To clear the contents but leave the emptied row in place, press the Delete key on your keyboard. To delete the contents *and* remove the row, choose Edit ➤ Delete from the menu bar. When you delete a row or column using the menu bar, **all** information is deleted, including cells that may not be visible in the part of the worksheet you are looking at.

TIP

There are some nifty keystroke combinations you can use to see if there is more data in a row or column. Select an occupied cell, hold Ctrl and press the → key. The cell pointer moves to the last occupied cell to the right of the original cell; in other words, it stops when it comes to a blank cell. If you press Ctrl+ → again, the cell pointer moves to the rightmost blank cell; it stops to the left of the first occupied cell. The other arrow keys work with Ctrl the same way. Using these key combinations, you can quickly zoom to the parts of the worksheet with cell entries. If you can zoom to the end of a row or column, you know it is empty from that point to the end of the worksheet.

EXERCISE 5.3 | **TO INSERT AND DELETE ROWS AND COLUMNS**

1. **Select the row or column where you want the new inserted column to appear.** In the *Payroll* worksheet, click the header for row 5 to select the row.

2. **Choose Insert ➤ Rows to insert a row** to separate the column headings and the data. **To insert a column, choose Insert ➤ Columns.**

3. Insert a column between the Rate and Gross Pay columns.

4. Insert a row between the data and the totals.

5. **To delete a column or row, first select it. Then, choose Edit ➤ Delete from the menu bar.** Delete the column inserted in step 2 above.

6. You've discovered that Buckley's name was misspelled. Change Beckley to Buckley.

7. Insert a row between Azimi and Buckley and another between Chiu and Jones.

SECTION 5.4: MOVING AND COPYING CELL CONTENTS

You can also move and copy ranges of cells (including columns and rows). When you **move** cells, the cells are deleted from their original location and placed in a new destination location. **Copying** cells leaves the originals in place and places a copy in the new location. In this section, you will learn to use cut/copy-and-paste to move and copy. The Cut, Copy, and Paste buttons are located on the Standard toolbar:

■ Moving a Range of Cells

Begin by selecting the cells to be moved. You can move a single cell, a range of cells, or one or more columns or rows. **Cut** the selection by clicking the Cut button on the Standard toolbar or choosing Edit ➤ Cut from the menu bar. The message "Select destination and press Enter or choose PASTE" appears in the status bar. Click on the destination cell. (If you are moving more than one cell, you only need to click the first cell in the destination range, as shown in Figure 5.5). Press Enter or click the Paste button to move the cells.

Name	23-Jun	24-Jun	25-Jun	26-Jun	27-Jun	28-Jun	29-Jun	
Azimi	0	5	5	6	4	8	0	28
Buckley	6	6	0	0	6	4	4	26
Chiu	2	2	5	5	5	6	0	25
Jones	4	5	0	0	0	6	6	21
Collins	0	3	3	6	4	9	0	25
Barzona	8	0	8	0	6	4	4	30
Retzloff	4	4	0	0	8	6	4	26

Figure 5.6
Moving a range
of cells

■ Copying a Range of Cells

To copy cells, you must first select them. Then, click the Copy button on the toolbar. The selected cells are copied to a location in the computer's memory called the **clipboard**. The copied selection remains on the clipboard until you copy a different selection or shut down Windows 95. The "Select destination" message will appear in the status bar.

Click on the destination cell, then press Enter or click the **Paste** button to copy the information from the clipboard and complete the copy operation. If you want to make more than one copy, move to the next destination and press the Paste button or choose Edit ➤ Paste from the menu bar.

When you insert a row or column above or to the left of existing data, Excel automatically adjusts the remaining data by moving it down or to the right.

CAUTION

If you paste cells on top of existing data, the existing data will be deleted, so it's advisable to make sure that there are enough blank cells to accommodate the selection you want to paste. If you make a mistake with cut/copy and paste, remember that you can immediately click the Undo button.

You can also access the cut, copy, and paste commands from the pop-up menu. Select the cells to be moved or copied. Make sure the mouse pointer is somewhere over the selected cells; then click the context button to open the pop-up menu.

EXERCISE 5.4 | **MOVING AND COPYING CELLS**

Follow the steps below to alphabetize the employees by last name:

1. Select Collins' name, hours, rate, and gross pay.

2. Click the Cut button, choose Edit ➢ Cut, or select Cut from the pop-up menu to cut Collins' data.

3. Move the pointer to column A of the empty row between Chiu and Jones. Paste Collins' data into the worksheet by clicking the Paste button, choosing Edit ➢ Paste from the menu bar, or choosing Paste from the pop-up menu.

4. Move Barzona's data to the empty row between Azimi and Buckley.

5. Delete the extra empty rows, leaving one blank row between the data and the totals.

SECTION 5.5: WORKSHEET LAYOUT

Once you are comfortable with Excel, you'll create most of your worksheets from "scratch." You will need to determine where text and numbers should be entered, where totals are required, and how numerical data should be formatted. There are some general rules you should observe when setting up worksheets:

■ Titles and column headings should be easily understandable to people using the worksheet. Use standard, easily recognized abbreviations.

- Numbers should be formatted as simply as possible. If a column contains only whole numbers, don't include trailing zeros. If the values in a column are currency, choose either no places or two places after the decimal.

- Columns must be wide enough for the data contained in the column.

- Use empty rows and columns to separate headings and totals from ranges of data.

EXERCISE 5.5	CREATING A WORKSHEET

The Wildlife Federation sells T-shirts at three booths at the week-long Alberta Provincial Fair each August. Booths are located on the Midway, near the West Gate, and in the Zoological Park.

The sales of shirts at the Midway for the week included: 119 Canada Goose SS, 251 Moose LS, 183 Moose SS, 34 Buzzard LS, 10 Snow Tiger SS, and 227 Endangered Species SS T-shirts.

The West Gate booth sold 67 Canada Goose SS, 189 Moose LS, 94 Moose SS, 27 Snow Tiger SS, and 184 Endangered Species SS.

Sales at the Zoo Park were as follows: 154 Canada Goose SS, 373 Moose LS, 191 Moose SS, 59 Buzzard LS, 114 Snow Tiger SS, and 150 Endangered Species T-shirts.

In the *Wildlife Federation* workbook, create an *ALT Fair* worksheet to present the data on fair sales. Include a title, column headings, and totals for each shirt type and each booth. Save *Wildlife Federation* when you have finished and printed the worksheet.

What You Have Learned

Text and numbers can be aligned left, center, or right within a cell, or across two or more columns. You can adjust the width of columns to reflect the data entered in the column. You can make other layout changes by inserting or deleting rows or columns and moving or copying cells or ranges of cells.

Focus Questions

1. Why is proper worksheet layout important?

2. What is alignment?

3. When should column widths be adjusted?

4. Describe the steps necessary to delete the data from column B and retain the empty column.

5. How would you move a heading from cell A3 to B3?

6. What is the difference between move and copy?

7. What are some rules for worksheet layout?

Reinforcement Exercises

Exercise 1   In the *Wildlife Federation T-shirts* worksheet, center the worksheet title across the columns. Edit the cells in column A to change each occurrence of SS to short sleeve and LS to long sleeve. Adjust the widths of all the columns. Right-align the Quantity and Cost column headings. Print the worksheet; then save *Wildlife Federation*.

Exercise 2   Open the *Personal Worksheets* file. The budget is John Sinkford's personal budget for June, 1996. Add three rows to the top of *Budget*. Use the new rows 1 and 2 to create an appropriate worksheet title, centered across the columns.

Insert a row below the row for Other Income. In column A of the new row, enter the label Total Income. Add a column heading, Totals, for column F. Enter a label for Total Expense in the row following Misc. Income. Leave a blank row below Total Expense. In the row following, put the row heading Net Savings.

Use AutoSum to total Hardware and Other for each of the four weeks. Use AutoSum to total all expenses for each of the four weeks. In column F, use AutoSum to total Total Income and Total Expenses. In the Net Savings row, enter a formula in column B to subtract John's Total Expenses from Total Income. (Hint: the correct Net Savings is a negative number since John spent more than he made the first week in June.) Don't enter Net Savings formulas for the other columns. Adjust column widths as necessary before saving and printing the *Budget* worksheet.

Exercise 3   Activate the *Order Response* worksheet in the *Wildlife Federation* workbook. Adjust column widths so dates are easily legible. Align titles and column headings as appropriate. Print and save the worksheet.

Formatting Text and Characters

IN THIS SESSION you'll learn about the variety of tools Excel provides to enhance the readability and style of your worksheet: boldface, underline, and italics; font types and sizes; and borders and color. You'll also learn about the convenient Format Painter and AutoFormat tools. At the end of this session you will be able to:

- Apply bold, underline and italics to text and numbers
- Change fonts and font sizes
- Use borders
- Apply color to parts of your worksheet
- Use the Format Painter and AutoFormat to format more efficiently

■ **Vocabulary**

- AutoFormat
- bold
- border
- font
- font color
- font size
- Format Painter
- italics
- point
- TrueType font
- typeface

57

SECTION 6.1: BOLD, UNDERLINE, AND ITALICS

Worksheets, like word processor documents or database reports, are constructed so that information can be used and communicated to others. Just as correct alignment and formatting of numbers makes a worksheet easier to read, text formatting gives those who use your spreadsheets visual clues, making your worksheet more "user friendly." Typically, titles, headings, and totals will be set off from data. Boldfacing and/or italicizing text visually separates it from other nonenhanced text and numbers. **Bold** text is darker than regular text. *Italic* text appears to lean to the right.

The two worksheets in Figure 6.1 present identical information. The worksheet on the left, formatted with tools from this and prior sessions, is easier to understand. Formatting makes the worksheet more accessible and inviting.

Figure 6.1

Sample worksheets

Michigan: 1997-98			Michigan: 1997-98	
			Placement Decisions:	
Placement Decisions:			Area	Amount
			Statewide	4,000
Area		**Amount**	Metro Detroit	6,000
			Out-State	5,000
Statewide		4,000	Local North	1,500
Metro Detroit		6,000	Total Budget	16,500
Out-State		5,000		
Local North		1,500		
Total Budget		**16,500**		

It's easy to dismiss the importance of good formatting as just "glitz"—a criticism usually rendered by people unwilling to take the extra effort needed to make a worksheet more usable. (These same people, however, make purchasing decisions about cars, beverages, even underarm deodorants based in part on the influence of an advertising industry that spends billions of dollars a year to attract their attention.) You won't often have a huge budget to market the ideas contained in a worksheet. Attractive formatting can catch a user's eye and focus it on the data with a minor investment of your time.

To boldface, underline, or italicize worksheet contents, begin by selecting the range or ranges you wish to affect. Click the Bold, Underline, or Italics button on the Formatting toolbar.

| EXERCISE 6.1 | TO ADD BOLD AND ITALICS TO A WORKSHEET |

Open the *Unicorn Software* workbook.

1. **Select the cells you want to format.** In the *Payroll* worksheet, select rows 1 and 2.

2. **Click the Bold or Italics button.** Click the Bold button on the Formatting toolbar.

3. Select and bold the column headings.

4. Bold the row title for totals.

5. Bold all totals in the worksheet.

6. In the *Time Sheet* worksheet, italicize the title and bold all headings.

SECTION 6.2: USING FONTS

A **font** is a specification for how text will appear on your screen and in a printed document like a worksheet. Fonts have three attributes: typeface (also known simply as face), size and style. A **typeface** is a set of characters that share a common design. Although typeface is only one of a font's attributes, the term *font* is also commonly used to refer to typeface alone. Figure 6.2 illustrates various typefaces or fonts.

Figure 6.2
Examples of
typefaces

ALGERIAN
Arial
Brush Script MT
Courier New
Footlight MT Light
Times New Roman
⊕⌘■℔☊⌘■℔♦ (Wingdings)

Typefaces

Fonts like Times New Roman, Arial, and Courier New that can be read easily in large blocks are called **text fonts** or **type fonts**. Fonts that are attention-grabbing (but tedious to read in large quantities) are called **display fonts.** Display fonts like Algerian and Brush Script MT are used for special purposes: logos or titles. Don't use them for columns of numbers.

Type fonts can also be separated into two groups: monospaced and proportionally spaced fonts. In a **monospaced font**, every character is allocated the same amount of space. Since the letter "w" and the letter "i" are given the same amount of space, a lot of white space separates the letter "i" from the characters before and after it. Monospaced fonts like Courier are directly descended from fonts used on typewriters. **Proportionally spaced fonts** (for example, Times New Roman and the type font in this book) have the same amount of white space between characters, no matter how large the characters are. **TrueType fonts**, designated with the TT symbol in a list of fonts, are designed for both the printer and the screen, so what you see on screen is what you get on your print out.

There is nothing that labels a font as "Easy to read: use for columns of numbers." In general, avoid display fonts for numbers. Proportionally spaced fonts are easier to read than monospaced fonts. When in doubt, choose the Excel default font, Times New Roman, a proportionally spaced TrueType font.

EXERCISE 6.2 **TO CHANGE A FONT USING THE FORMATTING TOOLBAR**

1. **Select the cells to which you want to apply the new font.** In the Payroll worksheet, select the entire worksheet by clicking the button to the left of column A's header.

2. **Click on the down arrow next to the font name (probably New Times Roman) to bring up a list of fonts:**

3. **Scroll through the list and select a new font.** Find Arial or Courier New. Click on the font name. The new font is applied to the entire worksheet. If the change in font makes the text too wide for the cells, adjust the column widths.

■ Font Sizes

The size of a font is measured in points, the measuring system used by type-setters and others in the printing industry. One **point** is 1/72nd of an inch. Most text you read in a newspaper, book, or magazine will be 10 to 12 points. That translates to characters that are 1/7 to 1/6 inch high. If you want your title to be twice the size of your 12-point text, you would make your title 24-point. See Figure 6.3 for examples of font sizes.

Figure 6.3
Examples of
font sizes

This is 8 point

This is 10 point

This is 12 point

This is 16 point

This is 24 point

The actual size of an individual character is a combination of its point size and typeface. If you compare text in one face to text the same point size in another face, you may find a great deal of variation in size and readability. In some typefaces, 12-point text is illegible; in others, it is very large and easy to read. Although you can't really compare sizes between fonts, you can compare sizes within a font.

Most fonts are fully **scalable**. You can change font sizes by selecting a new size from the drop-down list in the Size control on the Formatting toolbar. If the size you want isn't listed, type the size you would like. For example, even though 13 point isn't normally listed, you can enter 13 for a 13-point font.

EXERCISE 6.3	TO CHANGE FONT SIZE

1. **Select the cells you want to format.** In the *Payroll* worksheet, select rows 1 and 2.

2. **Click on the down arrow next to font size to bring up a drop-down list of font sizes.**

3. **Select a font size from the list.** Choose 14.

4. In the *Time Sheet* worksheet, change the font size for the titles in rows 1 and 2 to 14.

5. Save *Unicorn Software* again.

SECTION 6.3: BORDERS, COLORS, AND FONT COLORS

Borders and colors provide further ways to draw interest to part or all of a worksheet. A **border** is a line drawn around part or all of a cell or group of cells. **Colors** can be used to highlight the background of part of a worksheet.

The Formatting toolbar also includes a button for **font color**. The default color is Automatic, so that Excel will use the color set for text in Windows 95, usually black. You can also specify one of sixteen colors (including black, just in case someone has changed the Windows 95 text color). If you use a color printer, the worksheet will be printed in color as it appears on the screen. If you print to a noncolor printer, the colored text and numbers will be printed in shades of gray.

Even if you don't have access to a color printer, you may still want to use color in worksheets that you or other users use frequently. Color adds interest and can be used to separate titles and totals from data. Color can also be used to distinguish between similar looking worksheets (the junior class budget has a blue title, senior a burgundy title). If you don't have a color printer, colors will be rendered in a shade of gray similar in intensity to the color; dark blue print on a burgundy background will be illegible.

The Border, Color, and Font Color buttons are found on the Formatting toolbar.

 All three buttons are combination buttons that include a drop-down list. Clicking the drop-down arrow attached to the button provides a **palette** or group of choices:

  There are borders that completely surround the selected cells, surround each cell individually, provide an underline, or double-underline the selected range. Selecting a border from the palette assigns it to the button and applies it to the selected cells. After you have assigned a border from the palette, the next time you click the Border button, the border displayed on the button will be applied to the selected cell(s). The Color and Font Color buttons also have attached palettes and are used in the same manner.

EXERCISE 6.4	ADDING BORDERS, COLORS, AND FONT COLORS

1. Highlight the title rows in *Payroll*.

2. Click the Font Color drop-down list. Select a dark blue from the color palette.

3. Highlight the cells containing the title in *Time Sheet*. Click the Color drop-down list. Select a yellow background for the title.

4. Select the last row of data (not totals). Apply a single underline border to separate the data from the totals.

If you have a lot of borders, colors, or font colors to apply, you can open any or all of the palettes as a separate window on your worksheet, as shown in Figure 6.4.

Figure 6.4

Palettes opened as windows

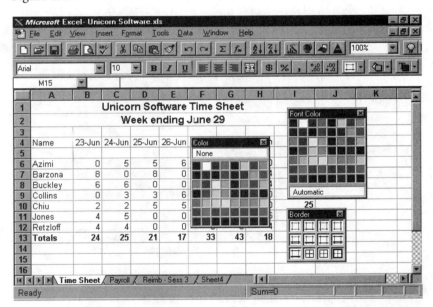

To open the border palette, click the Border button's drop-down arrow to open the palette. Release the mouse and point at the frame of the palette window. Drag the palette into the worksheet and release the mouse button. When you are done using the palette and want to close it, click the Close button on the palette window title bar.

TO OPEN A PALETTE WINDOW

1. Click the drop-down arrow on the Font Color button.

2. Drag the Font Color palette into the worksheet window.

3. Change the color of the column headings in the worksheet.

4. Click the Close button on the Font Color window to close the palette.

Number formats, fonts, alignments, and borders can all be set at one time in one location—the Format Cells dialog box. If you need to apply several formatting changes to a group of cells, you may find it easier to use the dialog box. After you have selected the cells to be formatted, choose Format ➢ Cells from the menu bar. The Font page of the Format Cells dialog box is shown in Figure 6.6. Click the page tabs to move from page to page and set the desired formats for the selected cells. When you are done, click OK to apply all the formats chosen to the selection. (Notice that some of the font names shown in Figure 6.5 are preceded with the "TT" TrueType symbol.)

Figure 6.5

The Fonts page of the Format Cells dialog box

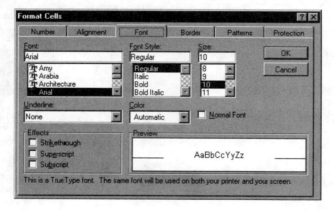

SECTION 6.4: USING THE FORMAT PAINTER

You've just changed the font, color, size, and numeric format for one column of numbers and want to format other columns the same way. You can use the Format Painter to copy the format to one or more cells or cell ranges. The Format Painter doesn't affect the contents of the cells, just the formatting.

To copy a format to another range of cells, begin by moving the cell pointer to a cell that already has the desired format—a source cell. Then click the Format Painter button on the Standard toolbar. The mouse pointer will include a picture of a paintbrush. Now, select the unformatted cell(s) you want formatted. When you release the mouse button, the format will be copied from the source cell to the cells you select, and the Format Painter will turn off.

If you know you want to format more than one cell range, *double-click* the Format Painter button. The Format Painter will remain on until you click its button again.

EXERCISE 6.6	TO USE THE FORMAT PAINTER

Activate the Payroll worksheet. Format Azimi's pay rate as follows: italics, gray background, burgundy font color.

1. **Place the cell pointer in the cell with the desired format.** Leave the cell pointer in the cell with Azimi's pay rate.

2. **Double-click the Format Painter button on the Formatting toolbar to copy the formatting in the current cell.**

3. **Select each of the cells you want to apply the copied format to.** Apply the format to all pay rates under $9 by clicking on each.

4. **Click again on the Format Painter button to turn format painting off.**

SECTION 6.5: AUTOFORMAT

Excel includes a number of "canned" formats that you can apply to a worksheet. The formats include formal business formats, colorful eye-catching layouts, and three-dimensional (3D) formats. AutoFormat can provide consistency in your worksheets. If you are in a rush, the predesigned formats allow you to create a professional look quickly.

Before AutoFormatting, select the cells to be formatted. This will probably include all the text and numbers in your worksheet. Then, choose Format ➢ AutoFormat from the menu bar. The AutoFormat dialog box, shown in Figure 6.6, includes choices of automatic formats. Clicking the Option button turns on the list of formats to apply. The first format, Simple, is selected. A worksheet in the Simple format is displayed in the Sample box.

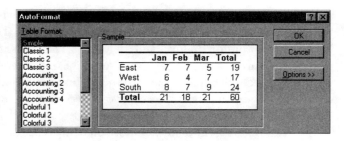

Figure 6.6
The AutoFormat
dialog box

To apply a format, click once to select the format from the Table Format list. If you wish, turn off parts of the format by deselecting some of the formats to apply. As you choose table formats and select/deselect format options, the sample will change to reflect your choices. When you are ready to apply the sample format to the selected area of your worksheet, click the OK button.

EXERCISE 6.7	**TO AUTOFORMAT A WORKSHEET**

1. **Select the worksheet or range you want to AutoFormat.** Select the occupied work area of the *Time Sheet* worksheet.

2. **From the menu bar, select Format ➢ AutoFormat.**

3. **Select a format from the list.** Select the List 3 format. Click OK.

4. **Save and print the worksheet.**

If the applied AutoFormat doesn't meet your expectations, click the Undo button to remove the format from your worksheet.

What You Have Learned

Bold, underline, italics, and font sizes and faces are tools for formatting both text and numbers in a worksheet. Borders and colors for fonts and cell backgrounds allow other types of visual distinction. Once you have formatted a cell, you can copy the format to other cells using the Format Painter. AutoFormat contains groups of formatting attributes that can be applied to an entire worksheet.

Focus Questions

1. Why is proper formatting important?

2. What are bold and italics typically used for in worksheets?

3. What is the difference between layout and formatting?

4. Why shouldn't you use a display font for numbers in a worksheet?

5. Describe the steps needed to change the font size for an entire worksheet to 14 point.

6. What steps would you use to copy the formats used in cell B7 to cells B8:B15?

Reinforcement Exercises

Exercise 1   Open the *Wildlife Federation* workbook. Apply formatting to the *T-shirts* worksheet to improve its appearance. Save and print the worksheet.

Exercise 2   Open *Personal Worksheets*. Using Font Color, Color, and Borders, format the *Budget* worksheet. Save and print the worksheet.

Exercise 3   Choose and apply an AutoFormat for the *Clearance* worksheet in the *Wildlife Federation* workbook. Save and print the worksheet.

Exercise 4   Activate the *Wildlife Federation Order Response* worksheet. Format titles and column headings. Apply a red font color to all the information for any orders that took more than five days to ship from the date the order was placed. Save and print the worksheet.

PART II

Advanced Worksheet Techniques

Printing in Excel

THE PRINT PREVIEW FEATURE allows you to see how a worksheet will look when printed. You can then modify print settings for the sheet to improve its appearance. Page Setup lets you change margins, center the worksheet on the page, and modify the headers and footers in your printed work. To eliminate typographical errors, you should check the spelling in your worksheet prior to printing. At the end of this session you will be able to:

- Preview a worksheet
- Change the print setup
- Select a printer
- Print one or more worksheets
- Use the Spelling tool to check spelling in a workbook

■ Vocabulary

- dpi
- footer
- gridlines
- header
- landscape
- margins
- orientation
- page setup
- placeholder
- portrait
- Print Area
- Print Preview
- scaling
- Spelling tool
- toggle

SECTION 7.1: PREVIEWING A WORKSHEET

Print Preview lets you see how a worksheet will be positioned on paper when printed. For example, using Print Preview you can determine whether the worksheet fits on one page. Print Preview saves paper and time. When you click the Print Preview button, the Preview window (see Figure 7.1) opens, displaying the current worksheet as it will appear when printed.

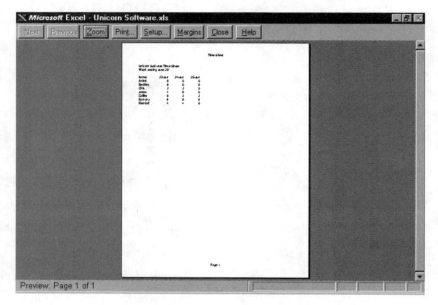

Figure 7.1
The Print Preview
window

The Print Preview window includes a toolbar. The Zoom button **toggles** (switches) between full-page view and a magnified view of the worksheet. The full-page view lets you see the general layout of the page; use the magnified view to look at specific details. If the worksheet is wider or longer than one page, the Previous and Next buttons let you move between pages. (If the worksheet fits on one page, these two buttons are dimmed out.)

You can't make changes to the worksheet in Print Preview. When you are done previewing the worksheet, click the Close button to close the Print Preview window and return to the worksheet.

EXERCISE 7.1	TO PREVIEW A WORKSHEET

Open the *Unicorn Software* workbook and choose the *Timesheet* worksheet.

1. Click the Print Preview button on the Standard toolbar.

2. Use Zoom to see the worksheet in magnified view.

3. When you have previewed the document, click the Close button to return to the worksheet.

SECTION 7.2: CHANGING PAGE SETUP

When you print a worksheet by clicking the Print button on the Standard toolbar, Excel prints using the default print settings, including settings for page orientation, margins, and headers and footers. **Page setup**, which includes these settings and others, determines how the printed worksheet will look. To change page setup, choose File ➢ Page Setup from the menu bar to open the Page Setup dialog box, shown in Figure 7.2. You can also open this dialog box from the Print Preview window by clicking the Setup button.

Figure 7.2
The Page Setup
dialog box

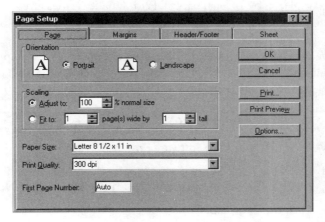

The Page Setup dialog box splits page layout into four tabbed pages:

Page: Lets you set paper size, print quality, page orientation, and scaling.

Margins: Lets you set margins or center the worksheet between the margins.

Header/Footer: Lets you choose existing headers and footers or create new ones.

Sheet: Lets you set the print area, repeat titles on multiple pages, add special print features, and specify print order for multiple-page worksheets.

■ Changing Page Settings

Orientation refers to the direction of print in relation to the paper it is printed on. **Portrait,** the default setting, places the short edge of the paper at the top and bottom. If your worksheet is wide, you might want to use **landscape** orientation, so that the long edge of the paper is at the top.

Scaling is used to reduce or enlarge the print. If you simply need to make the print larger (perhaps for a colleague who needs larger print), use the Adjust To control and choose a size greater than 100%. The Fit To control instructs Excel to reduce a worksheet that exceeds a specific number of pages so it will fit. For example, in previewing your worksheet you might see that the rightmost column prints by itself on a second page. Choose Fit To settings of 1 page wide by 1 page tall, and Excel will reduce the worksheet to fit.

Use the Paper Size control if you are using a different paper size (for example, 8½ by 14 legal paper). Print Quality is measured in **dpi**: dots per inch. Higher dpi means higher quality, but there is a trade-off: it takes longer to print at higher dpi. With a draft copy of a long worksheet, you might want to print at a lower dpi, and then change to a higher dpi to print your finished worksheet. The First Page Number control is used to set an initial page number other than 1.

EXERCISE 7.2   **TO CHANGE PAGE SETTINGS**

Make sure the *Unicorn Software Timesheet* is still open.

1. **Open the Page Setup dialog box by choosing File ➢ Page Setup or clicking the Setup button in the Print Preview window.**

2. **Click the Page tab.**

3. **Change settings for Orientation, Scaling, Paper Size, Print Quality, or First Page Number.** Change Orientation to Landscape. Click OK.

4. **Click the Print Preview button to view the changes.**

5. **Click Close to return to the worksheet.**

■ Headers and Footers

A **header** appears at the top of each page of a document. **Footers** are printed at the bottom of the page. By default, Excel places the sheet name (from the sheet tab) in the header, and the page number in the footer. If you don't want a header/footer, or want something other than the default, you must change it in the Header/Footer page of the Page Setup dialog box, shown in Figure 7.3.

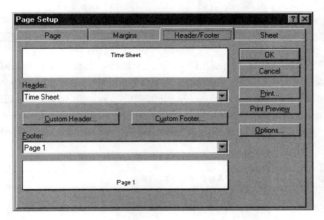

Figure 7.3
The Header/Footer page of the Page Setup dialog box

The current header and footer are displayed in the two preview panes. To choose no header or an existing header, click the Header drop-down list. No header (none) is at the top of the list, so you will have to move up the list to turn off the header. Choose a footer the same way, using the Footer drop-down control. When you select a new header (or footer), the preview pane will reflect the change.

You aren't limited to the headers and footers that are included in the list. To create a new header, click the Custom Header button to open the Header dialog box, shown in Figure 7.4. The header is separated into three sections: left, center, and right. Click in any section to place information in the header. You can enter text (like your name) or insert a **placeholder** for a page number, date, time, filename, or sheet (tab) name. When the file is printed, Excel will replace the placeholder with the actual page number, date, and so on.

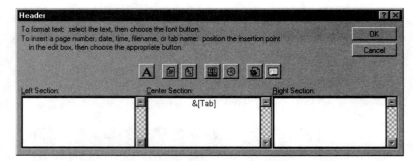

To format text, including placeholders, select the text and then click the Font button (with the letter "A") to open the Font dialog box. When you are finished creating the header, click OK to return to the Header/Footer page of the Page Setup dialog box. The new header will also be added to the list of headers available from the Header drop-down list. You create custom Footers the same way.

EXERCISE 7.3   **TO ADD HEADERS AND FOOTERS**

Select the *Unicorn Software Timesheet.*

1. **In the Page Setup dialog box, select the Header/Footer page.**

2. **Click the Header drop-down list and select a header, or click Custom Header to create a header.** Select (none) from the Header drop down.

3. **Click the Footer drop down and select a footer, or click Custom Footer to create a footer.** Create a custom footer. In the right pane, enter your name, press Enter, and insert a placeholder for the current date. Press Enter to return to the Page Setup dialog box.

4. **Choose Print Preview to view the header and footer changes.**

5. **Close the Print Preview window.**

■ Setting Margins

Margins are the empty spaces between the printed worksheet and the edges of the paper. The default margins are 1" top and bottom, and ¾" on each side. The Preview in the Margins page of the Page Setup dialog box (see Figure 7.5) displays the margins as dotted lines.

Figure 7.5
The Margins page
of the Page Setup
dialog box

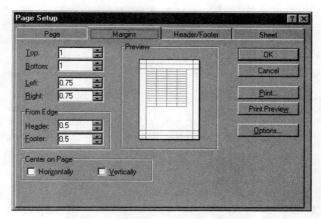

Headers and footers print in the top and bottom margins at the specified distance from the edge of the paper. Unless you have set headers and footers to None, the top and bottom margins need to be larger than the From Edge distance for headers and footers, or the headers and footers will print over part of the worksheet.

There is also a limit on side margins. Most printers require at least ¼" side margins. With smaller margins, some of your worksheet will not be printed. While the printer can physically handle a ¼" margin, your worksheet will definitely look crowded on the paper if you set your margins below ½".

Use the Center on Page control to center the printed worksheet horizontally between the side margins or vertically between the top and bottom margins. As you change settings on the Margins page, the Preview will change to reflect the new margin settings.

EXERCISE 7.4   **TO CHANGE MARGINS**

Open the *Unicorn Software Timesheet* if it is not already open.

1. **In the Page Setup dialog box, select the Margins page.**

2. **Using the spin box controls, set the top, bottom, left and right margins.** Change the left and right margins to 1".

3. **If you are using a header or footer, set the distance From Edge for the header and footer.** Leave the default From Edge settings.

4. **Use the Center on Page controls to center the printed worksheet.** Center the worksheet horizontally and vertically.

CONTINUES ON NEXT PAGE

5. **Click Print Preview to view the margin setup.**

6. **Close the Print Preview window.**

■ Changing Sheet Settings

The Sheet page (see Figure 7.6) contains settings that relate to individual worksheets. Settings changed in the Sheet page affect the current worksheet only.

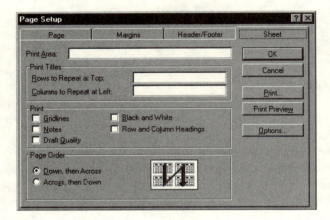

Figure 7.6
The Sheet page of
the Page Setup
dialog box

By default, Excel prints from the home cell (A1) to the last occupied cell in a worksheet. You can choose to print less than the entire worksheet. If, for example, you want to print only cells A1 through G20 (leaving out figures in columns H and I), you can enter *A1:G20* in the **Print Area** control. After clicking the Print area control, you can type the range in the control or select the range with the mouse. When you print, only A1:G20 will print. The Print Area setting will remain in effect until you set a new print area. If the print area includes noncontiguous cells, each contiguous range will print on a separate page.

You can also set the print area directly from the worksheet. Select the cells to be printed; then choose File ➤ Print Area ➤ Set Print Area from the menu bar. When you want to print the entire worksheet again, choose File ➤ Print Area ➤ Clear Print Area.

If the worksheet prints on more than one page, you might want to have titles for columns or rows print on each page of the printout. For example, the *Wildlife Federation Order Response* worksheet will eventually fill several pages as new orders are entered. The first two rows contain the worksheet title. Column headings are in row 4: Order, Placed, Shipped, Days. To begin each printed page with the titles and column headings, you would enter 1:4 in the Rows to Repeat at Top control. To include only the column headings, you would enter 4:4. (Excel requires a *range* of rows for this entry, even if it's only one row.)

If a printed worksheet is wider than one page, you may wish to repeat row headings by entering the range of columns to repeat. You can also enter the columns or rows using the mouse. To have columns A and B repeated on each page, click in the Columns to Repeat at Left control, then drag to select columns A and B in the worksheet. Excel will enter $A:$B in the control. (Ignore the dollar signs for now; you'll learn about them in Session 8.)

Gridlines are the lines that separate cells in the worksheet. If you don't want all your entries surrounded by little boxes, you can turn gridlines off. (Figure 7.1 shows an example of printing without gridlines.) You can switch to draft quality on this page (affecting only the current worksheet) instead of setting a lower dpi on the Page page, which changes the setup for the entire workbook. In draft mode, Excel prints the worksheet without gridlines or graphics. If you used colors in the worksheet but won't be printing on a color printer, click the Black and White control to speed up the print process.

If you turn on Row and Column Headings, the row and column numbers will be included in the printout. If you are trying to edit or find an error in a worksheet, this can be a useful feature. The Page Order setting establishes the order in which multiple-page worksheets are printed.

EXERCISE 7.5   **TO CHANGE SHEET SETTINGS**

1. With *Timesheet* open, **open the Sheet Page of the Page Setup dialog box.**

2. **Specify ranges for Print Area and rows and columns to be repeated.** In the *Timesheet* worksheet, enter A1:I4 (the titles) and A12 through I12 (Retzloff's information) as the print area. If you want to select the ranges and the dialog box is in the way, click and drag the dialog box title bar to move the dialog box out of the way. Remember to use the Ctrl key to select noncontiguous areas. To enter the ranges from the keyboard, separate the two ranges with a comma.

3. **Set rows 1–4 to repeat on the top of each page.**

CONTINUES ON NEXT PAGE

4. **Enter settings in the Print and Page Order sections.** Turn Gridlines on.

5. **Click Print Preview to view the changes.** Preview both pages of the worksheet.

6. **Close the Print Preview window.**

SECTION 7.3: CHANGING PRINT SETTINGS

The Page Setup dialog box lets you change the appearance of the printed worksheet. You use the Print dialog box, shown in Figure 7.7, to choose a printer and set a number of copies to be printed. Page Setup, Print Preview, and Print are all interrelated. If you click the Print button in Page Setup or Print Preview, the Print dialog box opens. (You can also open this dialog box from the File menu by choosing Print.) If you click the Preview button in this dialog box or in Page Setup, you open the Print Preview window. Many users begin the print process with Print Preview to get a quick look at the document, and then open either Setup or Print.

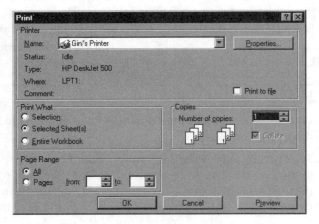

Figure 7.7

The Print dialog box

Click the Name drop-down list to open a list of all the printers connected to your computer (including any network printers or devices such as fax/modems).

In the Print What control, specify what part of the worksheet or workbook you want to print. Use the Number of Copies spin box to print more than one copy of the selection, worksheet, or workbook. Select specific pages to print in the Page Range control.

EXERCISE 7.6	TO CHANGE PRINT SETTINGS

Complete this exercise in the *Timesheet*.

1. Choose File ➢ Print to open the Print dialog box.

2. Select a printer from the Printer Name drop-down control.

3. Select what you wish to print. Choose Selected Sheet(s).

4. Set the number of copies (1) **using the Copies spin box.**

5. Accept All or specify a Page Range. Print from Page 2 to Page 2 to print Retzloff's information.

6. Click OK to print the specified worksheet or workbook and return to the worksheet.

7. Choose File ➢ Print Area ➢ Clear Print Area to reset the print area to the entire *Timesheet*.

SECTION 7.4: CHECKING WORKSHEET SPELLING

Misspelled words detract from the appearance of a worksheet; they also cast doubt on the accuracy of the numbers in the worksheet. Excel includes a **Spelling** program so you can ensure that the text in a worksheet is error-free. (Of course, you still need to examine all the numbers in a worksheet to verify that you've entered the data and formulas correctly.) To check spelling in a worksheet, move the cell pointer to A1 and click the Spelling button on the Standard toolbar, or choose Tools ➢ Spelling from the menu bar. Excel opens the Spelling dialog box (see Figure 7.8) and immediately begins checking the worksheet, comparing each word with a list of words in the Microsoft dictionary. When it encounters a word that is not included in the dictionary, Excel stops and asks you to take action.

Figure 7.8
The Spelling
dialog box

The word is selected in the worksheet and displayed in the Change To control in the dialog box. First, decide whether the word is spelled correctly. If it is correctly spelled, you can instruct Excel to:

Ignore: The word doesn't require correction and will only occur once in this worksheet.

Ignore All: The word is correctly spelled but appears more than once in the worksheet. This tells Excel not to stop at any other occurrences of the word in this Spelling check, speeding up Spelling.

Add: This is a word or proper name you will use frequently. Adding it to the dictionary will speed up spelling checks in the future.

If the word is incorrect, you can choose to:

Change: If the correct spelling is included in the Suggestions list, select it and click the Change button. If the correct spelling isn't shown, correct the spelling in the Change To control, and then click the Change button.

Change All: The same as Change, but applies the change to all occurrences of the word in this worksheet.

AutoCorrect: The word is incorrectly spelled, and it is a mistake you make frequently. If you add the word to the AutoCorrect list, Excel will correct this occurrence and automatically correct it as you type from now on.

If you are not in the home cell when you begin the spelling check, Excel will check from the cell pointer to the end of the worksheet, and then ask if it should go back to the top of the worksheet and finish checking. When the

Spelling check is complete, Excel will notify you that it has finished checking the entire sheet. The Spelling tool is a feature of all Microsoft Office products. Words you add to the dictionary or AutoCorrect are added to the common custom dictionary you use with Word, PowerPoint, and Access.

EXERCISE 7.7	TO CHECK SPELLING

1. **Move to the cell you want to check.** Here, move the cell pointer to cell A1 of the *Timesheet*.

2. **Click the Spelling button on the Standard toolbar.**

3. **Choose the appropriate action for each word Excel identifies that is not included in the dictionary.** Ignore proper names in the worksheet.

What You Have Learned

After you preview a worksheet, you can use Page Setup to modify page setup. The Print dialog box is used to specify a destination printer, number of copies, and specific pages or sheets to be printed. The spelling checker lets you eliminate typographical errors before you print.

Focus Questions

1. Why would you use Print Preview?

2. What are the default header and footer?

3. What is page orientation?

4. When would you use Fit To scaling?

5. How do margins and headers/footers interrelate?

6. What is the default print area?

7. What options can you choose for a misspelled word? When would you use each option?

8. What are the options for correctly spelled words that are not included in the dictionary?

Reinforcement Exercises

Exercise 1 In all worksheets in the *Wildlife Federation* workbook:

- Change the left and right margins to 1".

- Create a header with your name and the current date in the right section.

- Create a footer with the sheet name in the center.

- Check Spelling.

Turn the gridlines off on the *T-shirts* sheet. Preview and then print *T-shirts*.

Exercise 2 In the *Personal Worksheets* workbook, check spelling in John Sinkford's *Budget*. Preview and print John's budget with gridlines and row and column headings on.

Exercise 3 Check the spelling for all worksheets in the *Unicorn Software* workbook. For each worksheet, create a header that includes the current date in the left section, the Sheet name in the center section, and your name bolded in the right section. Change the footer to (none). Preview and then print the *Payroll* worksheet.

Streamlining Worksheet Construction

OW THAT YOU KNOW how to create, format, and print a worksheet, it's time to increase your efficiency. Excel includes tools that make it easy to do repetitive tasks like entering dates or formulas. Pop-up menus place formatting commands like Move and Copy at your fingertips (of the hand that holds the mouse). At the end of this session you will be able to:

- Enter labels and numbers using AutoFill
- Fill formulas
- Construct formulas using absolute cell references
- Move and copy cells using drag-and-drop
- Use pop-up menus to quickly copy cell contents

■ Vocabulary

- absolute reference
- AutoFill
- drag-and-drop
- fill handle
- mixed reference
- relative reference

83

SECTION 8.1: USING AUTOFILL TO ENTER LABELS AND NUMBERS

AutoFill is one of Excel's best time-saving features. Using AutoFill, you can quickly enter a series of labels, numbers, days, or dates. Before using AutoFill, we need to look closely at the relationship between the mouse pointer and the cell pointer.

Excel places a cell pointer around a selected cell or group of cells. The cell pointer is a thick border around the cell. There is a square box in the bottom right corner of the cell pointer. This box is called the **fill handle**.

Inside the worksheet window, the mouse pointer is shaped like a large plus sign (or "chubby cross"). When you click on a cell with the chubby cross pointer, the cell is selected. If you point to any part of the selected cell's border except the fill handle, the pointer changes shape to an arrow. You'll use the arrow pointer to move or copy the cell's contents (see Section 8.3). If you point at the fill handle, the mouse pointer changes to a thin plus sign ("skinny cross"), used in AutoFill. Whether you are using AutoFill, copying, moving, or selecting cells, it is important to point to the correct part of the cell or cell border. Minor changes in pointer position determine whether you are selecting, moving, or filling.

■ Automating Label Entry with AutoFill

Excel contains four lists of AutoFill entries: groups of labels that are used together in a particular sequence. If, for example, you enter the label *Monday* in a cell, you can use AutoFill to add *Tuesday, Wednesday, Thursday, Friday,* and so on. Enter *January*, and you can AutoFill the other months of the year. You can also enter *Mon* or *Jan* (or any other month or day abbreviation) and AutoFill the other days or months.

EXERCISE 8.1	TO AUTOFILL DATES OR DAYS

1. **Enter the name of the first day or month in a cell.** In a new worksheet in a new workbook, enter Jan in cell B2.

2. **Select the cell.** Select B2.

3. **Point to the cell's fill handle.** The mouse pointer will change shape to a skinny cross.

4. **Hold the left mouse button and point to the last cell you want labeled. Release the mouse button to fill the cells.** Move to cell G2; then release the mouse button.

> **5.** For practice using AutoFill, label cells A4:A10 with the days of the week, beginning with Monday. Fill cells B4:B15 with the months of the year, beginning with March and ending with February.

AutoFill can also be used to fill numbers. If, for example, you want to number a series of rows beginning with the number 101 and 102, you can have AutoFill number 103, 104, and so on. The trick is to establish a clear pattern for Excel to repeat. If you put the number 101 in cell D5, and then fill cells D6:D10, all the cells in D5:D10 will be filled with the number 101. One cell doesn't establish a clear sequence. It takes at least two cells to set a pattern. Enter 101 in D5, 102 in D6. Then select D5 *and* D6. Drag the fill handle down the column, and Excel will increment each filled number by one: 103, 104, 105…

You can fill even numbers (enter 2 and 4 to set the pattern), count by fives (5, 10), number beginning with a negative number or count backwards. There are only two limits to AutoFill: the growth between numbers in the pattern has to be additive (or linear), not exponential; and it must be constant. If you use 2, 4, and 8 (2^1, 2^2, and 2^3) as a fill pattern, Excel won't "make the leap" and put 16 (2^4) and 32 (2^5) in the next two cells. Similarly, you can't use a varying pattern like a Fibonacci series (1, 2, 3, 5, 8, 13). But when you need to fill a range with the same number or a simple series of numbers, AutoFill handles it efficiently.

EXERCISE 8.2	**TO FILL A RANGE WITH NUMBERS**

1. Enter the first number in the fill pattern. Enter *100* in cell C5.

2. If you want to increment or decrement the number, enter the next number in the series in the next cell. Enter *101* in cell C6.

3. Select the cell(s) that include the pattern. Select C5 and C6.

4. Point to the fill handle on the selected cell(s). Hold the left mouse button and drag the handle to the last cell you want to fill (C14) **before releasing the mouse button.**

5. To practice filling numbers, number cells D5:D14 with odd numbers beginning with 5. Fill cells E5:E10 with the number 100. Fill cells F5:F14 with the numbers 0 through −9.

6. Name the sheet *Fill*. Save the workbook as *Fill Practice*.

SECTION 8.2: USING AUTOFILL TO FILL FORMULAS

AutoFill is even more impressive with formulas. In Figure 8.1, AutoSum has been used to calculate total tree sales for the week ending December 2. The formula in B11 that adds the individual sales is =SUM(B6:B10). There is another way to look at the formula. From the perspective of cell B11, the formula instructs Excel to sum the block of numbers beginning with the number five rows up in the same column, and ending with the number one row up in the column. The same relationship would apply to the formula for the week of December 9. The formula would be the same, except that the column letters (B) in the original formula would have to be changed to C.

With the change in the column letter, the same formula also works in columns D, E, F, and G. **Relative** to (as viewed from the perspective of) the cells containing the formulas, these six formulas are identical. As the column that contains the SUM formula changes, the column portion of the cell address also needs to change.

Excel automatically adjusts relative cell references in formulas when you use AutoFill. If you grab the fill handle in cell B11 and move it to cell G11, the formula will be copied to each of the cells and adjusted so that the relationship between the cell containing the formula and the cells referenced in the formula is maintained.

EXERCISE 8.3	TO FILL FORMULAS

Begin the exercise by opening a new workbook. Create the worksheet shown below. Enter *2-Dec* and *9-Dec* to establish a pattern; then AutoFill the other column heading dates. Use AutoSum to create the formula in cell B11. Name the sheet *Dec Cut*.

	B11	▼	=SUM(B6:B10)			
	A	B	C	D	E	F	G
1	Traverse Tree Sales						
2	Cut Trees: December, 1997						
3							
4	Week Ending	2-Dec	9-Dec	16-Dec	23-Dec	30-Dec	Totals
5							
6	Scotch Pine	57	77	54	112	14	
7	Blue Spruce	33	59	71	66	9	
8	White Pine	114	136	191	83	0	
9	White Spruce	22	45	51	47	17	
10							
11	Totals	226					

> 1. **Click on the cell containing the formula.** Select B11.
>
> 2. **Using the fill handle, move to the last cell that you want to fill with the formula** (G11).
>
> 3. Create a formula in cell G6 to total Scotch Pine sales for the month. Fill the formula to cells G7:G9.
>
> 4. Save the workbook as *Traverse Tree Sales*.

■ Absolute Cell References

Traverse Tree Sales needs to know what percentage of sales was attributable to each type of cut tree. In Figure 8.1, a formula has been entered to divide the total number of Scotch Pines sold into the total trees sold (=G6/G11). The result (.2496…) was then formatted as a percentage (25%). This formula works well—until we use it to fill. The result of the fill in cells H7:H9 is not a number, but #DIV/0! This is an error message, saying that we tried to divide a number by zero (which always results in an error).

Figure 8.1

A worksheet with division-by-zero errors

H6		=G6/G11					
	A	**B**	**C**	**D**	**E**	**F**	**G**	**H**
1	Traverse Tree Sales							
2	Cut Trees: December, 1997							
3								
4	Week Enc	2-Dec	9-Dec	16-Dec	23-Dec	30-Dec	Totals	Percent
5								
6	Scotch Pir	57	77	54	112	14	314	25%
7	Blue Spruc	33	59	71	66	9	238	#DIV/0!
8	White Pine	114	136	191	83	0	524	#DIV/0!
9	White Spru	22	45	51	47	17	182	#DIV/0!
10								
11	Totals	226	317	367	308	40	1258	

The formula in H6 was =G6/G11. When it was AutoFilled to cell H7, Excel changed the formula to maintain the relationship between the cell with the formula and the cells referenced in the formula, just as it did with the totals you filled earlier. The formula in H7 was changed to =G7/G12. The problem is, there is no value in G12. We wanted G6 to change to G7, but didn't want G11 changed. The reference to G6 should be changed relative to the new location; the reference to G11 should be **absolute**—not changeable. Absolute cell references are preceded by dollar signs: =G6/$G$11. The dollar sign "locks in" the cell reference so Excel doesn't change it if you fill or copy the formula to another cell. The dollar sign in front of the G instructs Excel not to change the column; the dollar sign in front of the 11 locks in the row.

You create the absolute cell reference when you construct the original formula. (If you never intend to fill or copy the formula, you don't need to use absolutes. Remember, the original formula in H6 was fine.) If you are typing the formula, just precede the column and row addresses with a $. There is a special technique using the F4 key to change the cell reference to an absolute that you will see in Exercise 8.4.

EXERCISE 8.4	TO USE AN ABSOLUTE CELL REFERENCE

1. **Place the cell pointer where you want the answer to appear** (H6).

2. **Begin entering the formula.** Press the =.

3. Click on the first cell in the formula: G6.

4. Type the division symbol: /.

5. Click on the second cell in the formula: G11.

6. **After you select the cell that contains the absolute value** (in this case, G11), **press the F4 key once to add $ to the cell reference in the formula bar.** The formula will read =G6/$G$11.

7. **When the formula is complete, press Enter or click the green check mark.** Click the check mark.

8. Hold the left mouse button and drag the fill handle to H11 to copy the formula to cells H7:H11. Select each cell in turn and view its contents in the formula bar. Notice that the relative cell address (G6) changes in each formula, but the absolute cell address ($G$11) remains the same.

9. Delete the unnecessary entry in cell H10.

10. Select and format column H for Percent by clicking the Percent button on the Formatting toolbar. Save *Traverse Tree Sales*.

TIP

The F4 key also works when you are entering cell references from the keyboard.

You can also create a **mixed reference**, making part of a cell address absolute and part relative by locking in either the column or the row. The Absolute key (F4) is a four-way toggle. The first time you press it, it locks both the column and row: $G$11. Press again, and only the row is locked: G$11.

The third time you press, the column is locked: $G11. Press a fourth time, and both row and column are relative (unlocked): G11.

SECTION 8.3: USING DRAG-AND-DROP TO MOVE OR COPY CELLS

In Session 5 you learned to move or copy cells using cut, copy, and paste techniques. If you can see both the cells you want to copy or move and the destination for the cells, you might prefer to use **drag-and-drop** to move or copy. (When the source and destination are on different worksheets or different screens of the same worksheet, cutting or copying still works best.)

To move one or more cells, first select the cells. Then point to any part of the cell border except the fill handle. The mouse pointer will change shape to an arrow. Hold the mouse button, and drag the outline of the cell(s) to its new location. Release the mouse button to drop the cell(s) and complete the move.

To copy cells with drag-and-drop, hold the Ctrl key and the mouse button. A plus symbol will be added to the mouse pointer to show that you are making a copy. Drag the outline of the cells to the new location. Release first the mouse button, and then the Ctrl key.

TIP

There is an important difference between copying and moving cells that contain formulas. When you copy a formula, the formula changes relative to its new location. When you move a formula, it does not change.

EXERCISE 8.5	TO MOVE OR COPY WITH DRAG-AND-DROP

Begin by inserting a blank row in row 8 (between Blue Spruce and White Pine). You will be moving Scotch Pine to alphabetize the list.

1. **Select the cells to be moved or copied.** Select row 6: Scotch Pine.

2. **Move the mouse pointer to the cell pointer. The mouse pointer will become an arrow.**

3. **Hold the mouse button and drag the outline of the selected cells to the destination. If you want to copy the selection, hold the Ctrl key on the keyboard.**

4. **Move the outline to the empty row you created (row 8).**

CONTINUES ON NEXT PAGE

> **5.** Release the mouse button to complete the move. Release the Ctrl key to complete the copy.
>
> **6.** Delete the empty row (row 6).
>
> **7.** In Page Setup, create a header that includes your name and the current date.
>
> **8.** Save and print *Traverse Tree Sales*.

SECTION 8.4: EDITING WITH THE CONTEXT MENU

When you move the cell pointer out of the current screen display, it forces the screen to scroll. Windows products have built-in scroll acceleration. As you move to the edge of the screen, the screen scrolls quickly, making it appear that the mouse has suddenly picked up speed. This makes it difficult to use drag-and-drop if the source and destination for the cells aren't both visible on the screen. If, for example, you are moving cells from A5:A7 to J32, it is best to use cut-and-paste. After you have selected A5:A7 you can either choose the Cut button on the Standard toolbar, or right-click and choose Cut from the pop-up context menu, shown in Figure 8.2.

Figure 8.2

A context menu

You used the pop-up menu in Session 4 to format cells. Many of the Edit menu selections are also included in the context menu. Copy, Paste, Insert, Delete, and Clear are only a right-click away whenever you work in Excel.

What You Have Learned

You can use AutoFill to speed up the entry of text and numbers. Once you have created one correct formula, other formulas that have the same relationship can be automatically filled. Excel adjusts filled formulas relative to their new location. You can lock part of a formula by using the Absolute key (F4) when you construct the formula. This way it will not change cell references when copied to a new location. Using the mouse, you can use drag-and-drop to move or copy cell contents. Many of the edit functions, including copy and cut, can also be accessed by right-clicking to open the context menu.

Focus Questions

1. What kinds of text can be automatically entered with AutoFill?

2. What is the result if you use a single cell containing a number to AutoFill other cells?

3. How many cells are needed to establish a pattern for AutoFill?

4. What is a relative cell reference?

5. What kind of cell reference locks a cell address so it will not be changed in an AutoFill operation?

6. Name three ways you can move a cell to another location in the worksheet.

7. What edit functions are available from the context menu?

Reinforcement Exercises

Exercise 1   Open the *Wildlife Federation* workbook. In the *T-shirts* worksheet, insert three rows between the column headings and the T-shirt data. In column A of the second new row, enter the title Short Sleeve Shirts. Enter Long Sleeve Shirts in the third row. Insert rows, drag-and-drop, and delete to reorder the inventory so that all short sleeve T's are listed alphabetically under Short Sleeve Shirts, and all long sleeve T's are listed alphabetically under Long Sleeve Shirts. Save the workbook and print the worksheet.

Exercise 2   In the *Personal Worksheets* workbook, create the *Stocks* worksheet shown below. The column headings are centered and wrapped.

PERSONAL STOCK PORTFOLIO

Symbol	Date Purchased	Shares	Cost per share	Total Cost	Shares % of Portfolio	Cost % of Portfolio
IOMG	2/28/95	100	3.000	$ 300.00	18%	2%
MSFT	11/19/95	50	84.375	$ 4,218.75	9%	35%
MXTR	5/5/95	200	5.500	$ 1,100.00	36%	9%
SUNW	12/21/95	100	46.625	$ 4,662.50	18%	39%
VCI	3/8/96	100	17.500	$ 1,750.00	18%	15%
Totals		550		$ 12,031.25	100%	100%

Use the following information to create formulas for columns E, F, and G. Use AutoFill to duplicate formulas in the three columns.

■ Total Cost for each stock is the number of Shares multiplied by the Cost per share.

■ Shares % of Portfolio is the number of shares of each stock divided by the total number of shares for all stocks included in the portfolio.

■ Cost % of Portfolio is the total cost of the stock divided by the total cost of all stocks in the portfolio.

Name the worksheet *Stocks*. Create a header that includes your name, the sheet name, and today's date. Turn off the footer. Save the workbook and print the worksheet.

Exercise 3   Open *Payroll* sheet in the *Unicorn Software* workbook. Add the column headings Taxes and Net Pay in columns E and F. Each employee is taxed at 19%. Create and fill formulas for Taxes and Net Pay (Gross Pay minus Taxes). Format the worksheet, including a header with your name, the current date, and the sheet name. Print the worksheet before saving *Unicorn Software*.

Using Excel Functions

N SESSION 3 YOU used the SUM function (AutoSum) to add numbers. Excel includes hundreds of other functions that you can use to calculate results used in statistics, finance, engineering, math, and other fields. You can name specific cells or ranges, then include the name as the cell reference in a formula. At the end of this session you will be able to:

- Use the Function Wizard
- Use statistical functions to calculate average, minimum, and maximum
- Name cells and ranges
- Use basic financial functions

■ Vocabulary

- arguments
- average (AVERAGE)
- function
- function name
- Function Wizard
- maximum (MAX)
- minimum (MIN)
- named cell
- syntax

93

SECTION 9.1: UNDERSTANDING FUNCTIONS

Functions are structured, miniature programs that calculate a specific result. For example, Excel has a function to calculate loan payments, and another to calculate interest rate. Each function has a specific order or **syntax** that must be used for the function to work properly. Functions are formulas, so all functions begin with the equal sign (=). After the = is the **function name**, followed by one or more **arguments** separated by commas and enclosed in parentheses.

The SUM function you have used to add numbers (by clicking the AutoSum button on the Standard toolbar) provides a good example of the syntax of a function. If you use AutoSum to add the contents of cells B5:B10, the formula bar will read =SUM(B5:B10). SUM is the function name. The arguments (in parentheses) for SUM are the cells or range of cells to be added: B5:B10. Arguments for some functions are more specific: the current year, an interest rate, or the number of values in a range.

Excel has hundreds of functions, grouped into 11 categories:

- Database and List Management

- Date and Time

- DDE and External

- Engineering

- Financial

- Information

- Logical

- Lookup and Reference

- Math and Trigonometry

- Statistical

- Text

You don't have to learn all the functions; most users regularly utilize fewer than a dozen. (Many of the functions are specific to an industry or discipline. Non-engineers, for example, rarely use the engineering functions.)

■ Getting Help with Functions

Excel provides specific information on its features, including groups of functions and individual functions. Choose Help ➤ Microsoft Excel Help Topics from the menu bar to open the Help dialog box. Click the Index tab to use the Help Index, shown in Figure 9.1.

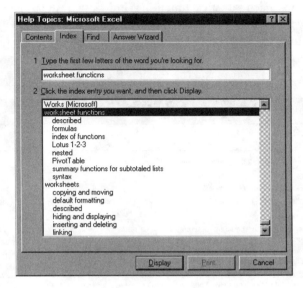

Figure 9.1
The Excel Help
Index

In the text box at the top of the page, enter *worksheet functions* as the topic you are looking for. The contents of the list box will change as Help searches for the information you request. Under *worksheet functions*, choose *index of functions* to see the categorized list of functions shown in Figure 9.2.

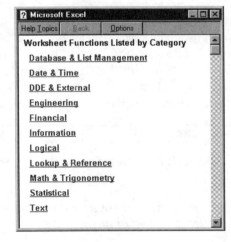

Figure 9.2
Worksheet
functions listed
by category

To see functions within a category, just click on the category name. For example, if you click on *Statistical,* Help will take you to the list of statistical functions. Each statistical function is individually documented. Click the name of any function to see more specific information, as shown in Figure 9.3. The Help topic explains the purpose of the function. The Syntax information defines the arguments required (or optional) by the function; Examples follow the Syntax section so you can see how the function works with specific values.

Figure 9.3
Help with the
AVERAGE function

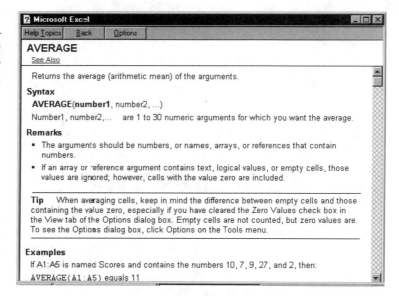

You can print any of the Help topics: the categorized list, the functions within a category, or help on a specific function. To print the current Help topic, click the topic's Options button, then choose Print Topic. To return to the Help Index at any time, click the Help Topics button. When you are done using Help, click the Close button on the Help title bar to return to Excel.

EXERCISE 9.1	TO GET HELP WITH A FUNCTION

1. Choose Help ➢ Microsoft Excel Help Topics from the menu bar.

2. Click on the Index tab.

3. Enter the name of the function or enter *worksheet functions* in the *Type the first few letters of the word you're looking for* control. Enter *worksheet functions.*

4. Click on the name of the function; if you entered *worksheet functions* in step 3, click on *index of functions*, then click the category in the index (Financial) that includes the function you want Help with. Click on the function name (PMT) in the category list.

5. Choose Options ➢ Print Topic to print the Help topic displayed on the screen.

6. When you are done using Help, click the Close button on the Help title bar.

TIP

If you want an overview of any part of Excel, the Contents section of Help provides general information arranged by subject area. Browsing the Help Contents is a good way to find out about features you aren't familiar with. When you are ready to use the new feature, return to the Index to search for specific information.

■ Using the Function Wizard

SUM is the only individual function included on the Standard toolbar. You can, however, access all the functions (including SUM) using the Function Wizard button. Before entering a function using the Function Wizard, make sure the cell where you want the results to be displayed is the active cell. Click the Function Wizard button on the Standard toolbar. (You can also enter an equal sign, and then click the Function button that appears in the formula bar.)

Figure 9.4
Selecting a function
in the Wizard

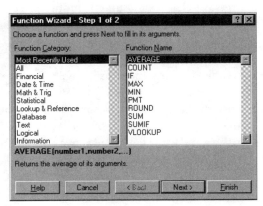

You select the function you want to use in the first step of the Function Wizard (see Figure 9.4). There are 12 categories listed. The first category, Recently Used Functions, contains the functions used last on your computer. Since most of us repeatedly use the same functions, the function you want will generally be on the list. If it is not, select a Category from the list, and then select the function from the Function list. (Clicking the Help button takes you directly to the Help topic for the selected function.) Click the Next button to continue to the next step of the Wizard, shown in Figure 9.5.

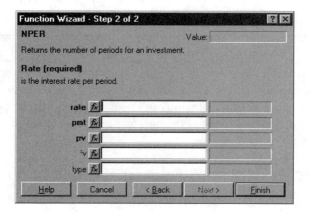

Figure 9.5

Entering function arguments

At the top of the Wizard, you'll see the definition of the function. Below are controls for each of the arguments required by the function. In Figure 9.5, the NPER function has three required arguments (*rate*, *pmt*, and *pv*) and two optional arguments (*fv* and *type*). Required arguments are displayed in bold. To enter an argument, click in the control for that argument. Then, either type the cell address (or range) or, using the mouse, select the cell or range of cells for the argument. If the Wizard window covers the cells you need to select, point to the Wizard title bar, hold the mouse button down, and drag the Wizard to a different location.

If there is more than one argument, as in Figure 9.5, continue to click the text box controls and enter each of the arguments. When you have entered all the arguments, click the Finish button to close the Function Wizard and enter the function in the active cell of the worksheet. As with any formula, the results of the function are displayed in the active cell; the function itself is displayed in the formula bar when the cell is active.

SECTION 9.2: USING BASIC STATISTICAL FUNCTIONS

The statistical functions include some of the most widely used Excel functions. If you want to determine an average price (AVERAGE), the number that occurs most frequently in a range (MODE), how many items are in a list (COUNT), or the largest (MAX) and smallest (MIN) values in a column, the statistical functions will meet your needs. There are also more advanced functions used to test how numbers are distributed, how a value is growing over time, or the validity and viability of statistical data. If your requirements for statistical analysis are complex, Excel is still a tool of choice.

EXERCISE 9.2   **USING STATISTICAL FUNCTIONS**

Open the *Traverse Tree Sales* workbook. In the *Dec Cut* worksheet, add the following labels: A12 and I4: Averages; A14: Maximum; A15: Minimum.

1. **Activate the cell where you want the result of the function to appear.** Move to B12.

2. **Click the Function Wizard button on the Standard toolbar.**

3. **Choose a function** (AVERAGE) **from the list in Step 1.**

4. **Click the Next button.**

5. **Enter or select the cell(s) for the required arguments.** Select B6:B9.

6. **Click Finish to close the Function Wizard and enter the formula.**

7. Use AutoFill to fill the formula to columns C through G.

8. Use the Function Wizard and AutoFill to calculate the maximum (MAX) and minimum (MIN) values in rows 14 and 15.

9. Use AutoFill and the Function Wizard to calculate the averages in column I. Be sure you don't include columns G or H in the average.

10. Preview and save *Traverse Tree Sales*.

SECTION 9.3: NAMING CELLS AND RANGES

You can apply a **name** to refer to a cell rather than using the cell's address as a reference. Using names has definite benefits:

■ Names are more descriptive than cell addresses.

■ When a cell moves, the name moves with it.

■ You can use a name in place of a cell or range address in a formula or function argument (see Exercise 9.5).

■ Formulas that use names add clarity to a worksheet. For example, =Hours*Rate is clearer than =B5*C5.

■ You can use one name to refer to an entire range of cells.

■ Names are easier to remember than addresses.

Names can be up to 255 characters long (also known as "too long") and can include letters, numbers, an underline, or period. You cannot use spaces, commas, exclamation points, or other special characters. The name must begin with either a letter or the underline character. Names cannot be valid cell addresses. (For example, A10 cannot be used as a name, since it is a cell address.) Names are not case-sensitive: GROSSPAY and grosspay are the same name. The traditional practice is to exclude spaces and to mix uppercase and lowercase, beginning each word within the name with an uppercase letter: GrossPay.

There are three ways to name a cell or range of cells. The easiest is to select the cell(s), then click in the Name box to the left of the formula bar. Click the box, not the drop-down arrow. Type the name for the cell(s); then press Enter.

EXERCISE 9.3	TO NAME A CELL USING THE NAME BOX

1. Select the cell(s) to be named. In *Traverse Tree Sales Dec Cut* worksheet, select the totals in column G.

2. Click the Name box.

3. Type a valid name for the cell(s) and press Enter. Name the range DecTotals.

You can quickly move to and select a named cell or range. Click the down-arrow in the Name box, and select the name from the list. Excel will move to the named range and select it.

You can name cells using the Define Name dialog box, shown in Figure 9.6. The dialog box displays a list of the names you are already using in any sheet in the workbook. This helps make sure you don't change a name already being used in another worksheet and lets you name cells consistently. Begin by selecting the cell(s) to be named. To open the dialog box, choose Insert ➤ Name ➤ Define. If there is a label near the selected cell(s), Excel will suggest a name. If you want to use a different name, simply type over it. Click OK to name the cells.

Figure 9.6

The Define Name dialog box

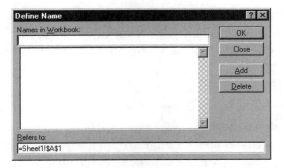

Use the Create Names dialog box (Figure 9.7) to apply existing labels to create a group of names. For example, the *Traverse Trees Dec Cut* worksheet has tree names in column A, and numbers of trees sold in columns B through F. The tree names in column A can be used to create names for the values in columns B through F. Begin by selecting both the labels to be used as names and the numbers to be named. Then choose Insert ➤ Name ➤ Create to open the Create Names dialog box.

Figure 9.7

The Create Names dialog box

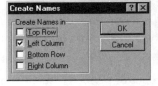

The labels are in the left column of the selection, so make sure Left Column is selected. Then click the OK button to close the dialog box and create names for each of the four rows. (If you want to see the names you have created, choose Insert ➤ Name ➤ Define to view the list of names used in the workbook or click the down-arrow next to the name box.

Excel edits labels as needed to make them valid names. If the label for a column or row contains spaces, Excel will replace the space with an underline: Blue_Spruce. Labels that begin with numbers are preceded by an underline: _2_Dec.

EXERCISE 9.4	TO CREATE NAMES

1. **Select the cells to be named and the cells that contain the labels to be used as names.** In the *Dec Cut* worksheet, select A4:F11.

2. **Choose Insert ➤ Name ➤ Create from the menu bar.**

3. **Select one or two name locations.** Select Top Row and Left Column.

4. **Click OK.**

5. Use the drop-down list in the Name box to select White_Pine, Dec Totals, and Scotch_Pine. Click anywhere in the worksheet to turn off the selection.

6. **Save the worksheet.**

Regardless of how you create a name, there is only one way to delete it. Choose Insert ➤ Name ➤ Define to open the Define Name dialog box (see Figure 9.6). Select the name to be deleted, and then click the Delete button.

SECTION 9.4: USING FINANCIAL FUNCTIONS

Excel has more than fifty built-in financial functions. Some of these functions are very useful, even if you don't work in the fields of accounting or finance. When you finance a purchase "on time," there are several variables that combine to determine your monthly payment: the amount you are financing, the interest rate, and the number of payments.

Monthly payment, amount, rate, and number of payments have a fixed relationship to each other. If you know any three, you can use Excel to calculate the fourth:

NPER calculates the number of periods (usually months);

PMT calculates the payment amount;

PV returns the present value for the amount financed; and

RATE returns the interest rate (usually expressed on an annual basis).

With these four functions, you can determine how expensive a car you can afford given the current interest rate, how many years it will take to pay off a student loan, or how many monthly payments you will need to finance a snowmobile or jet ski to keep each payment within your budget. The worksheet in Figure 9.8 uses named cells and calculates a monthly payment using the PMT function.

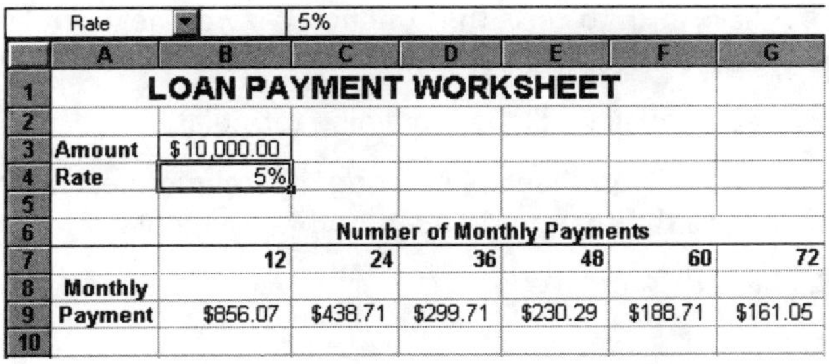

Figure 9.8

The Loan Payment worksheet

	Rate ▼		5%				
	A	B	C	D	E	F	G
1	LOAN PAYMENT WORKSHEET						
2							
3	Amount	$10,000.00					
4	Rate	5%					
5							
6			Number of Monthly Payments				
7		12	24	36	48	60	72
8	Monthly						
9	Payment	$856.07	$438.71	$299.71	$230.29	$188.71	$161.05
10							

EXERCISE 9.5   **CREATING THE LOAN PAYMENT WORKSHEET**

Open *Personal Worksheets*. Name a blank worksheet *Loan Pmt*.

1. Enter the labels as shown in Figure 9.8. Add borders and other font formatting as shown. Format B3 for currency with two decimal places, and B4 for percent.

2. Select cells A3:B4. Choose Insert ➤ Name ➤ Create from the menu bar. Choose Left Column and click OK to name the Amount and Rate cells.

3. Move to cell B9.

4. Click the Function Wizard button on the Standard toolbar.

5. Choose PMT from the list of Financial functions, then click Next. The PMT function has three required arguments that you will be entering in Steps 6, 7, and 8. (You can click the Help button to read more about this function before proceeding. If you do, close Help when you are finished to return to the Function Wizard.)

6. In the Rate control, enter the monthly interest rate. The rate entered in B4 will be an annual interest rate, so you need to divide it by the 12 months in a year. Either type *Rate/12* or click the Name box down-arrow, select Rate from the drop-down list, and type */12*.

CONTINUES ON NEXT PAGE

7. Click in the NPER control, then select cell B7.

8. Click in the PV control. The amount entered as a loan amount in cell B3 will be entered as a positive number. The amount is, however, really negative since it is money borrowed. Type a minus sign (−), and then either type *Amount* or choose it from the Name drop-down list.

9. Click Finish to close the Function Wizard. The formula in cell B9 will read *=PMT(Rate/12,B7, −Amount)*.

10. Use AutoFill to fill the remaining formulas.

11. Test the worksheet by entering different interest rates and amounts. Notice the changes in the monthly payments.

12. Save *Personal Worksheets*.

Excel includes a wealth of functions. Spend some time browsing Help for categories and types of functions so you can find specific functions when you need to use them.

What You Have Learned

Functions are programs that perform calculations. Excel includes 11 categories of functions for you to use. Each function has specific arguments that are required to complete the calculation. You can name cells or ranges and use the names later in functions or other formulas. The Function Wizard walks you through creating formulas using a function.

Focus Questions

1. What is a function?

2. What is a cell or range name?

3. What are some of the advantages of using names rather than cell addresses?

4. What is the general syntax for a function?

5. What is an argument?

Reinforcement Exercises

Exercise 1   Open *Wildlife Federation*. In the *T-Shirts* worksheet, add a row label for Average under the Totals row. Use Create Names to name the four columns. Using names and the Function Wizard, calculate averages for Quantity, Cost, and Total. Save the workbook.

Exercise 2   Open *Personal Worksheets*. Activate the *Stocks* worksheet. Using the labels in column A and the column headings, create names for values in columns A–G. Add a label for Averages below the Totals row. Using the Function Wizard and the Name box, calculate averages for Shares, Cost per Share, and Total Cost. Print and save the worksheet.

Exercise 3   Open *Unicorn Software*. In *Time Sheet*, leave a blank row under the Totals row and add labels for Average, Lowest, and Highest in column A. Use the Function Wizard and AutoFill to calculate AVERAGE, MIN, and MAX for each day. Format the results. Print and save the worksheet.

Exercise 4   In the *Wildlife Federation* workbook, open the *Order Response* worksheet. Calculate the average number of days orders take to be shipped. Format the result. Print and save the worksheet.

PART III

Creating Charts and Managing Data

Using Charts to Express Information Graphically

Vocabulary

- bar chart
- chart
- Chart Wizard
- column chart
- data points
- data series
- handles
- legend
- pie chart
- series chart
- X-axis
- Y-axis
- Z-axis

T'S BEEN SAID THAT a picture is worth a thousand words. It is certainly true that many people prefer pictures to numbers. By presenting numerical information in a chart, you make numbers friendlier and more accessible. In this session, you will learn how to create basic charts in Excel. Session 11 focuses on special formatting techniques for charts. At the end of this session you will be able to:

- Choose an appropriate chart type
- Select data for a chart
- Create a chart using the Chart Wizard
- Add titles and labels to a chart
- Print a chart as part of a worksheet
- Print charts separately

SECTION 10.1: USING CHARTS TO PRESENT DATA

Charts are graphical representations of numeric data. Charts used to be called "graphs"; now, the term "graphic" is used to mean any picture, including charts. Charts make it easier for users to compare and understand numbers, so they have become a popular way to present numerical data.

Every chart tells a story. Stories can be simple: "Look at how our sales have increased" or complex: "This is how our overhead costs relate to the price of our product." Whether simple or complex, the story should be readily understandable. If you can't understand what a chart means, it isn't a good chart.

Excel includes three basic types of charts. Each type is used for a different purpose–to tell a different kind of story. Before you begin charting, there are some fundamentals you need to understand so you can create excellent graphical representations of your data.

Charts are constructed with **data points**—individual numbers in a worksheet and **data series**— groups of related data points within a column or row. In the *Traverse Tree Sales Dec Cut* worksheet (see Figure 10.1), each number is a data point. There are many possible sets of data series in this worksheet: one set includes a data series for each of the four types of trees sold; each data series is a row. Another set includes a data series for each week in December; each data series in this set falls in a column. You could also have a single data series of the values in the Totals column or the Totals row.

Figure 10.1

The Dec Cut Trees worksheet

Traverse Tree Sales							
Cut Trees: December, 1997							
Week Ending	**2-Dec**	**9-Dec**	**16-Dec**	**23-Dec**	**30-Dec**	**Totals**	**Percent**
Blue Spruce	33	59	71	66	9	238	19%
Scotch Pine	57	77	54	112	14	314	25%
White Pine	114	136	191	83	0	524	42%
White Spruce	22	45	51	47	17	182	14%
Totals	226	317	367	308	40	1258	100%

SECTION 10.2: PIE CHARTS

Use **pie charts** (see Figure 10.2) to show the relationships between pieces of an entity. The implication is that the pie includes *all* of something: all the office expenses, all income, all trees sold the first week in December, all Scotch Pines sold in December. The pie chart isn't appropriate for illustrating *some* expenses, *some* income, etcetera.

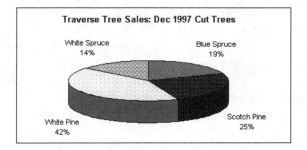

Figure 10.2

A pie chart from the *Cut Trees* worksheet

Pie charts almost always show relationships at a fixed point in time—the end of the year, a specific month, day, or week. It is unusual (but not impossible) for a pie chart to include more than one time frame. For example, you could chart Blue Spruce sales for all of December, including each week as a separate data point. But most pie charts represent a specific point in time.

A pie chart can only include one data series. When you create a pie chart, Excel totals the data points in the series, then divides the value of each data point into the series total to determine how large each data point's pie slice should be. Don't include a total from the worksheet as a data point; this doubles the total Excel calculates, resulting in a pie chart with one large slice (50% of the pie), as shown in Figure 10.3.

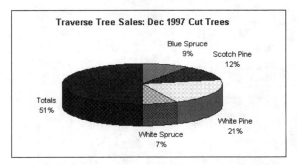

Figure 10.3

An incorrect Cut Trees chart

■ Selecting Data for a Pie Chart

Begin the charting process by selecting the data to be used in the chart. Remember that you can hold the Ctrl key to select noncontiguous ranges of data. Make sure that the ranges you select are symmetrical: if you select four labels in rows 9–12 of column A, select four data points that are in the same rows.

■ Using the Chart Wizard

Excel's Chart Wizard walks you through the process of creating a chart. Select the numbers and labels to include in the chart, then click the Chart Wizard button on the Standard toolbar. The mouse pointer will change to a set of crosshairs with a chart attached. The words *Drag in document to create chart* appear on the status bar. You will be dragging to construct a temporary location for the chart you create. The chart can be moved or enlarged after it is created, so the size and location aren't vital. Move the mouse pointer into the upper-left corner of the worksheet. Hold the mouse button down, and drag to the right and down to create an outline about the size of an index card. Release the mouse button to open the Chart Wizard.

The first step of the Chart Wizard lets you verify that you selected the correct cells. If you did not, Cancel the Chart Wizard, select the correct cells, and click the Chart Wizard button again. Click Next to continue.

Select a chart type in the second step (see Figure 10.4). There are two types of pie charts, which differ only in appearance: Pies and 3-D Pies. Pies are two-dimensional flat circles: a top view of a pie. 3-D pies appear to be tipped on edge, giving them a three-dimensional look. Other chart types are discussed later in this session. Click Next to continue.

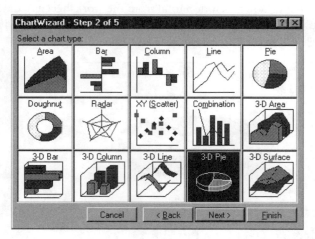

Figure 10.4
Selecting a
chart type

In the third step, shown in Figure 10.5, select a style for the chart. Style samples that include letters (A,B,C) will include the labels next to the pie slices. Samples that include a percent sign will print the size of each pie slice as a percentage of the whole.

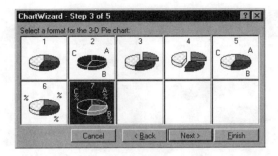

Figure 10.5
Data series
formatting

Excel now has enough information to provide a sample of your chart in step 4, shown in Figure 10.6. This step includes settings assumed by Excel; you need to double-check that they are correct. (If the settings are incorrect, pie slices will be missing or there will be no slices at all in the sample—just one big pie.) If you selected the correct data but the sample is incorrect, this is the only place to fix it. The data series can be either a row or a column. Based on this setting, Excel needs to know how many columns or rows are used for labels, and whether you selected one or more rows for a chart title. As you change settings in this step, the sample will change to reflect the new settings. When the sample has the correct number of slices, click Next to continue.

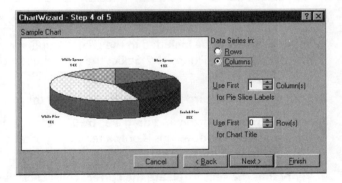

Figure 10.6
Verifying chart
settings

In the final step (see Figure 10.7), you can add a legend and chart title. (Pie charts have no axes, so you can't add axis titles.) A **legend** is a guide to let users relate colors and patterns to labels. If the chart formatting includes labels already, you don't need to add a legend. If you didn't include labels around the pie slices, you must include a legend or your readers won't know what each slice represents.

Figure 10.7
Adding a legend
and title

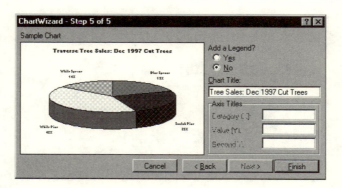

Every chart must have a title. The title provides information that is not already included in the graphical portion of the chart. The chart's picture, legend, and title should, taken together, answer any user questions about the timing, location, or contents of the chart. In Figure 10.2, the title *Traverse Tree Sales: Dec 1997 Cut Trees* places the chart in time (Dec 1997) and location (Traverse Tree Sales). After you have entered a title, click the Finish button to place the chart in the worksheet.

EXERCISE 10.1   **TO CREATE A CHART USING THE CHART WIZARD**

Open the *Traverse Tree Sales* workbook. Activate the *Dec Cut* worksheet.

1. Select the cells to be included in the chart. Your first chart will be the pie chart shown in Figure 10.2. Select the four labels in cells A6:A9, then hold the Ctrl key and select the total sales in G6:G9.

2. Click the Chart Wizard button on the Standard toolbar.

3. Hold the mouse button and drag a 3" by 5" rectangle for the chart in the worksheet window. This is only a temporary location for the chart. You'll be moving the finished chart later in this session.

4. Verify that the cells listed are the correct cells. Click Next.

5. Choose a chart type from the samples. Select a 3-D Pie. **Click Next.**

6. Choose a chart style from the samples shown. Choose type 6, which includes percentages but not labels. **Click Next.**

7. **Look at the sample and verify that there is a slice for each data point. If there are no slices, change the Rows/Columns setting for the data series. If there are not enough slices, check to see how many columns or rows Excel has allocated for labels and the chart title. When settings are correct, the sample will include a slice for each data point.** The data series you selected is in a column. The first column selected is labels, not data points. No rows were selected for a chart title. **Click Next.**

8. **Choose whether or not to include a legend.** (Yes, you want one.) **Click in the Chart Title text box and enter a title for the chart.** Type *Traverse Tree Sales: Dec 1997 Cut Trees.*

9. **Click Finish.**

■ **Moving and Sizing a Chart**

To see how the worksheet and chart will appear when printed, click the Print Preview button. (There is another reason to preview: after you print or preview, Excel marks the page breaks with a dotted line. This lets you know where each printed page of the worksheet starts and ends.) You will probably want to move or resize the chart. It may cover part of the worksheet. Or, if the chart isn't large enough, some of its text (titles or labels) may not be displayed. Even if you had dragged a larger space initially, it would still probably need some tweaking, which is why it's easiest to create the chart in a relatively small space, then adjust the size and location.

Clicking once on the chart selects it. A selected chart has square boxes on the corners and each side called **handles**. (To return to the worksheet, click once on part of the worksheet that isn't covered by the chart.) You can move or size any chart that is selected. If you double-click on the chart, you activate it for editing. An activated chart has a fuzzy border with handles. To turn off activation, click once in the worksheet. (You'll learn more about activating and editing charts in Session 11.)

You need to move the chart so the worksheet is visible, and size the chart so the legend and titles aren't cut off. Once the chart is selected, you can move it by pointing to the center of the chart, holding the mouse button down, and dragging the chart to its new location. If any part of the chart crosses the dotted lines that mark the page breaks, the chart will be cut off and the remainder will print on another page. If you want the chart to print on a separate page, drag the chart past a page break.

To change the chart's size, move the mouse pointer to one of the chart's handles. Press the mouse button and drag the handle to stretch or shrink the chart. Handles on the sides of the chart change the size in one direction (width or height). To increase width and height in proportion, hold Shift and use a corner handle.

EXERCISE 10.2	TO MOVE AND SIZE A CHART

1. Click once on the chart to select it.

2. To move the selected chart, point to the center of the chart. Hold the mouse button and drag the outline of the chart to its new location. Release the mouse button to drop the outline and move the chart. Move the chart below row 15 of the worksheet.

3. To size the chart, move the mouse pointer to one of the handles. Hold the mouse button and drag the handle to change the size of the chart. Use the handle in the lower-right corner of the chart. Size the chart so it is clear but does not extend beyond the boundaries of the page.

SECTION 10.3: SERIES CHARTS

In a **series chart**, you can chart multiple data series. This lets you compare more than one group of data points. Series charts are open-ended: there is no requirement that the data shown is all the data included in an entity. There are several types of series charts. You can give the same set of data a very different look by simply changing the chart type.

Line and Area Charts

The chart shown in Figure 10.8 is a type of series chart called a **line chart**. It shows the relationship between sales for each type of tree during the five weeks in December. Each tree is an individual data series contained in a row of the worksheet. Line charts are available in 2-D (as shown) or in a 3-D version that is sometimes called a ribbon chart. An area chart is a line chart with the area below the line filled. Line charts and area charts are typically used to show one or more variables (sales, income, price) changing over time.

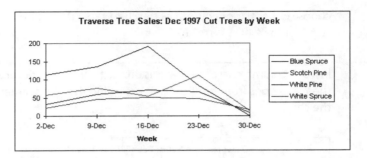

Figure 10.8

A line chart

■ Column and Bar Charts

Figure 10.9 shows the same information presented as a **bar chart**. The bars give added substance to the chart. In the line chart (Figure 10.8), what the reader notices is the trend up or down in each line and the gaps between the lines. The bar chart makes sales for each tree seem more substantial, but also makes the difference in sales between each type even clearer.

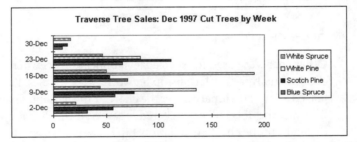

Figure 10.9

A bar chart

Most two-dimensional series charts share a common layout. The horizontal line is called the **X-axis**, and the vertical line is the **Y-axis** (the same X- and Y-axes you may have learned about in an algebra class when plotting data points). In a bar chart, however, the axes are turned 90 degrees so the X-axis is on the left side.

Column charts are the same as bar charts, but with the X-axis at the bottom. There are three-dimensional varieties of bar and column charts, which add depth to the regular chart. Excel also offers another style of bar and column chart—the stacked 3-D column chart, shown in Figure 10.10 (another representation of the same data used in Figures 10.8 and 10.9). In a stacked chart, parallel data points in each data series are stacked on top of each other. Stacking adds another dimension to the chart, since it allows the user to compare sales between as well as within time periods. To create a stacked chart, choose either bar or column as the chart type; then choose a stacked style in step 3 of the Chart Wizard.

TIP

In a 3-D column chart, the X-axis is on the bottom. The vertical axis is the Z-axis; the Y-axis goes from front to back, providing the "third dimensional" depth in the chart.

Figure 10.10

A stacked 3-D column chart

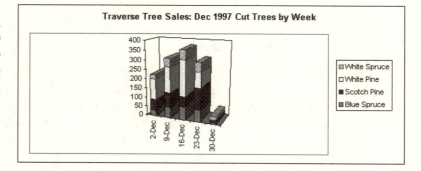

■ Other Charts

Other charts are used for specialized applications. Scatter charts are used to check visually for a relationship between two variables. Each data point is displayed as an individual dot on the chart. If the variables have a strong relationship, the dots will be clustered together. If the dots are scattered randomly throughout the chart, the relationship between the variables is weak or nonexistent. Scatter charts are widely used in the social sciences and in product testing and marketing.

Donuts are similar to pie charts, but can include more than one data series. Radar charts are series charts, but the Y-axis has been condensed to a single center point. Higher-value data points are located farther from the center point. Both donuts and radar charts are used more in Europe and Asia than in North America.

Surface charts are similar to topographical maps or color weather maps. Data points with similar values share a color or fill pattern.

Combination charts combine two types of series charts: a line and a column or area and a bar. Combination charts are useful when you want to show actual values in comparison to a standard: actual test scores compared to the average test score, departmental sales and corporate sales targets.

EXERCISE 10.3   **CREATING A SERIES CHART**

Open the *Traverse Tree Sales* workbook if it is not already open, and activate the *Dec Cut* worksheet.

1. **Select the cells to be included in the chart.** Select A4:F4 and A6:F9 (column headings, labels, and data points).

2. **Click the Chart Wizard button on the Standard toolbar. Hold the mouse button and drag a rectangle for the chart in the worksheet window.**

3. **Verify that the cells listed are the correct cells. Click Next.**

4. **Choose a chart type from the samples.** Select 3-D column. **Click Next.**

5. **Choose a chart style from the samples shown.** Choose type 2, the stacked column chart. **Click Next.**

6. **Look at the sample and verify that there is a column for each data point.** Use the first row for X-axis labels. Use the first column for legend text. Change the data series from Rows to Columns, and note the effect on the Chart Wizard sample. Change back to Rows.

7. **Click Next.**

8. **Choose whether or not to include a legend.** (Yes, you want one.) **Click in the Chart Title text box and enter a title for the chart. Add axis titles if you wish.** Title the chart *Traverse Tree Sales: Dec 1997 Cut Trees*. Do not include axis titles.

9. **Click Finish.**

10. For more practice, move the chart onto a new page, below the pie chart you created in Exercise 10.1. Size the chart so it looks good.

11. Preview the worksheet and charts.

12. Save *Traverse Tree Sales*.

SECTION 10.4: PRINTING CHARTS

Charts are separate graphic objects that are included in, and print as part of, a worksheet. You can also print charts separately. To print a chart by itself, double-click on the chart to activate it. Then select Print Preview to preview the chart. The chart only will be presented in landscape mode on a full page. Click Print to print the chart.

When a chart is not activated (when either the chart or part of the worksheet is selected), the worksheet including charts will print. When a chart is activated, the chart alone prints.

TIP

Remember that you single-click to select a chart, and double-click to activate it.

EXERCISE 10.4	TO PRINT A CHART

1. **Activate the chart you want to print.** Double-click the *Traverse Tree Sales* Pie Chart.

2. **Preview, then click Print to print the activated chart.**

What You Have Learned

You create charts to present numbers in a graphic form that is easy to understand. There are three basic types of charts. Pie charts are limited to one data series. Series charts can encompass multiple data series. Other charts are used for special purposes. The Chart Wizard helps you create charts. Charts can be moved and resized after they have been created. A chart can be printed as part of a worksheet or separately.

Focus Questions

1. What is a chart?

2. What is the difference between a data point and a data series?

3. What are pie charts typically used for?

4. Name and describe three types of series charts.

5. How do you print a worksheet and the charts embedded in the worksheet?

6. How do you print a chart without printing the chart's worksheet?

Reinforcement Exercises

Exercise 1   Open the *Wildlife Federation* workbook. Create a pie chart showing the number of T-shirts of each type in stock. Include a title and either labels or a legend. Position and size the chart on the worksheet. Save and print the worksheet and chart.

Exercise 2   Open the *Personal Worksheets* workbook. Using John Sinkford's budget, create a line chart comparing Total Income to Total Expense for the four weeks in June. Include a title, X-axis labels, and a legend. Position and size the chart. Save the worksheet. Print the line chart without the worksheet.

Exercise 3   Use the *Payroll* worksheet in the *Unicorn Software* workbook to create a bar chart showing the Gross Pay for each employee. Include a title and appropriate labels. Position and size the chart. Save and print the worksheet.

Exercise 4   Use the *Time Sheet* worksheet to create a 3-D pie chart showing the Total Hours worked by each Unicorn Software employee the week ending June 29. Title and label the chart, then position and size it within the worksheet. Save and print the worksheet.

PROJECT A: PERSONAL BUDGET

For this project, you will create a personal or household budget like John Sinkford's budget in the *Personal Worksheets* workbook. You'll illustrate the budget with charts.

Gathering Information

Gather information on your personal or household income and expenses. Pay stubs, check registers, money order receipts, and similar records are useful in this process. You will need at least three columns of data for your charts to be meaningful. John pays expenses and receives income every week, so a month of information will yield four or five columns of data, depending on the number of paydays in a specific month.

- If, like John, you receive income and/or pay expenses every week, gather one month (four or five weeks) of income and expense information.

- If you receive income and/or pay expenses twice a month or every other week, collect two consecutive months of income and expense information.

- If you receive income and/or pay expenses monthly, collect three consecutive months of income and expense information.

Organize the income and expense information you have gathered. The budget you construct in this project becomes more useful as the accuracy of your gathered data increases.

Try to track down expenses and income wherever feasible. If you cannot specifically account for all expenses, include a Miscellaneous Expense category when you construct the worksheet.

Creating the Worksheet

In a new workbook, create a *Project A* worksheet. See John Sinkford's *Budget* (Session 2, Figure 2.11) for ideas on worksheet layout. Include your name and the time periods encompassed by the worksheet in the worksheet title. Include column and row totals. Use appropriate formats for the numbers and text in the worksheet. Save the workbook as *Excel Projects*.

Creating the Charts

Create two charts: a pie chart to illustrate total expenses, and a series chart to compare total income to total expense. Both charts must include chart titles, labels, and legends as needed.

Printing

Move both charts to a page other than the page(s) used by the data in the *Project A* worksheet. Place your name and the current date in the worksheet header. Change the footer to (none). Turn off gridlines. If the worksheet is wider than one page, change page orientation to landscape and change the scaling to fit the new page width. Print the worksheet, and print each chart as a separate page.

PROJECT B: CMC RECORDING STUDIOS: FORMULAS AND CHARTS

For this project, you will create a statement of income and expenses for CMC Recording Studios. The information in the statement will be illustrated with charts.

Business Information

CMC Recording Studios rents studio time and technical support for audio recording. Founded in 1992, CMC is still a relatively small business. CMC has two sources of income: studio rental, and charges for a technician's time. Many of CMC's clients spend several consecutive days in the studio. Some bring their own technicians, others use technicians supplied by CMC. CMC's income and expenses for the second quarter of 1997 are shown in Figure B.1.

Creating the Worksheet

In the *Excel Projects* workbook (created in Project A), create a *Project B* worksheet. See John Sinkford's *Budget* (Session 2, Figure 2.11) for ideas on general worksheet layout for income, expense, and gross profit or loss (income minus expenses). Include your name in the worksheet footer. Use column totals for each month. In column E, calculate the quarterly total for each item. Use a function in column F to calculate the average for each row. Use appropriate formats for the numbers and text in the worksheet. Save *Excel Projects*.

Creating the Charts

Create three charts: a pie chart to illustrate total expenses for the quarter, a series chart to compare total income to total expense, and a series chart illustrating gross profit or loss for each month. All charts must include chart titles, labels, and legends as needed.

Printing

Print the worksheet, and print each chart as a separate page.

CMC Recording Studios
Spokane, Washington
Income and Expenses, Second Quarter 1997

Income	April	May	June
Studio Rental	44,800	48,000	46,400
Technical Support	16,800	18,000	17,400
Expenses			
Salaries	13,688	13,688	13,688
Technicians	11,200	12,000	11,600
Bldg. Rental	10,500	10,500	10,500
Utilities	647	543	482
Advertising	1,200	2,998	1,200
Office Expense	754	391	465
Depreciation	854	854	854
Taxes	2,364	2,440	2,402

Figure B.1
CMC Recording Studios income and expenses

Editing and Formatting Charts

EXCEL INCLUDES SPECIFIC **formatting** you can use with charts. You can enhance the basic charts you created in Session 10 by formatting data series and points. Charts can be modified by adding or removing data series or changing chart types. At the end of this session you will be able to:

- Add or remove data series and points
- Edit chart elements
- Format a data series
- Format individual data points
- Choose patterns and colors for chart elements
- Change chart type and style

■ Vocabulary

- chart area
- elements
- explode
- plot area
- tick marks

SECTION 11.1: ADDING OR DELETING CHART DATA

Excel's charting tools allow you to modify charts quickly and easily. You can, for example, create a simple chart, and then add data to it using drag-and-drop. The column chart shown in Figure 11.1 illustrates five weeks of sales for Blue Spruce.

Figure 11.1

The Blue Spruce sales chart

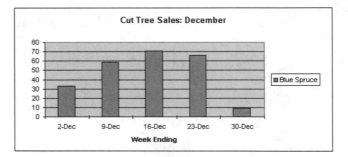

To add White Spruce to the chart, select the worksheet's corresponding label and numeric data for White Spruce. Drag the selection and drop it on the chart (as if you were moving it within the worksheet), and Excel will add the data range to the chart, as shown in Figure 11.2.

Figure 11.2

The sales chart with White Spruce added

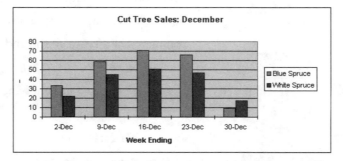

To delete a data series, begin by double-clicking to activate the chart. Click once on any column (slice, line) in the data series you want to delete. A handle will appear on each column in the series, as shown in Figure 11.3. Press the Delete key to remove the data series from the chart.

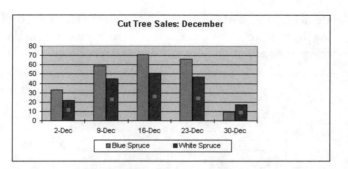

Figure 11.3
Selecting a
data series

EXERCISE 11.1	**TO ADD A CHART DATA SERIES**

Open *Traverse Tree Sales* and activate the *Dec Cut* worksheet. Select the column headings and data for Blue Spruce in columns A–F. Use the Chart Wizard to create the column chart shown in Figure 11.1. Enter the Chart and X-axis titles as shown. Position the chart directly below the worksheet figures.

1. **Select the data series you want to add to the chart.** Select the data for White Spruce.

2. **Point to the border of the selected cells. Drag-and-drop the cells into the chart.**

EXERCISE 11.2	**TO DELETE A CHART DATA SERIES**

1. **Double-click to activate the chart.**

2. **Click once on the series you wish to delete.** Click once to select the White Spruce data series.

3. **Press the Del key to delete the selected series.**

4. **Click the Undo button to undo the deletion and keep both series in the chart.**

SECTION 11.2: FORMATTING CHARTS

In Session 10, you changed the size and location of a chart by selecting the chart window, and then sizing and moving that window. You size or move any graphic object the same way. A chart is a collection of graphic objects or

elements, shown in Figure 11.4. To access the elements, begin by double-clicking the chart to activate it. Click once on any element in the activated chart to select it. Excel puts handles on the selected element.

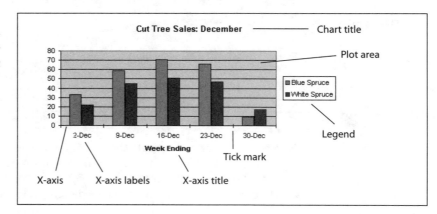

Figure 11.4
Elements of a chart

■ Editing Elements

The **chart area** is a rectangular area within the chart window bounded by the chart border. Changing the size of the chart window changes the size of the chart area. All elements in a chart must be within the chart area. The **plot area** is bounded by the axes, and contains the columns, lines, or other elements used to represent the data points. Elements within the plot area have fixed locations and cannot be moved or sized. You can, however, resize all the elements in the plot area by increasing or decreasing the plot area itself. (There's an exception to this rule; see "Exploding Pies" later in this section.)

Elements on an axis have specific locations relative to the axis. For example, the X-axis labels must be located near the X-axis. You can't move the X-axis labels to the right end of the plot area.

Elements outside the plot area and axes can be sized or moved to other locations in the chart area. The title and legend can be placed above, below, or in the plot area. Any element in a chart can be selected and deleted.

EXERCISE 11.3	TO EDIT CHART ELEMENTS

1. **Activate the chart.** Double-click to select the chart you created in Exercise 11.1.

2. **Select the element you want to edit.** Select the X-axis title, Week Ending.

3. **Drag the selected element by its center to move it, or by a handle to size it. Press Del to delete the element.**

4. **For more practice, delete the X-axis title.**

5. **Select the legend and move it to the bottom of the chart. Size the legend so that its elements appear horizontally, as in Figure 11.3.**

■ Exploding Pies

You can **explode** a pie chart, moving one or more pieces of the pie farther from the center. Usually, you will move one or two individual slices to emphasize specific data series in the chart. In Figure 11.5, the White Pine slice has been exploded.

To explode all pie pieces, begin by double-clicking to activate the chart. Click once on the pie; Excel will put handles on the outside edge of the slices. Drag any slice of the pie away from the center to explode all the pie slices.

Figure 11.5
An exploded
pie chart

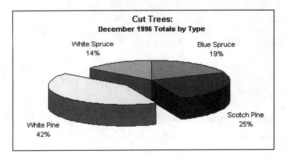

The exploded pie chart provides a good illustration of the downside of 3-D charts. Because the chart is rotated to simulate three dimensions, it isn't easy to visually compare the sizes of the slices. While 3-D pie charts are impressive looking, you lose some clarity in the presentation. When creating 3-D pies, it's a good idea to include percentage labels to help the user compare data points.

CAUTION

To explode a single slice, click once on the activated chart to select the chart. Click again to select the slice you want to explode. Drag the slice away from the center.

When you explode all slices in a pie, the slices get smaller as you increase the space between the slices. If you explode slices individually, the rest of the pie remains centered in the plot area.

■ Formatting Data Series

Appropriate formatting is available for each type of chart element. Double-click on any element to open the formatting dialog box for the element. For example, double-clicking any column in a data series opens the Format Data Series dialog box, shown in Figure 11.6.

Figure 11.6

The Format Data Series dialog box

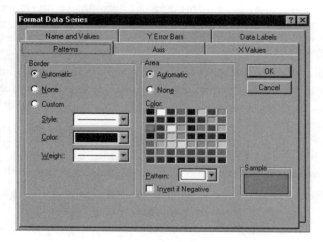

There are six pages in this dialog box. Each contains a group of settings for the selected data series:

Names and Values: contains the range selected for the series, separated into labels (Names) and numbers (Values).

X Values: the range used for X-axis labels.

Axis: lets you add a second Y-axis at the right end of the plot area with values specific to this data series.

Y Error Bars: adds a graphic display of the standard error; used to approximate sampling error when the data in a chart is a statistical sample being applied to a larger population.

Data Labels: displays a descriptive label or the numeric value for each data point in the series next to the column or line representing the data point.

Patterns: used to set the color and pattern used for the series.

Excel assigns colors and patterns to each data series. Colors that look different on screen may look very similar when printed, making it difficult to read the chart. Many users change the patterns for data series to ensure that each series looks different when printed. (In Session 14 you will learn how to change the default colors Excel uses for charts.)

For more information on a specific control within any of these pages, click the dialog box Help button; then click on the control.

EXERCISE 11.4	TO FORMAT A DATA SERIES

1. **Activate the chart.**

2. **Double-click on the series you want to format to open the Format Data Series dialog box.** Double-click the Blue Spruce data series.

3. **Change the series' formatting.** Change the color and pattern for this data series.

4. For more practice, select a different color and pattern for the White Spruce data series.

5. **Click OK to apply the formatting changes.**

▮ Formatting Data Points

You can also format individual data points. To select an individual data point, first select the data series. Then, click once on the data point to select it. You might change the pattern of a data point slightly to make it stand out from other elements in the series. Be cautious about changing data points: if you change a point's formatting too much, it looks like it is no longer part of the series, defeating some of the purpose of the chart.

▮ Formatting Titles

You can add a chart title or axis titles. With the chart activated, choose Insert ➤ Titles from the menu bar, or point to part of the chart area that doesn't include another element and right-click to open the context menu; then choose Insert Titles. The Titles dialog box (see Figure 11.7) will open. Check the title(s) you want to add or remove check marks from titles you want to delete. Excel will insert a placeholder for each added title.

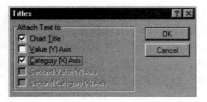

Figure 11.7
The Insert Titles
dialog box

You can edit or format titles (including placeholders) in the activated chart. To change the text in a title, click once to select the title, then edit the selected text. To format a title into multiple lines, place the insertion point where you want the second line to begin. Hold the Ctrl key and press Enter to insert a line break in the title.

Double-click on a title (or select the title, right-click, and choose Format Title from the context menu) to open the Format Title dialog box. Use the controls in the Pattern, Font, and Alignment pages to format the title as you would format other text in Excel.

TIP

To change all the fonts used in a chart, double-click on an unoccupied portion of the chart and change fonts in the Format Chart Area dialog box.

■ Formatting Axes

Double-clicking any axis opens the Format Axis dialog box, shown in Figure 11.8. Use the Patterns page to set the color and style of the axis. **Tick marks** are the lines that cross at regular intervals perpendicular to the axis (see Figure 11.4). You can turn off tick mark labels or change their position.

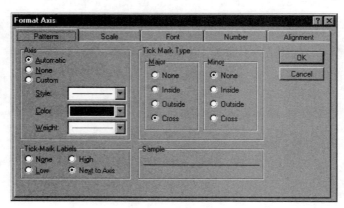

Figure 11.8
The Format Axis
dialog box: Patterns

You can change the range and scale of the axis in the Scale page of the Format Axis dialog box, shown in Figure 11.9. By default, Excel will set the minimum value to 0; if there is a data point with a negative value, the minimum value will be slightly lower than the lowest data point value. The maximum will be slightly larger than the largest value plotted. Double-click on the axis (usually the Y-axis) that has the numeric values you want to format, and then click the Scale tab. Use this page to set the major and minor intervals and the starting and ending point for the axis scale. The Minimum and Maximum values are the smallest and largest numbers you want to appear on the scale. The Major Unit is the interval between major tick marks and gridlines. If you also have minor tick marks or gridlines turned on, they will appear at the intervals you specify for Minor Units. You can also change the Y-intercept for the X-axis.

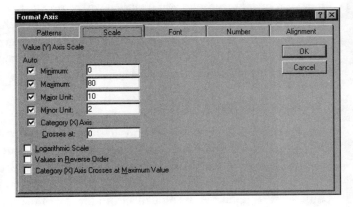

Figure 11.9
The Format Axis dialog box: Scale

Use the Font and Number pages to format the labels for an axis just as you would other labels and numbers within the worksheet. To change the orientation of the labels, use the Alignment page.

If your chart has long labels on the X-axis, change the labels' alignment to avoid crowding.

TIP

■ Adding Gridlines

You can add or remove horizontal gridlines at the major intervals of a chart by clicking the Gridlines button on the Chart toolbar. If the toolbar was not displayed when you activated the chart, choose View ➤ Toolbars and select the Chart toolbar. To add other gridlines, choose Insert ➤ Gridlines from the menu bar to open the Gridlines dialog box, shown in Figure 11.10. Gridlines intervals, both major and minor, are set in the Format Axis dialog box.

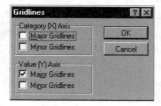

Figure 11.10
The Gridlines
dialog box

■ Adding Legends

Click the Legend button on the Chart toolbar to add a legend to the active chart or remove the legend you included when you created the chart. (The Legend button is a toggle. When the selected or activated chart has a legend, the button is depressed.) You can also choose Insert ➤ Legend to add a legend. If you are in the middle of editing a chart, you can simply select the legend and press Del to remove the legend.

■ Plot Area and Chart Area

You can assign patterned backgrounds to the plot area and the chart area. Double-click on the plot area or chart area to open the appropriate formatting dialog box. The plot area border can also be formatted. If you choose None for the plot area border, the plot area seems larger since you have removed the boundary that separates the plot area from the rest of the chart area.

EXERCISE 11.5	FORMATTING A CHART
	Change the current chart title to the two-line title: *Cut Spruce Sales, December 1996.* Use the chart to practice formatting chart elements. When you have finished, print the chart by itself and save the workbook.

SECTION 11.3: CHANGING CHART TYPE AND STYLE

After you have created a chart, you may decide to see how the same data could be represented differently. You can easily change the type and style of a chart. Clicking the drop-down arrow on the Chart Type button opens a palette of chart types. Select any type from the palette and Excel will redraw the chart in the new type.

Excel keeps track of settings for one default chart type. The original default type is a 2-D column chart that includes a legend. (In Session 14 you will learn how to change the default setting.) To change the selected chart to the default chart type, simply click the Default Chart button on the Chart toolbar.

If you want to change type and style, first activate the chart. Then choose Format ➢ Chart Type from the menu bar to open the Chart Type dialog box, shown in Figure 11.11. In this dialog box, chart types are separated by Dimension: 2-D and 3-D. Select a dimension and choose a type from the thumbnail samples. Click the Options button to view the chart styles and other formatting available within the selected chart type. Click OK to apply changes or Cancel to close the dialog box and retain the current chart type and style.

Figure 11.11
The Chart Type
dialog box

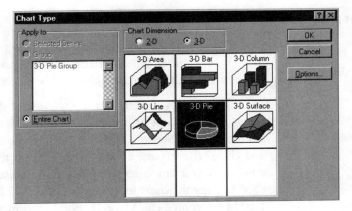

EXERCISE 11.6 | **TO CHANGE CHART TYPE**

1. **Select the chart.** Select the Spruce chart.

2. **Click the drop-down arrow attached to the Chart Type button.**

3. **Select a new chart type from the palette.** Select 3-D Column.

What You Have Learned

You can add or delete data series from a chart. Excel gives you lots of tools for formatting individual chart elements. Elements outside the plot area can be moved and sized. You can format colors, patterns, fonts, and other element attributes to improve the quality of a chart.

Focus Questions

1. How do you add a data series to a chart?

2. What is the difference between selecting and activating a chart?

3. Why might you change the patterns or colors used for a data series?

4. How do you select a chart element and open the element's formatting dialog box?

5. What type of chart can be exploded? Why would you explode a chart?

Reinforcement Exercises

Exercise 1   Open *Wildlife Federation.* Activate the T-shirt pie chart created in Session 10. Explode the slice that represents Anteater Long Sleeve T-shirts. Print the chart. Save the workbook.

Exercise 2   Open *Personal Worksheets.* In the *Budget* worksheet, select and copy (click the Copy button or choose Edit ➢ Copy) the line chart created in Session 10. Select a cell below the current chart, and click Paste to paste a copy of the chart in the worksheet. (If you prefer, you can select the chart, hold Ctrl, and use drag-and-drop to copy the chart to its new location.) Change the chart type in the copied chart to 2-D column. Format the chart elements to improve chart appearance. Print the new chart and save the workbook.

Exercise 3   Open *Unicorn Software.* Format the *Payroll* worksheet chart you created in Session 10. Save the changes, and print the worksheet with the embedded chart.

Exercise 4   Open the *Time Sheet* worksheet in the *Unicorn Software* workbook. Explode all slices of the 3-D pie chart created in Session 10. Change the font used for the chart title. Change the alignment of the X-axis labels so there is more space between the labels. Preview the chart. Choose new colors or patterns for pie slices if necessary. Print the chart and save the workbook.

Tracking Data with Excel

Vocabulary

- ascending order
- AutoFilter
- criteria
- database
- database management system (DBMS)
- descending order
- field
- field name
- filter
- list management
- null set
- primary sort
- record
- secondary sort
- sort
- subset
- subtotal
- tertiary sort

XCEL IS A RICHLY FEATURED program. In previous sessions you have worked with Excel's spreadsheet and charting features. In Sessions 12 and 13, you will use Excel's database capabilities to create and manage lists. At the end of this session you will be able to:

- Create an Excel database
- Sort records in a database
- Filter data in Excel
- Print filtered records

SECTION 12.1: CREATING AN EXCEL DATABASE

A **database** is a list with a specific structure, defined by its **fields**: the categories of information it contains. A telephone directory, for example, is a printout of a computer database whose fields include last name, first name, middle initial, address, and telephone number. Each entry in the phone book corresponds to a **record** in the database, containing a single set of the fields (one phone user's last name, first name, middle initial, address, and telephone number). Each field must have a unique **field name**: LastName, last name, LASTNAME, and LastNameforListing are all possible field names for a field containing last names.

The Traverse Tree Sales database (shown in Figure 12.1), is an example of a database created in Excel. Each field is a separate column. Field names (*Month, County, Type, Quantity,* and *Bundles*) are used as column headings. Each individual row is a record.

Figure 12.1

The Traverse Tree Sales database

TRAVERSE TREE SALES
County Cooperative Tree Orders
Deliver for Distribution 15th of Month

Month	County	Type	Quantity	Bundles
Oct.96	Genesee	Concolor Fir	6500	13
Apr.96	Genesee	Frazier Fir	7500	15
Sep.96	Kalkaska	Concolor Fir	9500	19
Apr.96	Oakland	Scotch Pine	11000	22
May.96	Lake	Concolor Fir	12000	24
Apr.96	Genesee	Blue Spruce	12500	25
Sep.96	Kalkaska	Frazier Fir	12500	25
Apr.96	Oakland	Concolor Fir	13500	27
May.96	Lake	Frazier Fir	14500	29
Apr.96	Oakland	White Pine	15500	31
Oct.96	Genesee	White Pine	16000	32
Oct.96	Genesee	Blue Spruce	17500	35
Apr.96	Oakland	Blue Spruce	22500	45
Sep.96	Lake	White Pine	26500	53
Sep.96	Lake	Blue Spruce	31000	62
May.96	Lake	White Pine	32000	64
Apr.96	Genesee	White Pine	37000	74
May.96	Lake	Blue Spruce	42500	85

Database management system (DBMS) software like Microsoft Access is designed specifically to create and use databases. It allows you to create and manage lists with many thousands of records. Databases you create in Excel are limited to the number of rows in a worksheet: under 17,000. DBMS programs can also easily control the types of data entered in a field, and they let the user easily work with information in more than one database at the same time. Despite its limitations, Excel's **list management** (database) features are powerful tools for creating small databases and manipulating sets of records from larger DBMS databases.

Creating a database is as simple as creating any other worksheet. Rules for creating databases include:

Blank rows: A blank row signals the end of a database. Don't leave a blank row between column headings and data records. DO leave a blank row after all records and before totals, averages, or other summary rows.

Field names: There can be only one row of column headings used by the database. Make sure each column heading is unique within the worksheet, since no two field names can be the same. Be consistent: either use headings for every column or don't use column headings at all.

A worksheet you have already created can be used as a database, but you may have to delete or add rows or rename column headings to meet these requirements.

EXERCISE 12.1	CREATING A DATABASE IN EXCEL

Open *Traverse Tree Sales*.

1. In a blank worksheet, create the Excel database shown in Figure 12.1. The values in the Bundles column are calculated: Quantity of Trees/500.

2. Name the sheet *County Sales*.

SECTION 12.2: SORTING A DATABASE

Database software must allow you to do two distinct things with data: organize (**sort**) the data in a specific order (for example, alphabetized by state), and separate (**filter**) the data to find specific information (for example, all your customers who live in Oregon).

To sort the data in a database, first select any cell in the database; then choose Data ➤ Sort from the menu bar to have Excel select the database (the records and column headings) and open the Data Sort dialog box, shown in Figure 12.2.

Excel will select all cells above, below, to the right, and to the left of the cell you selected until it encounters a blank column and row. Excel will examine the top row of the database and assign it as a record or deselect it, assuming it is a row of column headings. If there is a unique text entry in each cell in the top row of the database, Excel will assume that the row contains headings. The last section of the Data Sort dialog box lets you correct an incorrect selection by specifying whether you have a header row.

Figure 12.2

The Data Sort
dialog box

TIP

If you didn't select a cell within the database before choosing Data ➤ Sort, Excel will open a dialog box and warn you that there was no list to select. Click the OK button in the dialog box, select a cell in the database, and choose Data ➤ Sort again.

In a telephone book, records are sorted initially by last name. This is called a **primary sort**. What if there is a tie: for example, all the people whose last name is Smith? In case of a tie, a **secondary sort** is done by first name. If there are two David Smiths, they will be sorted by middle initial in a **tertiary sort**. Notice that the secondary and tertiary sorts occur only in case of a tie at a higher (primary and secondary) level of sorting.

You can sort up to three levels using the Data Sort dialog box. Records can be sorted in **ascending order** (A–Z or 1–100) or **descending order** (Z–A or 100–1). In the Sort By text box, enter (or use the drop-down to select) the field name you want to sort by. Choose ascending or descending sort order. If some of the records have the same value in the Sort By field, use the first of the two Then By text boxes to select the field you want to sort by when there is a tie in the primary sort field. For databases with many similar records, you may also want to add a tertiary sort in the last Then By control. When you have made all the sort selections, click the OK button to sort the database according to the specifications you entered.

EXERCISE 12.2 | **TO SORT A DATABASE**

Make sure the *County Sales* worksheet is active.

1. **Select any cell within the database.**

2. **From the menu bar, choose Data ➤ Sort.**

3. **Select the field you want to sort by from the Sort By drop-down list.** Select Type.

4. **Use the Then By drop-down lists to select secondary and tertiary sort fields.** Choose County as a secondary sort, and Month as a tertiary sort.

5. **Click the OK button to sort the database.**

    You can conduct a primary sort on a database using the sort buttons on the Standard toolbar. Select any cell within the database in the column you want to sort by. Click the Ascending Sort or Descending Sort button to sort the database. This is an easier way to sort, but it has two drawbacks: you can only sort by one field, and Excel doesn't allow you to verify that the correct cells have been selected as the database. It's best to sort each database once using the Sort ➤ Data dialog box and ensure that the correct rows have been selected before using the toolbar. (If Excel uses an incorrect selection to sort the database, you can always choose Edit ➤ Undo Sort or click the Undo button.)

CAUTION

When sorting, it is vital that you select all the *columns* of a database. If some are not selected, the selected columns will be sorted but the unselected columns will not be, ruining the integrity of the data by mixing up the records. Always check to be sure that all columns were included before proceeding to another task. Click Undo immediately if they were not.

EXERCISE 12.3 | **TO SORT USING THE TOOLBAR**

1. **Select any cell within the database records in the column you want to sort by.** Choose any cell under Quantity.

2. **Click the Ascending or Descending Sort button.** Click the Descending Sort button to put the largest orders at the top of the sorted database.

SECTION 12.3: FILTERING A DATABASE

At times you will want to work with a database **subset**: a group of records in the database. A **filter** is used to select a subset of records that meet a specific criterion and temporarily hide the remaining records. (What's a criterion? *Webster's* calls it "a standard on which a judgment or decision may be based." In filtering it means a value or range of values that some field should contain for the record to be displayed—for example, State = Oregon. It's a Latin word; the plural is **criteria**.) You can manipulate the filtered records as you would the entire database. AutoFilter is Excel's built-in filtering system. Select any cell in the database and choose Data ➢ Filter ➢ AutoFilter to have Excel set up an AutoFilter. Excel reads every record for each field in the database and creates a filter criteria list for each field. You click the drop-down arrow that appears next to each field name (see Figure 12.3) to access the field's criteria list.

Figure 12.3
A database with an AutoFilter

	A	B	C	D	E
1	TRAVERSE TREE SALES				
2	County Cooperative Tree Orders				
3	Deliver for Distribution 15th of Month				
4					
5	Month	County	Type	Quantit	Bundle:
6	Oct-96	Genesee	Concolor Fir	6500	13
7	Apr-96	Genesee	Frazier Fir	7500	15
8	Sep-96	Kalkaska	Concolor Fir	9500	19
9	Apr-96	Oakland	Scotch Pine	11000	22
10	May-96	Lake	Concolor Fir	12000	24
11	Apr-96	Genesee	Blue Spruce	12500	25
12	Sep-96	Kalkaska	Frazier Fir	12500	25

The default criteria setting in each field is (All), meaning that the contents of the field are not being used to limit the records displayed. (Top 10) is used in numeric fields to display a range of values. You use (Custom) to select filter criteria that do not automatically appear on the field criteria list. For example, to view the records for one county only, select the county by name from the criteria list. To see those records where this field has been left blank, choose (Blanks).

When you apply a filter, all the records that are not included in the subset are hidden, as shown in Figure 12.4. The number of records found (and the total number of records in the database) are displayed on the status bar. Each record retains its original row number; the row numbers of filtered records appear in blue. The field criteria drop-down arrow for the filtered field turns blue, to show that it is being actively used to filter the database.

	A	B	C	D	E	F	G	H	I	
1	TRAVERSE TREE SALES									
2	County Cooperative Tree Orders									
3	Deliver for Distribution 15th of Month									
4										
5	Month ▼	County ▼	Type ▼	Quantit ▼	Bundle: ▼					
6	Oct-96	Genesee	Concolor Fir	6500	13					
7	Apr-96	Genesee	Frazier Fir	7500	15					
11	Apr-96	Genesee	Blue Spruce	12500	25					
16	Oct-96	Genesee	White Pine	16000	32					
17	Oct-96	Genesee	Blue Spruce	17500	35					
22	Apr-96	Genesee	White Pine	37000	74					
24										

Figure 12.4

Filtering a database

You can filter on more than one field to select, for example, all the Scotch Pine sales in Oakland County. Set the criteria using each field's drop-down list. Only records that meet all the criteria you selected will be included in the filtered subset.

To redisplay the entire database, change the filter criteria for all filtered fields back to (All). A quick way to know that all filters are set to (All) is that all drop-down arrows are the same color again.

EXERCISE 12.4 **TO APPLY AND USE AUTOFILTER**

1. **Select any cell in the database.** Select any cell in *County Sales.*

2. **Choose Data ➢ Filter ➢ AutoFilter.**

3. **Click on the column heading drop-down arrow for the field you want to use to filter.** Click the County drop-down arrow.

4. **Choose a filter from the field criteria drop-down list.** Choose Genesee. View the filtered records.

5. Change the filter to Lake County.

6. Reset the Quantity filter to (All). Use the County and [Month] filters to view the Apr-96 records for Oakland County.

7. Reset all filter criteria to (All).

■ Creating a Custom Filter

When you filter using the drop-down criteria, you are always looking for records that are blank, in the Top 10, or exactly equal specific criteria. Custom filters give you access to other ways to set criteria:

■ All records with fields that are NOT equal to a criterion

- Records that are greater than or less than a criterion

- Records that meet one condition OR another

To create a custom filter, choose Custom from the drop-down criteria list to open the Custom AutoFilter dialog box, shown in Figure 12.5.

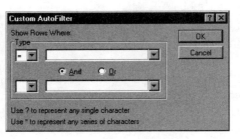

Figure 12.5
The Custom
AutoFilter
dialog box

The left drop-down (under Show Rows Where) opens a list of operators:

=	equal to
>	greater than
<	less than
>=	greater than or equal to
<=	less than or equal to
<>	not equal to

The right drop-down lists the record entries in the field from the field criteria list. To find all records that are NOT in Lake County, choose <> as the operator, and select Lake from the drop-down.

You can also enter text in the criteria control. To find all orders for Oakland and Ottawa counties, you could use the wildcard character (*). The entry O* will find all records that begin with the letter O. This same task can be accomplished using the second set of controls. Enter =Oakland in the top set of controls, and =Ottawa in the second set. Set the And/Or option to Or, to indicate that you are looking for records where the county is Oakland OR Ottawa. If you set this option to And, only records where the county is Oakland AND Ottawa will be selected. The resulting subset will be a **null set** (a set with no records in it), since no single record has both counties listed.

AND is used to filter for a range of records and is almost always used on numeric fields. For example, you might want to select all orders above 10000 and below 20001, or all sales made between April and October 1996. Set the lower limit as the first criteria (>10000), select And, and set the high end of the range (<20001 or <=20000) as the second criteria. For a record to be included in the filtered subset, both criteria must be true, eliminating quantities equal to or less than 10000 and greater than 20000. (If you use Or instead of And in this example, the filtered subset will include all records.)

EXERCISE 12.5	TO CREATE A CUSTOM FILTER

1. **Choose Custom from the filter criteria drop-down list to open the Custom AutoFilter dialog box.**

2. **Set the operator for the first criteria.** Select greater than or equal to (>=).

3. **Enter or select the first criterion from the drop-down list.** Enter 15000.

4. **Set an operator and enter or select the second criterion.** Set the criteria as <=25000.

5. **Make sure that AND, not OR, is selected.**

6. **Click OK to apply the custom filter.**

■ Using the Top 10 Filter

You can also filter columns that contain values for records that fall at the top or bottom of the database. To use the Top 10 Filter, choose Top 10 from the drop-down filter criteria list to open the Top 10 AutoFilter dialog box, shown in Figure 12.6.

The first control is used to choose records from the Top or Bottom. The second (spin box) control is used to set the interval. The default setting is 10, but you can choose to see the top 5 records, the bottom 25 records, or any other interval greater than 0. The third control has two drop-down entries: Items or Percent. By setting this to Percent, you can filter those records in the bottom 25 percent rather than the bottom 25 records.

Figure 12.6
The Top 10
AutoFilter
dialog box

Top 10 can only be used on values. If you try to apply a Top 10 filter to a field with text entries, the dialog box will not open.

The filter criteria drop-downs don't appear when you print a database, so there isn't usually a reason to turn AutoFilter off until you are done working with a database. To turn AutoFilter off, choose Data ➤ Filter ➤ AutoFilter again.

SECTION 12.4: WORKING WITH FILTERED RECORDS

After you have filtered a database, you can work with the filtered subset in a number of ways. If you print the database while it is filtered, only the filtered records will print. Filtering is also useful when you need to create charts using part of the data in the database. Filter the records you want to chart, then select and chart the information as you would normally. When you create a chart based on a filter, you need to print the chart *before* changing the filter criteria. Changing the criteria changes the chart. If you need to create a permanent chart, see the following section on creating a subset database.

■ Creating a Subset Database

There are times when you will want to work with or distribute a subset of the database. For example, you might have a database with 5000 records—but only 700 of them pertain to your current project. It would be easier to work with a smaller database that included only the 700 records you need. You can copy the filtered subset to the clipboard and paste it in a new location. This creates a new database containing only records from the filtered subset.

EXERCISE 12.6   TO CREATE A NEW DATABASE FROM A FILTERED SUBSET

1. **Filter the active database to create a filtered subset.** Set filter criteria to select the county orders from Oakland County.

2. Print Preview the filtered subset.

3. **Select the filtered database.** Select the worksheet titles, column headings, and filtered subset.

4. **Click the Copy button on the Standard toolbar.**

5. **Select the first cell where you want the new database to appear.** Click the sheet tab of an empty sheet in *Traverse Tree Sales*. Select cell A1.

6. **Press Enter to paste the database.** The pasted database includes only the records in the filtered subset.

7. Name the new sheet *Oakland*. Save *Traverse Tree Sales*.

SECTION 12.5: CREATING SUBTOTALS

You can create subtotals based on any field in the database. A subtotal is not necessarily a sum. A **subtotal** can be an average, count, minimum, maximum, sum, or other basic statistical calculation based on a group of records. Before subtotaling, you need to sort the database on the field you wish to subtotal on. For example, if you want to subtotal each month's orders, first sort by Month. To subtotal by county, first sort the database by county. Then, select a cell anywhere in the database and choose Data ➤ Subtotals to open the Subtotals dialog box, shown in Figure 12.7.

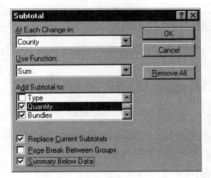

Figure 12.7
The Subtotals
dialog box

In the At Each Change In control, select the field the database is sorted on. This is an important step. The "trigger" for Excel to insert a subtotal is a change in the value of the At Each Change In field. If you choose an unsorted field, you'll get a multitude of meaningless subtotals. Select a type of subtotal (Sum, Average, or Count, for example) from the Use Function drop-down. In the Add Subtotals To control, select each field you want to subtotal.

Use Replace Current Subtotals if you have subtotaled earlier and want to create a different set of subtotals to replace the former set. If you want both sets of subtotals to appear (for example, sums and averages), deselect this option. If you are going to print the worksheet with subtotals and want each subtotaled set of data to print on a separate page, insert a Page Break Between

Groups. Summary Below Data places a summary grand total row at the bottom of the database. When you have entered the information for subtotals, click the OK button to add subtotals to the database, as shown in Figure 12.8.

Figure 12.8

Traverse Tree
Sales subtotals

1 2 3		A	B	C	D	E
	1	TRAVERSE TREE SALES				
	2	County Cooperative Tree Orders				
	3	Deliver for Distribution 15th of Month				
	4					
	5	Month	County	Type	Quantity	Bundles
	6	Oct-96	Genesee	Concolor Fir	6500	13
	7	Apr-96	Genesee	Frazier Fir	7500	15
	8	Apr-96	Genesee	Blue Spruce	12500	25
	9	Oct-96	Genesee	White Pine	16000	32
	10	Oct-96	Genesee	Blue Spruce	17500	35
	11	Apr-96	Genesee	White Pine	37000	74
	12		Genesee Total		97000	194
	13	Sep-96	Kalkaska	Concolor Fir	9500	19
	14	Sep-96	Kalkaska	Frazier Fir	12500	25
	15		Kalkaska Total		22000	44
	16	May-96	Lake	Concolor Fir	12000	24

To remove subtotals from a database, open the Subtotals dialog box again (see Figure 12.7) and click the Remove All button.

EXERCISE 12.7 | **TO ADD SUBTOTALS TO A DATABASE**

1. **Sort the database on the field you wish to subtotal by.** Sort the *County Sales* database by county.

2. **Select any cell in the database.**

3. **Choose Data ➤ Subtotals from the menu bar.**

4. **Select a field from the At Each Change In drop-down list.** Select County.

5. **Select a type of subtotal.** Select SUM.

6. **Select the numeric fields to be subtotaled when the value of the At Each Change In field changes.** Select Quantity and Bundles.

7. **Check and, if necessary, change the settings for Replace Current Subtotals** (yes), **Page Break Between Groups** (no), **and Summary Below Data** (yes).

8. **Click OK to generate subtotals.**

9. Print *County Sales* with subtotals.

10. **Choose Data ➤ Subtotals, then click Remove All to turn subtotals off.**

Your worksheet with subtotals is displayed in an outline form. You will learn more about Excel outlining in Session 18.

What You Have Learned

You create databases in Excel in much the same way you have created other worksheets. Databases don't have empty rows. Column headings are used as field names; each field name must be unique within a worksheet. You can sort databases, using up to three levels of sorts. You can filter a database to work with records that meet a specified criteria. Filtered databases can be printed or copied to create other databases. Excel can generate different types of subtotals for numeric values in the database.

Focus Questions

1. What is a database?

2. How do Excel's rows and columns relate to database records and fields?

3. How does a database differ from other Excel worksheets?

4. What is the result of applying a filter?

5. How would you select records in a numeric range: for example, all records where Price was more than $10.00 but less than $20.00?

6. What types of database subtotals can be created using the Subtotals dialog box?

Reinforcement Exercises

Exercise 1   Open *Wildlife Federation*. Activate *T-shirts*, and make the following changes so that the worksheet conforms to the rules for Excel databases:

■ Delete the subsection headings for Long Sleeve Shirts and Short Sleeve Shirts.

■ Delete the blank row between the column headings and the records and any blank rows between database records.

■ Make sure there is a blank row between the records and the summary (totals) section.

Sort the *T-shirts* worksheet by Quantity in descending order. Sort the worksheet by Item name. Use a filter to select those t-shirts with more than 50 in stock. Print the filtered worksheet. Add a column between Item and Quantity for Type. Enter LS or SS in the Type column for each item. Sort the database on the Type field. Create SUM subtotals for each change in Type of t-shirts. Print the worksheet. Remove the subtotals.

Exercise 2   Open *Personal Worksheets*. Move to the *Stocks* worksheet. Delete the row between the column headings and the stocks so you can use the column headings as database field names. Sort the records so that:

- The stock with the highest Cost % of Portfolio is on top;

- They are arranged in descending order based on Cost per Share;

- Stocks are shown in ascending order based on Shares % of Portfolio;

- Stocks are listed alphabetically by symbol.

Apply a filter to show only those stocks that comprise more than 15% of the Cost % of the Portfolio. Print the worksheet. Save and close *Personal Worksheets*.

Exercise 3   Open *Unicorn Software*. Sort the *Payroll* worksheet three separate times by the following primary sort fields:

- Hourly Rate, ascending

- Gross Pay, descending

- Employee name, ascending

Close the workbook without saving changes.

Exercise 4   Open *Wildlife Federation*. In the *Order Response* worksheet, find and print the records for orders that took more than three days to ship, sorted in descending order by Days. Close the workbook without saving changes.

Analyzing Data with Excel

N THIS SESSION YOU will learn to enter data using a data form. You then will create a pivot table to summarize and analyze a database. You'll work with more database and analysis Tools in Sessions 15, 18, and 19. At the end of this session you will be able to:

- Use a data form to enter records
- Search for data using the data form
- Create a pivot table using the PivotTable Wizard
- Add and remove pivot table fields

Vocabulary

- calculated field
- data form
- drill down
- field button
- PivotTable

SECTION 13.1: USING THE DATA FORM

Excel's **data form** lets you enter or search for records in a database. Select any cell in a database, and choose Data ➤ Form to open a data form. The first record in the database will be displayed in the data form. The data form for *Traverse Tree Sales* is shown in Figure 13.1.

Figure 13.1

The *Traverse Tree Sales* data form

Use the scroll bar or the up- and down-arrow keys to browse database records. You can change the contents of a field by editing the text box next to the field name. If a field's contents are the result of a formula, you can't edit it. The contents of **calculated fields** (like entries in the Bundles field) are displayed without a text box. However, if you change the value in the Quantity field, the value shown for Bundles in the data form will be recalculated just as it is in the worksheet. To discard changes made to a record, click the Restore button before moving to another record. If you may want to restore the former value, remember to use the Tab key to move between fields (or leave a field you have just edited). Clicking the Enter key moves to the next record.

■ Adding and Deleting Records

Click the New button to open the New Record form so you can add a record. (You can also scroll to the last record of the database to open the New Record form.) Enter each field in the appropriate text box control. To move from control to control, press the Tab key or click the text box. When you have entered information for the last field, press Enter or click the New button again if you want to keep entering new records. Press the up arrow or click the scroll bar when you finish entering records.

To delete the record currently displayed in the data form, click the Delete button. A dialog box will appear, warning that the record will be permanently deleted. Click the OK button to delete the record's row from the database.

EXERCISE 13.1	TO ADD RECORDS WITH A DATA FORM

Open *Traverse Tree Sales* and select the *County Sales* worksheet.

1. **Select any cell in the database.**

2. **Choose Data ➢ Form from the menu bar to open the data form.**

3. **Click the New button or scroll to the end of the database to add a record.**

4. **Enter the record using the data form text box controls. Tab between controls. Press Enter on the last field of a record to open another New Record form.** Add the following records for trees delivered to Kalkaska County in May 96: Concolor Fir, 10000; Frazier Fir, 7500; and Blue Spruce, 13500.

5. **Press the up arrow or scroll the database to close the New Record form.**

It isn't always more convenient to use the data form. Excel's AutoComplete feature doesn't work with the data form, so you have to fully type the name of each county and each type of tree in *Traverse Tree Sales*. The data form is most useful when the database is wider than the worksheet window and the contents of records vary widely. For example, the fields in a mailing list can easily be wider than the screen. While state or zip code may repeat frequently within a list, names and addresses will differ. Using the form allows you to see all the database fields at once without scrolling horizontally, and AutoComplete will not be helpful with the names and addresses.

■ Searching for Records

You can use the data form to search for individual records that meet a criterion. This is like filtering, but you view the records one at a time. Click the Criteria button to open the Criteria form (which looks just like the data form, but has "Criteria" at the top). A Form button replaces the Criteria button. Enter the field contents you are searching for in the appropriate text box. Click the Find Next button to return to the form and find the first record that matches the criteria. Each time you click Find Next, you move to the next record that is a match. (If you need to delete specific records, this can be a good way to locate them.) The Find Prev (Previous) button lets you move back to the last record that matches the search criteria.

When you have criteria entered, you can use the Find Next and Find Prev button to move between records based on criteria, and the scroll bar or up and down arrows to move between all the records in the database. If you want to erase the search criteria, click the Criteria button again. Delete the criteria from the text box; then click the Form button to return to the form.

You can enter criteria in more than one text box. Excel joins the two criteria with AND, so will only find records that meet both criteria. You can't search for records that meet either criteria (OR). You should only enter logical operators like greater-than or less-than for numeric fields in the Criteria form. For advanced searching, use a filter. When you are finished using the data form, click the Close button to return to the worksheet.

EXERCISE 13.2	TO SEARCH FOR RECORDS

1. **Open the data form if it is not already open.**

2. **Click the Criteria button.**

3. **Enter the search criteria for one or more fields in the text box controls.** Enter *Genesee* in the County control.

4. **Click Find Next to find the first record that meets the criteria. Use Find Next and Find Prev to view the records that meet the search criteria.**

5. **Click the scroll bar to view all records in the database.**

SECTION 13.2: CREATING PIVOT TABLES

Pivot tables provide a powerful tool for data analysis. A **pivot table** summarizes the columns of information in a database in relationship to each other. *Traverse Tree Sales—County Sales* is a small database, but it would still take time and effort to accurately answer the following questions:

- How many trees of each type were delivered each month?

- How many Blue Spruce were delivered each month?

- What quantities of White Pine were delivered in 1996?

- How many trees did each county purchase?

- What was the average number of each type of tree sold to a single county?

You could filter the list, and then calculate totals and averages to answer any one of these questions. Then, to answer any other question, you would have to filter again, and look at the new totals. A single pivot table will allow you to answer all of the above questions, and more.

■ Using the PivotTable Wizard

Select any cell in a database, and choose Data ➤ PivotTable to launch the PivotTable Wizard. In the first step, shown in Figure 13.2, you tell Excel what kind of data you have: data in a single Excel database, data from an external source (like Access), or data that you want to consolidate from several worksheets or sources. In this session, all the pivot tables you construct will be created from Excel databases. At the bottom of the Step 1 dialog box is a reminder that you can get more information on pivot tables in Excel's Answer Wizard, part of Help. Clicking Next moves you to the second step.

Figure 13.2

Step 1 of the PivotTable Wizard

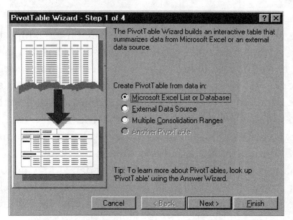

In step 2, you verify the range of the database. A flashing dotted line appears around the suggested range of cells. Use the scroll bars to verify that the entire database—including the field names—is selected before clicking the Next button to continue to step 3.

A pivot table contains four areas: the Page number, the Column labels, the Row labels, and the Data. Each area has a corresponding layout area in Step 3's dialog box, shown in Figure 13.3. At the right side of the dialog box is a group of **field buttons,** one for each field name in the database. In this step you design the pivot table layout by dragging the field buttons into one of the four sections of the layout area. The Row, Column, and Data areas must have fields assigned to them; Page is an optional area that you can leave blank. You can change the layout of a pivot table after it has been created, so the initial layout isn't critical.

Figure 13.3

Step 3 of

the PivotTable

Wizard—layout

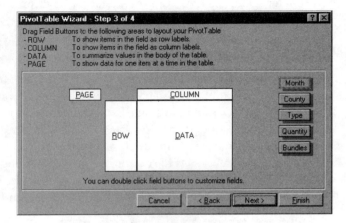

The Row and Column areas are somewhat interchangeable, since the entries in both areas will be labels for the summary data in the Data area. However, your pivot table is easier to use if it isn't too wide. When the table is created, Excel will examine each entry in a column of the database. Each unique (different) entry in a column becomes an entry in the pivot table, just as each unique entry was included in the filter criteria list for the field. If you have four counties, but ten types of trees, placing the County field in the column will result in four columns of data in the pivot table. If you put Type in the Column, you will have ten columns of data: too wide to view without scrolling. You should, therefore, place the button for the field with the fewest unique entries in the Column area. Place another field button in Row.

If you plan to filter the data in the table based on one or more fields, drag those field buttons to the Page area. If, for example, Traverse Tree Sales wants to be able to view the data for each county separately, then County should be moved to the Page area.

Information in the data area is mathematically summarized, so numeric fields are generally placed in the Data layout area. (You could place a non-numeric field and COUNT the number of entries rather than totaling or averaging.) For *Traverse Tree Sales*, we could place either Quantity, Bundles, or both in the data area. As you drop a field button in the Data area, Excel will indicate the type of summary that will be done with the data. SUM is the default. You can choose to have averages, minimums, maximums, or other summaries instead of, or as well as, the totals.

To change the type of summary, drag the field button to the Data area, and then double-click on the field button to open the PivotTable Field dialog box, shown in Figure 13.4. Choose the type of summary you want to use from the scroll list.

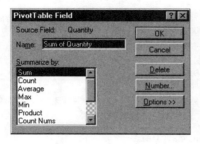

Figure 13.4
The PivotTable Field
dialog box

The default numeric format in a pivot table is General. You can click the Number button in this dialog box to format the numbers for this field. (You can also format the completed pivot table.) Click OK to close the dialog box and return to the PivotTable Wizard. When you are finished with the pivot table layout, click the Next button to continue to the final step of the PivotTable Wizard.

In Step 4 (see Figure 13.5), specify the final layout and destination for the pivot table. In the PivotTable Starting Cell control, enter a cell address for the upper left corner of the pivot table. Choose a cell to the right or below the database. If you leave this control blank, Excel will add a worksheet to the current workbook and create the pivot table in the new worksheet.

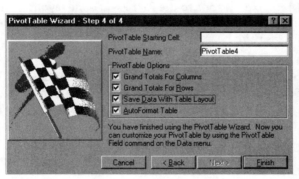

Figure 13.5
Step 4 of
the PivotTable
Wizard—finishing

If you wish, you can name the pivot table just as you name any other range of cells. The four PivotTable options instruct Excel to add column totals, row totals, save the database with the pivot table, and format the table when it is created. All four options are turned on by default. Click Finish to close the PivotTable Wizard and create the pivot table, as shown in Figure 13.6.

Figure 13.6

The finished County

Sales pivot table

	A	B	C	D	E	F
1	County	(All) ▼				
2						
3	Sum of Quantity	Month				
4	Type	4/1/96	5/1/96	9/1/96	10/1/96	Grand Total
5	Blue Spruce	35000	56000	31000	17500	139500
6	Concolor Fir	13500	22000	9500	7500	52500
7	Frazier Fir	6500	22000	12500	0	41000
8	Scotch Pine	11000	0	0	0	11000
9	White Pine	52500	32000	26500	16000	127000
10	Grand Total	118500	132000	79500	41000	371000

EXERCISE 13.3   **TO CREATE A PIVOTTABLE**

Select the *County Sales* worksheet in *Traverse Tree Sales*. You will be creating the pivot table shown in Figure 13.6.

1. **Select any cell in the database.**

2. **Choose Data ➤ PivotTable from the menu bar.**

3. **Select the type of data source you will be using for the table.** Choose Microsoft Excel List or Database. **Click Next.**

4. **Verify that the entire database is selected. If it is not, enter the correct range for the database. Click Next.**

5. **Drag field buttons to the four PivotTable layout areas.** Place County in the Page area; Month in the Column area; Type in the Row area; and Quantity in the Data area.

6. **To choose another type of data summary, double-click the field button in the data area to open the PivotTable Field dialog box. Select a summarization method from the Summarize By list, then click OK to return to the PivotTable Wizard.** Don't change the summarization method for this pivot table. Click OK to return to step 3.

7. **Click Next to proceed to the final step of the Wizard.**

8. **Enter a starting cell location for the table, or leave the location blank to have Excel insert a new worksheet for the table. Enter a name for the table or leave the default name.** Leave the Starting Cell control blank; name the table "County Analysis."

9. **Select the PivotTable options you want to use.** Leave the default options.

10. **Click the Finish button to close the Wizard and create the pivot table.**

11. **Double-click the pivot table's sheet tab.** Name the sheet *County Pivot*. Save the workbook.

SECTION 13.3: CHANGING PIVOT TABLE LAYOUT

A pivot table summarizes the data in an easily understandable form. In Figure 13.6, you could use the County drop-down list to filter the data and view sales for just one county. Different departments in a business may want to view summary data in different ways. The Nursery may be interested in viewing the separate types of trees that were shipped, while the Accounting department wants to view and bill individual counties.

A single pivot table lets both departments work with the data. The field buttons you placed in the Page, Column, and Row areas are visible as buttons in the pivot table. The pivot table is **dynamic**—attached directly to the underlying data, so that changes in the database are reflected in the table. This also means you can change the pivot table by dragging a field button to another area; Excel will update the table. For example, to view the data by county and date, filtered by type, you can drag the County button to the Column area, Month to the Row area, and the Type column to the Page area. The pivot table will change to reflect the new layout, as shown in Figure 13.7.

Figure 13.7
The rearranged
pivot table

	A	B	C	D	E	F
2	Type	(All)				
4	Sum of Quantity	County				
5	Month	Genesee	Kalkaska	Lake	Oakland	Grand Total
6	4/1/96	56000	0	0	62500	118500
7	5/1/96	0	31000	101000	0	132000
8	9/1/96	0	22000	57500	0	79500
9	10/1/96	41000	0	0	0	41000
10	Grand Total	97000	53000	158500	62500	371000

To remove a field from the pivot table, drag the field button out of the pivot table area. A large X will appear on the button. Release the mouse button to drop and delete the field. You can click the Undo button if you change your mind.

If you include two field buttons in either the Row or Column area, Excel will create subtotals for the first field, as shown in Figure 13.8.

Figure 13.8
The pivot table
with subtotals

	A	B	C	D	E	F	G
4	Sum of Quantity	County	Type				
5		Genesee				Genesee Total	Kalkaska
6	Month	Blue Spruce	Concolor Fir	Frazier Fir	White Pine		Blue Spruce
7	4/1/96	12500	0	6500	37000	56000	0
8	5/1/96	0	0	0	0	0	13500
9	9/1/96	0	0	0	0	0	0
10	10/1/96	17500	7500	0	16000	41000	0
11	Grand Total	30000	7500	6500	53000	97000	13500

TIP

It is difficult to chart an entire database, but you can easily select and chart part of a pivot table. Don't begin selecting with a cell that includes a field button, since the button itself can be moved. You can, however, include a field button at the end of a selection. If you change the layout of the pivot table, the chart will be changed as well, so you might want to print the chart before changing pivot table layout.

EXERCISE 13.4	TO CHANGE PIVOT TABLE LAYOUT

Select *County Pivot*.

1. **Rearrange the table by dragging field buttons from one area to another.** Move Type to the Page area. Move County to the Column area. Move Month to the Row area. Examine the new layout.

2. Move Month from the Page area to the Column area, to the right of County. Excel will include subtotal columns for each county. Print the *County Pivot* worksheet.

3. Rearrange the fields so the pivot table is in its original configuration.

4. **To delete a field, drag the field button from the table and drop it in the worksheet.**

If you need to add a field to the pivot table, select any cell in the table and choose Data ➢ PivotTable to reopen the layout page of the PivotTable Wizard. Add, delete, or rearrange the field buttons; then click the Finish button to return to the pivot table.

■ Creating Individual Pages

You might want to separate the pivot table data, creating individual tables for each value in a field. For example, it might be useful to create and print a pivot table for each individual county. Before you can create individual County tables, you need to make sure that County is in the Page area of the table. (It need not be the only field button in the Page area.) Select any cell in the pivot table and right-click to open the context menu. Select Show Pages from the menu to open the Show Pages dialog box. Choose the field for which you want to create individual pages; then click the OK button. Excel will insert new worksheets and create a pivot table for each value in the selected field. (The values will appear on the new worksheet's sheet tabs.)

■ Viewing Pivot Table Detail

Even though the cells in the Data area contain summary information, you can "**drill down**" through a pivot table: view all the detail that underlies an individual summary figure. Double-click on any nonzero value in the Data area, and Excel opens a new worksheet to display the records that were used to create the summary. The worksheet shown in Figure 13.9 was created by double-clicking on the pivot table cell that contained the summary for White Pine deliveries in April 1996.

Figure 13.9

Drilling down to
pivot table detail

	A	B	C	D	E
1	Month	County	Type	Quantity	Bundles
2	4/1/96	Oakland	White Pine	15500	31
3	4/1/96	Genesee	White Pine	37000	74

EXERCISE 13.5 | **TO DRILL DOWN A PIVOT TABLE**

1. **Double-click on the Data area cell that contains the summary you want to examine in more detail.** Double-click on the September figure for Scotch Pines.

2. **If you want to delete the detail worksheet after reviewing it, choose Edit ➣ Delete Sheet; then click OK.** Delete the detail worksheet.

■ Updating a Pivot Table

A pivot table is dynamically linked to the database used to create the table. If you edit values within the database, simply choose Data ➣ Refresh Data and Excel will update the pivot table to reflect the database changes.

If you add records or fields to the database, you cannot simply refresh the data. You must return to the PivotTable Wizard and identify the new range of records that should be included in the table. If you don't, the pivot table values will not include the values in the added records.

To update the range being used by the pivot table, select any cell in the table and choose Data ➣ PivotTable from the menu bar. The PivotTable Wizard will open at Step 3. Click the Back button to go to Step 2, where you select cells to be included in the table. Excel will move to the currently selected database range (changing to another worksheet, if necessary). To add rows or columns, you can reselect the entire database, or hold the Shift key and use the down- and right-arrow keys to extend the current selection. Click the Finish button to close the PivotTable Wizard and return to the updated pivot table.

What You Have Learned

Data forms can streamline data entry. The data form can also be used to browse all records, or just the records that meet your criteria. A pivot table is Excel's database summary and analysis tool. You create pivot tables using the PivotTable Wizard. After you've constructed the table you can rearrange the layout, creating new data summaries. Double-clicking lets you examine the detail behind any cell in the Data area.

Focus Questions

1. Why might you use a data form to enter data?

2. When would you choose not to use a data form to enter data?

3. What is a pivot table used for?

4. How is the Data area of a pivot table similar to subtotaling?

5. When do you need to update a pivot table?

6. How do you view the detail underlying a pivot table summary value?

Reinforcement Exercises

Exercise 1   Open *Wildlife Federation*. After studying the preliminary results of the *Order Response* worksheet, the Wildlife Federation decided to install a new tracking system in the Warehouse and Shipping areas in both regions. A Help Desk was established to answer calls from employees needing assistance with the tracking system. Help Desk staff tracked information on calls over a four month period. Create and format the *Help Desk* database shown in Figure 13.10.

Figure 13.10

The *Help Desk*

database

	A	B	C	D
1	WILDLIFE FEDERATION			
2	HELP DESK USAGE			
3				
4	Department	Region	Month	Calls
5	Warehouse	East	Sep-96	61
6	Warehouse	East	Oct-96	54
7	Warehouse	East	Nov-96	32
8	Warehouse	East	Dec-96	13
9	Warehouse	West	Sep-96	77
10	Warehouse	West	Oct-96	61
11	Warehouse	West	Nov-96	45
12	Warehouse	West	Dec-96	20
13	Shipping	East	Sep-96	38
14	Shipping	East	Oct-96	30
15	Shipping	East	Nov-96	19
16	Shipping	East	Dec-96	7
17	Shipping	West	Sep-96	93
18	Shipping	West	Oct-96	68
19	Shipping	West	Nov-96	33
20	Shipping	West	Dec-96	36

Construct a pivot table so Help Desk personnel can analyze their results. Name the pivot table worksheet *Help Pivot*. Print *Help Desk* and *Help Pivot*. Save the workbook.

Exercise 2   Open the *County Pivot* worksheet in *Traverse Tree Sales*. Move the Type field to the Page area and move County to the Row area of the pivot table. Select any cell in the table, and choose Show Pages from the context menu to create a separate page for each Type of tree. Print the *Blue Spruce* worksheet. Delete the separate pivot table pages created in this exercise before saving the workbook.

Exercise 3   Open *Traverse Tree Sales*. Rearrange *County Pivot* so that the pivot table layout includes:

■ Month in the Page area

■ Type in the Row area

■ County in the Column area

■ Average of Quantity and Sum of Quantity in the Data area

Since some cells have zero values, division by zero errors will occur with some of the averages. Change the layout so you can get details on the Genesee County information for April, 1996.

Create a 3-D pie illustrating Genesee County's detail worksheet. Print the pie; then close *Traverse Tree Sales* without saving changes to delete the detail worksheet and return the pivot table to its original layout.

Exercise 4   Open *Wildlife Federation*. Select the *Help Pivot* worksheet created earlier in this session. (If you do not have this worksheet, complete Exercise 1 above before proceeding.) Rearrange *Help Pivot* so you can create a stacked column chart to illustrate help desk calls for all departments separated by region. Format and print the column chart; then close *Wildlife Federation* without saving changes to return *Help Pivot* to its original layout and discard the chart.

PART IV

Customization, Functions, and Macros

Customizing Excel

ANY OF THE FEATURES of Excel can be changed to keep close at hand the tools you use frequently. You can select the toolbars you wish to display or create custom toolbars with buttons for functions you use frequently. You can alter other features in the Options dialog box. At the end of this session you will be able to:

- Show or hide toolbars
- Customize toolbars
- Create personal toolbars
- Change options using the Options dialog box

Vocabulary

- automatic calculation
- custom lists
- customize
- manual calculation
- options

SECTION 14.1: DISPLAYING TOOLBARS

Excel includes predesigned toolbars: sets of buttons grouped by function. In previous sessions you have worked with the Standard, Formatting, and Chart toolbars. To see all the toolbars available in Excel, choose View ➤ Toolbars to open the Toolbars dialog box, shown in Figure 14.1.

Figure 14.1
The Toolbars
dialog box

Toolbars currently displayed have a check mark; to turn a toolbar off, click to remove its mark. To display a different toolbar, click on its check box. Below the toolbar list are three display options that affect all toolbars:

Color toolbars: The use of color always takes a bit of computer memory, but it makes buttons easier to distinguish.

Large buttons: Fewer large buttons fit on a toolbar, but they are useful if you have difficulty seeing the buttons as normally displayed.

Show ToolTips: When you point to a button, the ToolTip shows the name of the button. This is very useful while learning new toolbars, but it uses some system resources.

When the toolbars you want to display are selected and you have chosen the display options, clicking the OK button closes the dialog box and displays the selected toolbars. Excel places no limit on the number of toolbars you can display at one time. There is, of course, a practical limit. Each additional toolbar you display reduces the amount of space available for the worksheet window. Too many toolbars, and you can't see the worksheet.

You can display a toolbar in a strip at the top or bottom of the window, or as a floating palette in the worksheet window. The "floating" style works best with toolbars you use while performing a specific task; use the "strip" style for toolbars you always display. You move a toolbar by dragging it from one location to another. To begin, point to part of the gray area of the toolbar that frames the buttons. Press and hold the mouse button. As you move the mouse, the outline of the toolbar will move. If you move the outline into the worksheet window, it will change to a palette shape. Drop the outline in the new location to move the toolbar.

You can quickly move any toolbar to the worksheet window by double-clicking on the gray frame. To restore the toolbar to its original location above or below the worksheet window, double-click on the toolbar title bar. Clicking the palette toolbar's Close button when it is being viewed as a palette closes the toolbar.

You can also display or hide toolbars using a context-sensitive menu. Point to any toolbar and right-click to open the Toolbar pop-up menu (see Figure 14.2). Choose a toolbar from the list, or select Toolbars to open the Toolbars dialog box.

Figure 14.2
The Toolbar
pop-up menu

EXERCISE 14.1   **TO DISPLAY TOOLBARS**

1. **Choose View ➢ Toolbars.**

2. **Select the toolbars that you want to display by clicking them so that a check mark appears in front of them.** For this exercise, turn on the Drawing toolbar.

3. **Turn off any displayed toolbar by clearing its check box.** Turn off the Formatting toolbar.

4. **Click the display options that you want on: Color Buttons, Large Buttons, Show ToolTips.** Here, turn off Color. Turn on the other two options.

5. **Click OK.**

CONTINUES ON NEXT PAGE

6. Drag the Drawing toolbar to the left side of the worksheet window. Double-click the Drawing toolbar title bar to move the toolbar above the worksheet window.

7. Right-click on any toolbar and choose Toolbars from the pop-up menu to open the Toolbars dialog box. Turn color back on; display the Standard and Formatting toolbars only. Undo the Large Button Display.

SECTION 14.2: CUSTOMIZING TOOLBARS

Over time, you will discover that there are Excel features you wish were on the toolbars you regularly use. There will be other buttons you rarely use. Excel allows you to **customize** (modify) toolbars, adding and deleting buttons to create one or more personalized toolbars.

■ Adding or Deleting Toolbar Buttons

When you remove a button from the toolbar, the toolbar will not include that button until you or another user restores the button to the toolbar.

TIP

If you share a computer with other users, you will need to restore the default toolbars and menu bar before ending this session.

First, display the toolbar you want to customize. Then open the Customize dialog box (see Figure 14.3), by choosing Customize from the toolbar pop-up menu; or by choosing View ➤ Toolbars, and then clicking the Customize button in the Toolbars dialog box.

Figure 14.3
The Customize dialog box

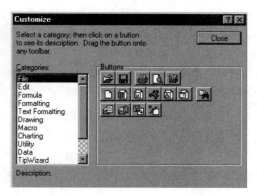

The Customize dialog box contains sets of buttons organized in the same categories as the menu bar. If, for example, you want to add a button to create PivotTables, you would select Data from the Categories list. The buttons displayed in the Buttons control relate to the options on the Data menu.

The meaning of some buttons is obvious; others require an explanation. Click on any button in the Buttons section, and a description of the button appears at the bottom of the dialog box:

> Description:
> Saves changes made to active document

To add a button to a toolbar, drag the button's outline from the Buttons section to the toolbar and drop it in place. You can also drag a button from one toolbar to another, or to another location on the same toolbar. To delete a button from a toolbar, drag the button off the toolbar and drop it in the worksheet window. (**Note:** The Customize dialog box must be open before you can customize a toolbar.) When you have finished customizing the open toolbars, click Close to close the Customize dialog box.

If you prefer the previous toolbar settings, use the Toolbars dialog box to restore the default settings. Choose Toolbars from the toolbar pop-up menu, or View ➤ Toolbars from the menu bar. Click the name of the toolbar you want to restore; then click the Reset button.

EXERCISE 14.2	TO ADD OR DELETE TOOLBAR BUTTONS

To make restoring the defaults easier, make sure that just the Standard and Formatting toolbars are open.

1. **Point to a toolbar and right-click to open the pop-up menu.**

2. **Choose Customize to open the Customize dialog box.**

3. **Drag buttons off the toolbar to delete them.** Remove Cut, Copy, and Paste from the Standard toolbar. Remove Color from the Formatting toolbar.

4. **To add buttons, select a button category from the Category list. Drag the buttons you want to add to the open toolbars.** Add a PivotTable button to the Standard toolbar. Select another button from Data and add it to the Standard toolbar.

5. **Click Close when you are finished editing the toolbars.**

6. Choose View ➤ Toolbars to open the Toolbars dialog box. Reset both the Standard and Formatting toolbars. Click OK when you are finished.

■ Creating a New Toolbar

Many people using this book share a computer with other users, but would still like to have custom toolbars of their own. Excel lets you create new toolbars that you can then customize, leaving the predesigned toolbars intact for others to use.

To create a new toolbar, open the Toolbars dialog box. Enter a name for the toolbar in the Toolbar Name text box control; then click the New button. Excel will create a new toolbar and open the Customize dialog box. Select the buttons you want and drag each onto your new toolbar.

TIP

Keep buttons chosen from the same category next to each other; this makes it easier to remember their purpose.

When you are finished creating the toolbar, click the OK button to close the Customize dialog box. You can place the new toolbar above or below the worksheet window with the other toolbars. The new toolbar will be added to the list in the Toolbar dialog box.

EXERCISE 14.3 **TO CREATE A NEW TOOLBAR**

1. **Choose View ➤ Toolbars to open the Toolbars dialog box.**

2. **Enter a name for the toolbar. Click New.** Enter your first or last name as the toolbar name.

3. **Drag the buttons you want to the toolbar.** Add at least five buttons to the toolbar. Group related buttons together.

4. **Click Close when you have finished creating the new toolbar.**

5. Choose View ➤ Toolbars to turn the new toolbar on or off.

SECTION 14.3: CUSTOMIZING AUTOCORRECT

Excel automatically corrects some misspellings as you enter text. You can customize AutoCorrect to handle other typing mistakes you make that aren't on the list. Choose Tools ➤ AutoCorrect to open the AutoCorrect dialog box, shown in Figure 14.4.

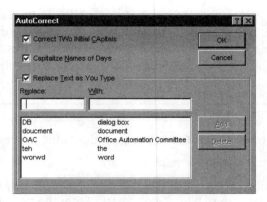

The first option, Correct Two Initial Capitals, fixes typos created when you do not release the Shift key quickly enough. When you enter two capital letters in a row (ONtario), AutoCorrect changes the capital N to lowercase. (It won't, however, change a word that is all caps, so you can still enter state or province abbreviations and acronyms like FYI or FOB.) When the Capitalize Names of Days option is enabled, Excel will capitalize the first letter of weekday names if you forget to. You can enable or disable either of these options.

The final option, Replace Text as You Type, is an AutoCorrect option that can save time when you are constructing worksheets. Skillful use of the replacements list can make real improvements in your efficiency. For example, you may often type *acounts* when you mean to type *accounts*. By including the mistake and the correction in the list, you can have Word fix this error on the fly. To enter an automatic correction, enter the misspelling in the Replace control and the corrected word in the With control.

Click the Add button to add the replacement to the AutoCorrect list. If you make a mistake creating an AutoCorrect entry, just select the mistaken entry and click the Delete button.

There are some errors that are not good candidates for AutoCorrect. If you type *form* instead of *from*, you may be tempted to create an AutoCorrect entry. But if you do, when you really want the word *form*, you'll have to turn off AutoCorrect.

You can use AutoCorrect to expand unique phrases and names you enter frequently. In the Replace control, enter a short string that stands for the phrase you want to expand; then enter the complete phrase in the With control:

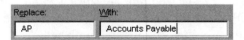

Click the Add button. Now, you can type *AP* and have Excel automatically replace it with *Accounts Payable*. AutoCorrect isn't just a feature in Excel—it is a Microsoft Office feature accessed by other Office products like Word, Access, and PowerPoint. Entries you add to AutoCorrect in Excel also work in other Office applications on your system, and vice-versa.

EXERCISE 14.4   **TO SET AUTOCORRECT OPTIONS**

1. **Choose Tools ➤ AutoCorrect to open the AutoCorrect dialog box.**

2. **Select options to turn them on or off.**

3. **In the AutoCorrect list, add words that you frequently misspell or that you wish to have Excel expand. Enter the misspelling or shortened form of the word in the Replace text box. Enter the correct or expanded spelling in the With text box.** Add *TTS* and *Traverse Tree Sales* to the list.

4. **Click OK to close the AutoCorrect dialog box.**

5. To test the AutoCorrect entry that you made, open a new blank worksheet. Type *TTS* and press the space bar. *TTS* should be replaced with *Traverse Tree Sales*.

SECTION 14.4: CHANGING EXCEL'S OPTIONS

Options provide another method of customizing Excel. Choosing Tools ➤ Options from the menu bar opens the Options dialog box. This section covers some of the options that determine how Excel responds to your instructions.

TIP

If you don't know what an option means, you can click on the Help question mark in the top-right corner of the Options dialog box and then click on an option to get a description of the option.

■ The General Options

The General Options page (see Figure 14.5) contains miscellaneous settings that affect the user interface. The most important General options and their default settings are:

Reference Style (A1): Columns are labeled with letters, and rows are labeled with numbers. In the R1C1 style used in a small number of worksheets, both rows and columns are numbered.

Menus: Recently Use File List (on): Displays recently used files on the File menu so you can open them directly from the File menu.

Menus: Microsoft Excel 4.0 Menus (off): When this option is off, the Excel for Windows 95 menus are displayed in the menu bar.

Sheets in New Workbook (16): The number of worksheets included in new workbooks.

Standard Font and Font Size (Arial 10 pt): The default font for new workbooks.

Default File Location (My Documents folder): Where files are saved (and opened from) if you don't specify another location.

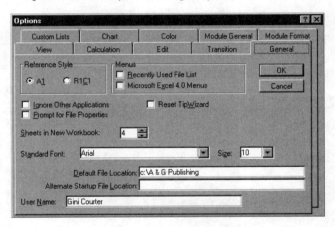

Figure 14.5
The General options

■ View Options

There are three categories of View Options:

Show: Determines which tools will be displayed within Excel.

Window: Sets the features you want to have displayed by default.

Objects: Lets you display (the default) charts and other objects, show them as placeholders, or hide them completely.

■ Edit Options

The Edit options (see Figure 14.6) directly affect Excel's response when you edit text and numbers. If you double-click on a cell and it doesn't open for editing, or if you try to drag-and-drop a selection and nothing happens, an option has been disabled on this page.

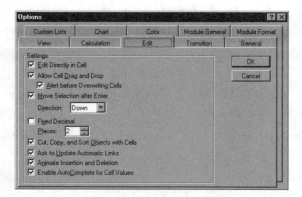

Figure 14.6
The Edit options

■ Color Options

The settings on the Color Options page determine the colors that are included on the Color and Font Color palettes and the default colors for charts. (All four categories of colors shown are used in the two palettes.)

You can replace any of the colors. If you frequently create charts, you might want to change the basic colors used for Chart Fills. Double-click the color you want to replace to open the Color Picker, shown in Figure 14.7. Using the mouse, move the crosshairs to select a new color. Use the intensity bar on the right edge of the Color Picker to adjust the color intensity; then click OK to add the color to the Color page.

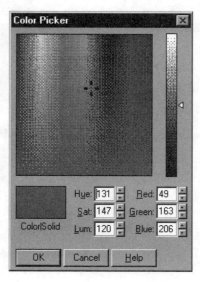

Figure 14.7
The Color Picker

■ Chart Options

The settings on the Chart Options page are dimmed out most of the time since they affect the currently activated chart. The options include how empty cells will be illustrated in the chart and whether hidden cells will be included.

■ Calculation Options

There are three ways that Excel can calculate the results of formulas and functions in worksheets. You control calculation on the Calculation Options page, shown in Figure 14.8. With **Automatic calculation** (the default setting), the worksheet is recalculated each time you enter a new formula, value, or name in the worksheet. Automatic Except Tables applies automatic calculation except for entries in PivotTables and other data tables.

Figure 14.8
The Calculation options

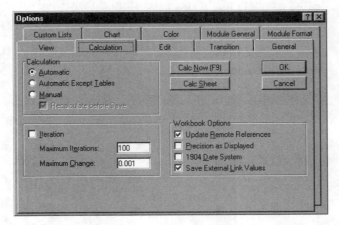

Both of the automatic methods work well until you are entering values in a large worksheet that includes many formulas. Then, having Excel calculate after each numeric entry will slow down worksheet performance (and your data entry). If you switch to **Manual calculation**, Excel won't recalculate the worksheet until you:

- Press F9, or

- Open the Calculation Options page and click the Calc Now button (to calculate all open worksheets) or Calc Sheet to calculate the active worksheet, or

- Change the calculation method back to automatic, or

- Save the worksheet.

TIP

When you begin working with Manual calculation, it is easy to forget to recalculate worksheets. If you print a worksheet without calculating, the results of formulas will be incorrect in the printout. Since worksheets are always calculated when you save, make a habit of always saving immediately before printing, regardless of your calculation method.

■ Custom Lists Options

In Session 8, you used custom lists with AutoFill. The four default **custom lists** are shown in Figure 14.9. You can create other Custom List entries which can then be AutoFilled when you construct worksheets. Custom lists should be entries that you always use in the same sequence. For example, a school district secretary might create a custom alphabetized list of buildings in the district; an accountant might create a custom list of account names. To create a custom list, type each entry in the List Entries text box. Press Enter after each entry in the list. When the list is complete, click the Add button to move the list to the Custom Lists scroll box.

Figure 14.9

Custom Lists options

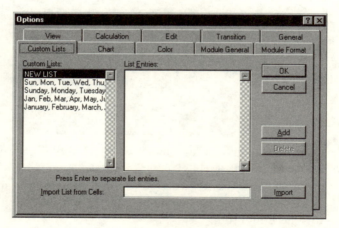

Custom lists you create are used just like the predesigned lists. Enter one or more of the list entries; then AutoFill the remaining entries.

■ Other Options

The Module General and Module Format pages are used by programmers. The changes made here affect the response and formatting for the Visual Basic programming language, which can be used with Excel. The Transition options can be set so that Excel will respond to Lotus 1-2-3 commands to help former Lotus 1-2-3 users work with Excel.

Excel contains many customizable settings and options. You don't need to set them all at once. In fact, many users never change most of the defaults. As you learn more about Excel, return periodically to tweak settings or change options to make Excel work most efficiently for you.

EXERCISE 14.5	TO SET OPTIONS

1. **Choose Tools ➢ Options from the menu bar.**

2. **Click on the tab that contains the option you want to change.** For this exercise, click on each tab and browse the available options. If you do not understand an option, use the Help question mark to get a definition. Do not make any changes at this time.

3. **Click the option to turn it on or off.**

4. **Click OK when you have finished setting the options.**

What You Have Learned

In this session, you have learned how to customize Excel to help you work more efficiently. You have learned how to add and delete buttons from toolbars and create custom toolbars to meet your needs. You now know how to set options for the AutoCorrect feature, including how to add words or shortcuts to the AutoCorrect dictionary. Finally, you have learned about the many options available to make working with Excel easier and more convenient.

Focus Questions

1. How do you move a toolbar to a different part of the screen?

2. List the steps you would take to add a File ➢ Close button to the Standard toolbar.

3. How do you restore toolbar defaults if the toolbar has been changed?

4. What steps would you take to customize Excel so that when you typed AR it automatically changed the abbreviation to Accounts Receivable?

5. What option would you set to turn off Gridlines in the worksheet window? Where is the option located?

Reinforcement Exercises

Exercise 1   Create a custom toolbar that you can use when you work in PivotTables. Name it *[your last name] Tools*. Add the following buttons: New PivotTable, Show Pages, Sort Ascending, Sort Descending, Show Data Detail (Drill Down).

Exercise 2   Edit the toolbar you created earlier in this session in Exercise 14.3. Add additional buttons to it so that you can use it in place of the Standard toolbar. Only include buttons for features that you use regularly.

Exercise 3   Add three to five words that you commonly misspell to the AutoCorrect dictionary. Add three abbreviations for phrases or names that you use regularly so that when you type them they are replaced with the full text.

Advanced Functions: IF and LOOKUP

THIS SESSION PROVIDES an in-depth look at the logical function IF and at lookup tables, used by many businesses to create and maintain lists that supply values and labels for other worksheets. Product information databases, customer databases, and other Excel lists can be easily used as lookup tables. At the end of this session you will be able to:

- Explain how the IF function operates
- Use IF in formulas
- Explain how lookup functions are used
- Create a lookup database
- Construct a worksheet using lookup functions

Vocabulary

- 3-D cell reference
- array
- HLOOKUP
- IF
- logical function
- logical operators
- logical test
- LOOKUP
- lookup functions
- lookup value
- VLOOKUP

SECTION 15.1: USING LOGICAL FUNCTIONS

Excel has hundreds of functions. This session focuses on three frequently used functions. Understanding how you can use these specific functions should help you understand how functions are generally used.

The microprocessor in a computer is capable of two types of operations: arithmetic operations and logical operations. In the worksheets you have constructed in previous sessions, all the formulas and functions used arithmetic: adding numbers, dividing to calculate an average, multiplying to calculate gross pay. **Logical operators** allow you to compare two or more numbers. You use logical operators (=, >, <, =>, <=, and <>) to create custom filters to find records that met specific criteria. Excel's **logical functions** let you place the selection power of a filter inside a formula.

You can use logical functions any time you want to apply a formula based on criteria. Payroll worksheets provide numerous opportunities to use logical functions: different tax rates depending on Gross Pay, different pay rates based on actual hours or days worked, different deductions. Unicorn Software's Payroll worksheet for July 6 is shown in Figure 15.1. Barzona took unpaid leave, so other employees worked overtime to cover Barzona's hours. Employees receive their regular rate for the first 40 hours worked in a week. Hours in excess of 40 are paid at time-and-a-half (a 50 percent increase in pay). As you'll see, this calculation requires us to use logical functions.

Figure 15.1

The *July 6 Payroll* worksheet

	A	B	C	D	E	F
1			Unicorn Software Payroll			
2			Week Ending July 6			
3						
4	Name	Hours	Rate	Gross Pay	Taxes	Net Pay
5	Azimi	48	$ 8.75	$ 420.00	$ 79.80	$ 340.20
6	Barzona	0	$ 9.00	$ -	$ -	$ -
7	Buckley	15	$ 8.00	$ 120.00	$ 22.80	$ 97.20
8	Chiu	42	$ 10.00	$ 420.00	$ 79.80	$ 340.20
9	Collins	45	$ 10.00	$ 450.00	$ 85.50	$ 364.50
10	Jones	29	$ 9.50	$ 275.50	$ 52.35	$ 223.16
11	Retzloff	30	$ 7.75	$ 232.50	$ 44.18	$ 188.33
12						
13	Totals	209		$ 1,918.00	$ 364.42	$ 1,553.58

Before proceeding, create the *July 6 Payroll* worksheet so you can use it as a reference for the rest of this section.

EXERCISE 15.1   **CREATING *JULY 6 PAYROLL***

Open *Unicorn Software*. The *July 6 Payroll* worksheet is similar to the *June 22* worksheet you created in Session 3 and modified in Session 8.

1. You can copy *Payroll* and paste it into a blank worksheet; then change the values in the Hours column. Or, you can create the worksheet as shown in Figure 15.1. Gross Pay = Hours * Rate; Taxes = Gross Pay * 19%; Net Pay = Gross Pay – Taxes.

2. Name the worksheet *July 6 Payroll*. Rename *Payroll* so that the new name is *June 22 Payroll*; save *Unicorn Software*.

3. Browse the formulas for Gross Pay, Taxes, and Net Pay in the *July 6 Payroll* worksheet; you'll be modifying the Gross Pay formula later in this session.

The Gross Pay formula in Column D (Hours * Rate) calculates the correct Gross Pay for Barzona, Buckley, and Jones. But the same formula will be incorrect for Azimi, Chiu, and Collins, since the formula doesn't reflect their overtime pay. There are at least two ways to correctly calculate Gross Pay for Azimi, Chiu, and Collins:

- Calculate all hours at the regular rate, then add 50 percent of the regular rate for the overtime hours:

$$(\text{Hours} * \text{Rate}) + (.5 * \text{Rate} * \text{Overtime Hours})$$

- Calculate Gross Pay for the 40 regular hours; then add 150% of the regular rate for the overtime hours:

$$(40 * \text{Rate}) + (1.5 * \text{Rate} * \text{Overtime Hours})$$

The regular formula underpays the employees who worked more than 40 hours. If you use an overtime formula for an employee who worked 15 hours, overpayment would result.

No single arithmetic formula lets you calculate both overtime and regular gross pay correctly. You could use a "non-overtime" formula for Barzona, Buckley, and Jones and create another new "overtime" formula for Azimi, Chiu, and Collins. However, each week you would need to look at each employee's hours and decide which formula to use. This system would be time-consuming and error-prone.

The logical functions are used for decision making. You can use the IF function to instruct Excel to use different calculations based on whether an employee worked more than 40 hours. If you selected the IF function in the first step of the Function Wizard, the second step looks like Figure 15.2.

```
┌──────────────────────────────────────────────────────────────┐
│ Function Wizard - Step 2 of 2                       [?] [X]    │
│ IF                                    Value: [              ]  │
│ Specifies a logical test to perform.                           │
│                                                                │
│ Logical_test (required)                                        │
│ is any value or expression that can be evaluated to TRUE or FALSE. │
│                                                                │
│     logical_test  fx [              ]    [              ]      │
│      value_if_true fx [              ]    [              ]     │
│     value_if_false fx [              ]    [              ]     │
│                                                                │
│   [ Help ]   [ Cancel ]   [ < Back ]   [ Next > ]  [ Finish ] │
└──────────────────────────────────────────────────────────────┘
```

The IF function has three arguments, separated by commas:

IF(logical test,value if true,value if false)

logical test: the condition that triggers a change in action. The result of the logical test will be either true or false.

value if true: the action to be taken if the result of the logical test is true.

value if false: the action if the result of the logical test is false.

All three arguments are required. As a simple demonstration of the IF function, we can create a formula for the Gross Pay column that checks to see whether the employee worked overtime: *=IF(B5>40, "Over", "")*. When Excel evaluates the formula, it begins by checking the contents of B5. If B5 is greater than 40, Excel will print "Over" in D5. If the logical test is false, D5 will be blank. Text strings like "Over" must be in quotations. The set of quotes "" are an empty string, instructing Excel to put nothing in the cell. (This third "empty" argument is necessary because all three arguments are required.)

EXERCISE 15.2 | **TO CREATE A FORMULA WITH IF**

1. **Click on the cell where you want the result of the formula to appear** (the cell for Azimi's Gross Pay).

2. **Click the Function Wizard button on the Standard toolbar.**

3. **Choose Logical from the Function Category list and IF from the Function Name list. Click Next to continue.**

4. **Enter values for the logical test** (B5>40), **the value if true** ("Over"), **and the value if false** ("").

5. **Click Finish.** (Since the formulas in columns E and F are based on the values in column D, error messages will appear after you change the values in column D. You'll be placing another formula in D in the next exercise. For now, just ignore columns E and F.)

6. Use AutoFill to copy the formula for the other employees' Gross Pay.

The results in the Gross Pay column clearly indicate which employees worked more than 40 hours. Now, we need to create a formula that will use a different calculation based on this distinction. We want a formula that says "If the employee worked more than 40 hours, use the overtime formula. If not, use the regular formula." The logical test is the same; the value if true and value if false will be different. In cell D5, the formula will be:

=IF(B5>40,((40*C5)+(B5-40)*1.5*C5),B5*C5)

as shown in Figure 15.3.

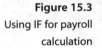

Figure 15.3
Using IF for payroll
calculation

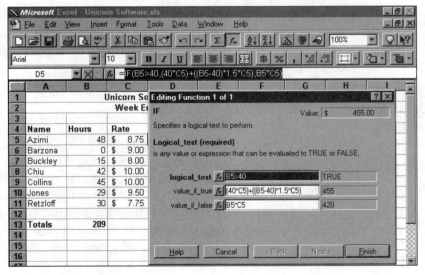

EXERCISE 15.3 | **CREATING THE OVERTIME FORMULA**

1. In *Payroll*, click on cell D5.

2. Click the Function Wizard button on the Standard toolbar. In Step 1, choose the logical function IF. The existing IF statement will automatically be displayed so you can edit it.

3. Enter B5>40 as the logical test.

4. For the value if true, enter (40*C5)+(B5−40)*1.5*C5.

5. For the value if false, enter B5*C5.

6. Click Finish.

7. AutoFill to copy the formula to the other Gross Pay cells. Columns E and F will once again show values.

Other logical functions include NOT, AND, and OR. By including these functions within a formula that uses the IF function, you can set up two or more logical tests within a single formula. For example, Unicorn Software tries to ensure all employees work between 20 and 40 hours a week. You can create and then fill a formula in column G to show which employees' hours were exceptions: =IF(OR(B6<20,B6>40), "Exception", ""). The OR function evaluates as true if either of the two logical tests (B6<20 and B6>40) are true. For more information on logical functions, see the Excel Help Index under the topic *worksheet functions*.

SECTION 15.2: USING LOOKUP FUNCTIONS

The **lookup functions** are used to find information within an array and return it to the cell that contains the function. An **array** is a special type of database in which one column or row contains unique values. You may need to sort the database on the unique column or row depending on how you intend to use lookup functions. The ticket price database for the Peach Hill Theatre shown in Figure 15.4 is an array with the first column, Tickets, sorted in numeric order. The sheet is named *Spring Promo*; the array is named *SpringPrices*.

	A	B
1	PEACH HILL THEATRE	
2	Spring Promotion Prices	
3		
4	**Tickets**	**Total**
5	1	$ 27.50
6	2	$ 52.25
7	3	$ 74.25
8	4	$ 93.50
9	5	$ 110.00
10	6	$ 132.00
11	7	Group Rate

Figure 15.4

The *Peach Hill Theatre* array

The **VLOOKUP** function is used to search vertically through the first column of an array until it finds a particular value. It then looks in a specified column of the value's row and returns the value in that column. VLOOKUP has three required and one optional argument:

vlookup(lookup value,array,col index number,range lookup)

lookup value: the value Excel searches for in the first column of the array (the number of tickets). The lookup value can be a number, text, or a cell reference. If there is no exact match, Excel will find an approximate match. This argument is required.

table array: the range of cells that contain the array (SpringPrices). This can be a named range, and is a required argument.

column index number: the column number in the array that contains the value that should be returned. The left column is column 1; to look for Price, you would look in column 2. This argument is also required.

range lookup: This optional field can either be TRUE or FALSE. If the argument is FALSE, the database doesn't have to be sorted, but VLOOKUP will find only exact matches for the lookup value.

To encourage ticket sales, the theater decreases the price for each additional ticket purchased. Requests for more than six tickets are forwarded to the Group Sales Office. Since each ticket is priced differently, the staff at the theater use a ticket order form with VLOOKUP to find the price for tickets. In the *Ticket Sales* worksheet (see Figure 15.5), an employee enters the customer's name, phone number, and the number of tickets the customer is purchasing. The formula in B7 is

=VLOOKUP(B6,SpringPrices,2)

Figure 15.5

The *Ticket Sales* worksheet

	A	B	C
1	PEACH HILL THEATRE		
2	TICKET ORDER FORM		
3			
4	Customer Name	**Margaret Marmot**	
5	Customer Phone	555-0000	
6	Number of Tickets	4	
7	Total Price	$ 93.50	

Excel uses the lookup value in B6 to search through the SpringPrices table array. When it finds a match for the lookup value in the first column, it returns the value found in the second column of the array (column index number 2). If there is no exact match, Excel will find an approximate match. When the lookup value is less than the smallest value in the left column, the error #N/A is returned. When the lookup value falls between two values in the left column, Excel finds an approximate match: the largest value that is less than the lookup value. If the lookup value is greater than the largest value listed, the largest lookup value will be returned.

CAUTION

If you set the optional range lookup argument to FALSE, Excel will return the contents of the column index number column only if there is an exact match for the lookup value in the left column of the array. Because Excel is looking for an exact match, the array does not have to be sorted. Use FALSE when the lookup value must be included in the table.

Spring Promo and *Ticket Sales* are separate worksheets. The Total Price formula in *Ticket Sales* refers to the array in *Spring Promo*. The formula uses a **3-D cell reference**—a reference to a cell or range in another worksheet.

EXERCISE 15.4   **CREATING THE THEATRE WORKSHEETS**

1. Open a new workbook.

2. Enter the text and values for the worksheet shown in Figure 15.4. Format the worksheet.

3. Select the range A5:B11. Name the range *SpringPrices*.

4. Name the sheet *Spring Promo*.

5. On another sheet, create the titles and column A labels for the *Ticket Sales* worksheet shown in Figure 15.5. Format the worksheet.

6. In cell B7, open the Function Wizard. Choose the lookup function VLOOKUP. Click Next to continue.

7. Click the lookup value control, then select cell B6.

8. Select the table array control. Click on the Name Box drop down and select SpringPrices.

9. In the column index number control, enter 2. Choose Finish.

10. Name the worksheet *Ticket Sales.*

11. Enter your name and phone in cells B4 and B5. Test the lookup by entering different values in B6.

12. Save the workbook as *Peach Hill Theatre.*

During the summer, the Peach Hill Theatre uses an outdoor amphitheater. Ticket prices differ based on seating: the closer the seats, the higher the ticket price. Peach Hill's summer ticket prices are shown in Figure 15.6. The array is named SummerPrices.

Figure 15.6
Summer ticket prices

	A	B	C	D	E
1	PEACH HILL THEATRE				
2	SUMMER TICKET PRICES				
3					
4			Sections		Lawn
5	Tickets	A	B	C	L
6	1	$ 27.50	$ 24.00	$ 20.00	$ 15.00
7	2	$ 55.00	$ 48.00	$ 40.00	$ 30.00
8	3	$ 82.50	$ 72.00	$ 60.00	$ 45.00
9	4	$ 110.00	$ 96.00	$ 80.00	$ 60.00
10	5	$ 137.50	$ 120.00	$ 100.00	$ 75.00
11	6	$ 165.00	$ 144.00	$ 120.00	$ 90.00
12	7	GROUP	GROUP	GROUP	GROUP

You use the HLOOKUP function when the lookup value is contained in the first row, rather than the first column, of an array. Rather than requiring a column index number, HLOOKUP uses a row index number. To look up the price for summer tickets, we need two pieces of information: the number of tickets, and the section code (A, B, C, or L). *Ticket Sales* will need to be modified to include the section code, as shown in Figure 15.7.

Figure 15.7
The modified
Ticket Sales
worksheet

	A	B	C
1	PEACH HILL THEATRE		
2	TICKET ORDER FORM		
3			
4	Customer Name	Margaret Marmot	
5	Customer Phone	555-0000	
6	Number of Tickets	3	
7	Section Code	A	
8	Total Price	$ 82.50	

The first row of the SummerPrices array (see Figure 15.6) contains the section codes. Using HLOOKUP, Excel can choose the correct column based on the section code entered in the Order Form. The second row of the array contains prices for one ticket, the third row is for two tickets, and so on—the row number is always 1 greater than the number of tickets. Therefore, the row index number will be the number of tickets plus 1. The formula for Total Price in cell B8 of the Order Form is:

=HLOOKUP(B7,SummerPrices,B6+1)

EXERCISE 15.5   MODIFYING THE *PEACH HILL* WORKBOOK

1. On a blank worksheet in *Peach Hill Theatre*, enter the titles, labels, and values for row 6 of the worksheet shown in Figure 15.6. Make sure that "Tickets," "Sections," and "Lawn" are in row 4, not row 5.

2. The figures in B7:E11 are the values in row 6 multiplied by the number of tickets in column A. Using either the keyboard or the point method, enter the formula =B$6*$A7 in cell B7.

3. Use AutoFill to copy the formula from B7 to C7:E7.

4. Use AutoFill to copy the formula in B7:E7 to B8:E11.

5. Enter GROUP in cell B12. Use AutoFill to copy B12 to the other cells in row 12.

6. Select A5:E12. Name the range SummerPrices.

7. Format the worksheet; name it *Summer*. Save the workbook.

8. Activate *Ticket Sales*. Insert a new row between Number of Tickets and Total Price.

9. Enter the label Section Code in cell A7.

10. In cell B8, use the Function Wizard and Name Box to enter the formula =HLOOKUP(B7,SummerPrices,B6+1). Test *Ticket Sales* by entering different values in cells B6 and B7. Save the workbook.

You can use Excel's horizontal and vertical lookup functions to search for information in any database where the contents of one field are unique.

SECTION 15.3: COMBINING LOGICAL AND LOOKUP FUNCTIONS

Excel lets you use functions as arguments for other functions. Using functions in combination unleashes the full power of Excel formulas.

The modified *Ticket Sales* form now works for summer ticket prices, but not for spring prices. You could create two separate order forms to be used for the two ticket seasons. Or, you can modify *Ticket Sales* to include a logical function. By using IF in combination with the lookup functions, you can have one formula that uses the vertical lookup for spring sales, and the horizontal lookup for summer sales. (If the Section Code is blank, the formula should use SpringPrices; if not, it should use SummerPrices.)

EXERCISE 15.6 **ADDING IF TO *TICKET SALES***

1. Activate *Ticket Sales*.

2. Modify the formula in cell B8 so that if the value in B7 is greater than a null string ("") Total Price will be calculated using the SummerPrices. If B8 is empty, the formula will use the SpringPrices array. Here's the completed formula; additions to the current formula appear in boldface:

=IF(B7>"",HLOOKUP(B7,SummerPrices,B6+1),VLOOKUP (B6,SpringPrices,2))

You can press F2 and edit the existing formula using the keyboard, or reconstruct the formula using the Function Wizard and the Name Box.

3. Test *Ticket Sales*. Save *Peach Hill Theatre*.

What You Have Learned

This session has provided deeper experience with three functions. As you learn more Excel functions, you will also gain greater breadth of experience. Remember that Help with functions is only a mouse-click away.

You can use IF to carry out different actions based on the results of a logical test. The lookup functions let you access information in array records, both horizontally and vertically. A formula can reference cells in another worksheet. You can use the results of a function as the argument in another function.

Focus Questions

1. When would you use the IF function?

2. What is a logical test?

3. What makes a cell reference 3-D?

4. What is an array?

5. What is the difference between HLOOKUP and VLOOKUP?

Reinforcement Exercises

Exercise 1   Open the *Wildlife Federation* workbook. In the Calls column of *Help Desk*, create a formula to average the number of calls received at the help desk. In column E, use the IF function to create a formula that prints "Over" if the number of calls was over the average. If the number of calls was under, leave the cell blank. (Hint: Seven of the records are over average.) Print *Help Desk*. Save *Wildlife Federation*.

Exercise 2   Open *Peach Hill Theatre*. Modify the *Summer Price* worksheet to add the information shown in Figure 15.8 below. Change the Total Price formula in *Ticket Sales* to reflect the change in *Summer Price*. Test the new formula by entering different numbers for both spring and summer ticket sales. Change the header and footer for all three worksheets to include your name and the current date. Print both *Summer Price* and *Ticket Sales* before saving *Peach Hill Theatre*.

Figure 15.8
The revised
Summer Price
worksheet

Tickets	Sections			Lawn
	A	B	C	L
6	$ 165.00	$ 144.00	$ 120.00	$ 90.00
7	$ 192.50	$ 168.00	$ 140.00	$ 105.00
8	$ 220.00	$ 192.00	$ 160.00	$ 120.00
9	$ 247.50	$ 216.00	$ 180.00	$ 135.00
10	$ 275.00	$ 240.00	$ 200.00	$ 150.00
11	$ 302.50	$ 264.00	$ 220.00	$ 165.00
12	$ 330.00	$ 288.00	$ 240.00	$ 180.00
13	GROUP	GROUP	GROUP	GROUP

Exercise 3   Open *Unicorn Software*. Using the hours worked in *Time Sheet*, create a new sheet for *June 29 Payroll*. Use IF to create a Gross Pay formula that accurately reflects both overtime and regular hours worked. Save *Unicorn Software*.

Exercise 4   Open *Wildlife Federation*. In the *Order Response* worksheet, insert four blank rows above the array. Use VLOOKUP to create two formulas that will look up the date an order was placed and the number of days it took to ship, as shown in Figure 15.9. Format *Order Response* appropriately. Enter various Order numbers to test the formulas. Print *Order Response* and save the workbook.

Figure 15.9

The *Order Response* worksheet

	A	B	C	D
1		Wildlife Federation		
2		Order Responsiveness Survey		
3				
4		Order -->	960002	
5		Placed	2-Jan-96	
6		Days	4	
7				
8	Order	Placed	Shipped	Days
9	960001	2-Jan-96	5-Jan-96	3
10	960002	2-Jan-96	6-Jan-96	4
11	960003	2-Jan-96	5-Jan-96	3
12	960004	2-Jan-96	10-Jan-96	8
13	960005	2-Jan-96	5-Jan-96	3
14	960006	2-Jan-96	7-Jan-96	5

Streamlining Your Work with Macros

A macro is a set of instructions that Excel executes on command. These instructions can be simple keystrokes or complex menu selections. If you have tasks you regularly perform that include the same series of steps, creating a macro to automate the task for you will save time and effort. At the end of this session you will be able to:

- Record a simple macro
- Examine the Visual Basic macro code
- Create a custom toolbar button to play a macro
- Assign a macro to a keyboard shortcut
- Play macros
- Delete a macro

■ Vocabulary

- execute
- global macro
- macro
- module
- play
- record
- Visual Basic
- workbook macro

SECTION 16.1: UNDERSTANDING MACROS

You create and use **macros** to complete repetitive tasks that involve several steps. You **record** the series of steps you want to repeat in the same document or another document. The next time you need to carry out the operation, you can **play** the macro to repeat the series of steps in the same order.

There are many occasions when you may want to use macros:

- To apply a standard format for all or part of a worksheet

- To create a process that checks spelling, and then sends the corrected worksheet to the printer

- To print and close a specific worksheet

- To automate any other task you perform frequently

SECTION 16.2: RECORDING A SIMPLE MACRO

When you begin recording, Excel records all the actions you take; it even records mistakes you make during recording. Before recording a macro, you should practice the steps you want to record. Next, determine what conditions your macro will operate under. Will you use the macro in a specific worksheet? If so, open the worksheet. Will the macro be used to change or format selected text or numbers? Then have a range selected before you begin recording the macro, just as you will when you play the macro back at a later time.

When you have practiced the steps and set up the same conditions the macro will run under, select Tools ➤ Record Macro ➤ Record New Macro to open the Record New Macro dialog box, shown in Figure 16.1.

Figure 16.1

The Record New Macro dialog box

Excel suggests the macro name Macro1. Click in the Macro Name control and enter a descriptive name for the macro. Macro names must follow these rules:

- They can be up to 255 characters long;

- They can contain numbers, letters, and underscores;

- They cannot contain spaces or any other punctuation;

- They must begin with a letter;

- They must be unique.

The default Description includes the user name and the current date. If you share your computer with others, the user name may be Preferred Customer, Guest, or someone else's name. Select the text in the Description control and enter a new description. Include the date as part of this basic documentation. If other users will have access to the macro, include your name, as well, as shown in Figure 16.2.

Figure 16.2
A macro name and
description

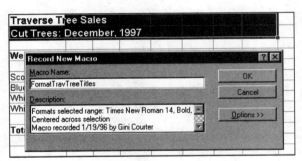

Click the OK button to begin macro recording. The message *Recording* is displayed at the left end of the status bar to show that you are recording a macro. The Stop Recording toolbar (a single button) will open. The macro recorder records the actions you take, but not the time in between actions. It does not matter if you wait before you enter a keystroke or mouse command, so take your time.

If you want the macro to enter text, enter the text now. Type carefully—if you make a mistake and correct it later, the same mistake and correction will be included when you replay the macro. If you want the macro to format text, choose the formatting options from the menu bar, the toolbar, or by using shortcut keys. Make menu selections as you normally would to include them in the macro.

When you are finished entering all the steps in the macro, click the Stop button on the Stop Recording toolbar. The toolbar will close automatically.

EXERCISE 16.1 | **TO CREATE A MACRO**

In this exercise, you will create the macro to format titles in the *Traverse Tree Sales* workbook.

1. **Create the same conditions that will be in effect when you play the macro.** For this exercise, make sure Excel is running and *Traverse Tree Sales* is open. Select the titles and the cells to center the titles across.

2. **Choose Tools ➢ Record Macro ➢ Record New Macro to open the Record New Macro dialog box.**

3. **Enter a Macro Name.** Type FormatTravTreeTitles.

4. **Type a description for the macro. Include the date and your name.** Enter the following description: Formats selected range: Times New Roman 14, Bold, Centered across selection. Macro recorded [today's date] by [your name].

5. **Click OK to begin recording the macro.**

6. **Perform the steps that you want included in the macro.** Choose Format ➢ Format Cells. Click the Alignment tab of the Format Cells dialog box and click Center Across Selection as the Horizontal alignment. Click the Font tab. Select Times New Roman from the font scroll list. Choose the Bold font style. Set the Size to 14. Click OK to close the Format Cells dialog box.

7. **Click the Stop button on the Stop Recording toolbar when you have finished recording the steps of the macro.**

8. **Save the workbook to save the macro.**

SECTION 16.3: MACRO PLAYBACK

It's always a good idea to save open workbooks (including the workbook that contains a macro) before you play a new macro. If you made a mistake during recording, the playback results may not be what you expected. If the macro does not work, you can click Undo, then record the macro again using the same name. To play a macro, choose Tools ➤ Macro to open the Macro dialog box, shown in Figure 16.3. Select the macro below the scroll list of macro names in the Macro Name/Reference control; then click the Run button.

Figure 16.3

The Macro dialog box

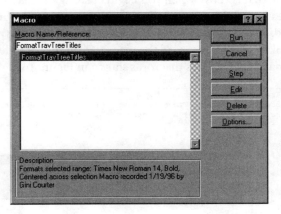

The macro will **execute** (play, run) one step at a time. You can't enter text or choose menu options while the macro is executing. When the macro is done playing, Excel will return control to you.

EXERCISE 16.2	TO PLAY A MACRO

Select A1:E3 (the title area) of the *County Sales* worksheet.

1. **Choose Tools ➤ Macro.**

2. **Select the macro from list of available macros and click Run.** Select FormatTravTreeTitles. Click the Run button to play the macro.

When you created the macro, you used the Format Cells dialog box rather than choosing the font, font style, size, and alignment by clicking toolbar buttons. If you had created the macro using the buttons, the playback results would be unpredictable because the toolbar buttons are toggle buttons. If the titles were already bold, clicking the Bold button would unbold them. If the titles were already centered across the selection, clicking would revert to left alignment. Whenever possible, don't use format toggle buttons in macros unless you can guarantee that the text you select for macro playback will be formatted exactly as the text was when you recorded the macro.

■ Examining the Macro

Excel macros are stored in workbooks. By default, macros are stored in the workbook that is active when you begin creating the macro. FormatTrav-TreeTitles is stored in *Traverse Tree Sales*, and was saved when you saved the workbook. A **module** worksheet (used to store macros) was added to the workbook when you recorded the macro. Click the Module1 sheet tab to view the FormatTravTreeTitles macro, as shown in Figure 16.4.

Figure 16.4

The FormatTrav-TreeTitles macro in its module

```
' FormatTravTreeTitles Macro
' Formats selected range: Times New Roman 14, Bold, Centered across selection
' Macro recorded 1/19/96 by Gini Courter
'
'
Sub FormatTravTreeTitles()
    With Selection.Font
        .Name = "Times New Roman"
        .Strikethrough = False
        .Superscript = False
        .Subscript = False
        .OutlineFont = False
        .Shadow = False
        .Underline = xlNone
        .ColorIndex = xlAutomatic
    End With
```

Visual Basic

◄ ◄ ► ►◄ Cnty Sls - 13 ╱ Dec Cut ╱ County Pivot ╱ County Sales ╲ **Module1** ╱ ◄ ►

Excel records macros in the **Visual Basic** programming language, which is used to create automated applications based on Excel and other Microsoft Office products. Programmers create macros and other procedures directly by typing Visual Basic code into a module window. You can scroll through the Visual Basic module to see the information recorded in a macro. The macro name and description appear at the top of the macro. Programming code follows, beginning with the word Sub.

TIP

If you want to learn about Visual Basic, recording macros and studying the resulting code is a good way to begin.

SECTION 16.4: MACRO RECORDING OPTIONS

Excel offers numerous options for controlling how macros will be recorded and stored. These options are of two types: those you must specify before recording, and those you can change after recording a macro.

■ Options You Must Specify Before Recording

All the macro options are available before recording begins, including the options you can change after you finish recording the macro. The options listed below (Cell References, Macro Storage, and Macro Language) must be selected *before* you choose Macro ➢ Record New Macro or in the Record New Macro dialog box. They cannot be altered once you begin recording.

Cell References

All cell references within a macro are absolute by default. If you click in a cell during macro recording, the macro will select that cell each time you play it back. You can instruct Excel to record all cell and range selections as relative rather than absolute cell references. For example, you might want to format cells, and then move to the cell below the selection. When you record the macro, the cell below the selection is J22. But each time you play the macro, you don't want Excel to select J22; you want to select the cell below the cells you just formatted.

To instruct Excel to use relative cell references, choose Tools ➢ Record Macro ➢ Use Relative References. Then select Tools ➢ Record Macro ➢ Record New Macro to record the macro. Choose Tools ➢ Record Macro ➢ Use Relative References again to turn relative references off and record future macros using absolute references.

Macro Storage

By default, macros are stored in a worksheet in the active workbook. This means the macro is only available when the workbook is open. Macros stored in the default location are called local macros or **workbook macros**. If you close *Traverse Tree Sales* and choose Tools ➢ Macro, the macro list will be empty. You can choose to store the macro as a **global macro**. Global macros are stored in the Personal Macro Workbook in the computer's hard drive. Macros in the Personal Macro Workbook are available from any workbook while you are using the computer the macros were created on. You can only change the storage location before the macro is recorded. In the Record New Macro dialog box (shown in Figures 16.1 and 16.2), click the Options button to display the recording options, shown in Figure 16.5. Choose Personal Macro Workbook from the Store In control to save the macro as a global macro.

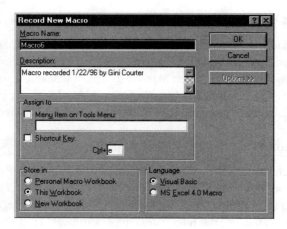

Figure 16.5

Macro Recording
Options

TIP

If you use more than one computer, accept the default location to store macros within the appropriate workbook on your floppy disk. Then, you will always have the macros in that workbook regardless of the computer you are using.

The Personal Macro workbook is created when Excel is installed. If you use Excel on a network, the Personal Macro workbook may be located on a network drive rather than the local hard drive.

Macro Language

Some prior versions of Excel used a macro programming language called XLM. Visual Basic replaced XLM as the programming language beginning with Excel version 5.0. Excel for Windows 95 supports both macro programming languages. If you have XLM macros, Excel will play them. Many Excel users are familiar with XLM and would prefer to record (and edit) macros in XLM. The Language control box lets users record XLM language macros.

EXERCISE 16.3	TO CREATE A GLOBAL MACRO

In this exercise, you are going to create a macro that opens *Peach Hill Theatre* and activates *Ticket Sales* so employees can respond quickly to ticket requests. You want this macro to be available from any worksheet. Before recording the macro, practice the activities in step 8.

1. **Create the same conditions that will be in effect when you play the macro.** For this exercise, make sure Excel is running and the *Peach Hill Theatre* workbook is not open. Since this macro will use absolute cell references, also check to be sure that Relative References is not checked on the Tools ➤ Record Macro menu.

2. **Choose Tools ➤ Record Macro ➤ Record New Macro to open the Record New Macro dialog box.**

3. **Enter a Macro Name.** Type SellTickets.

4. **Type a description for the macro. Include the date and your name.** Description: Opens Peach Hill Theatre; activates Ticket Sales; selects the Customer Name cell. Created [today's date] by [your name].

5. **Click the Options button.**

6. **Change the Store In option to Personal Macro Workbook.**

7. **Click OK to begin recording the macro.**

8. **Perform the steps that you want included in the macro.** Choose File ➤ Open. Select the *Peach Hill Theatre* workbook on your floppy disk. When the file opens, click once on the Ticket Sales sheet tab to activate the sheet. (Do this even if the sheet is already active.) Click in cell B4.

9. **Click the Stop button on the Stop Recording toolbar when you have finished recording the steps of the macro.**

10. Save and close the *Peach Hill Theatre* workbook. Choose Tools ➤ Macro to open the Macro dialog box. Test the macro by playing it.

■ Options After Recording

Before or after recording, you can assign a macro to the Tools menu or a shortcut key combination. You can also add a toolbar button that plays a macro. If you don't assign a macro to any of these locations, it will still be accessible from a list of macros. Obviously, seldom-used macros shouldn't be assigned prime space on the Tools menu, so you'll want to think about how important a macro is when you create it.

TIP

While you can assign macros to shortcut keys, you should use extreme caution when making assignments. Excel will not notify you if the key you assign is already used for another Excel function. Most of the Control key combinations are already in use. It's safer to assign frequently used macros to the Tools menu or a toolbar.

To alter the options that can be changed after a macro has been recorded, choose Tools ➤ Macro, select the macro from the Macro dialog box, then click the Options button. To add a macro to the Tools menu click the Menu Item on Tools Menu check box in the Assign To control. In the text box below the control, enter the name you would like displayed on the menu. Click the OK button to close the Options and return to the Macro dialog box. Click Close. The macro will be added to the bottom of the Tools menu, as shown in Figure 16.6. To play the macro, choose Tools and then select the macro.

Figure 16.6
A macro added to the Tools menu

| EXERCISE 16.4 | TO ASSIGN A MACRO TO THE TOOLS MENU |

1. **If the macro is not global, open the workbook that contains the macro.** Make sure *Traverse Tree Sales* is open.

2. **Choose Tools ➤ Macro from the menu bar.**

3. **Select the macro from the scroll list.** Select FormatTravTreeTitles.

4. **Click the Options button.**

5. **Click the Menu Item on Tools Menu check box in the Assign To control.**

6. **Enter a menu name for the macro.**

7. **Click OK to add the macro to the Tools menu.**

8. **Close the Macro dialog box.**

■ Assigning a Macro to a Toolbar

Some macros you create may be used frequently—five or six times in a session. Excel lets you place these macros on a toolbar button. Macros that you anticipate using regularly can be placed on a toolbar you always display, such as the Standard or Formatting toolbars. You could also create a group of related macros that you use for some special purpose and place them together on a toolbar of their own. (Refer to Session 14 for more information on creating a toolbar.)

Figure 16.7
The Customize dialog box

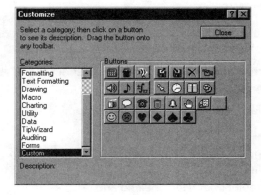

Choose View ➢ Toolbars; then click the Customize button to open the Customize dialog box, shown in Figure 16.7. Select Custom from the Customize toolbars dialog box, and Excel displays a palette of buttons that can be assigned to macros. Select a button from the palette and drag it to the toolbar. When you drop the button, you'll see the Assign Macro dialog box, shown in Figure 16.8.

Figure 16.8
The Assign Macro dialog box

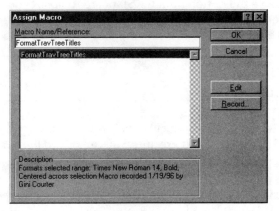

Select the macro you want to assign from the list, then click OK. You will be returned to the Customize dialog box. Click Close. Now, you can play the macro by clicking a toolbar button.

TIP

If you know you are going to add a macro to a toolbar, you can add it when you record it. Begin by selecting View ➤ Toolbars. Drag a button from the Custom palette to the desired toolbar. When the Assign Macro dialog box opens, click Record to open the Record New macro dialog box and start recording the macro.

EXERCISE 16.5	TO ASSIGN A MACRO TO A TOOLBAR BUTTON

1. **If the macro is not global, open the worksheet that contains the macro.**

2. **Choose View ➤ Toolbars; then click Customize.**

3. **Choose Custom from the Categories list.**

4. **Drag a button from the custom palette to the toolbar and drop the button in its desired location.** Drag the yellow happy face to the Standard toolbar between Spelling and Cut.

5. **Select the macro from the Macro Name/Reference list.** Select SellTickets.

6. **Click OK to assign the macro to the button, then Close the Customize dialog box.**

7. Test the button.

8. To remove the button from the Standard toolbar, choose View ➤ Toolbars. Select Standard from the scroll list (make sure you don't click the check box and turn off the toolbar) and click the Reset button.

SECTION 16.5: DELETING MACROS

There are two ways to delete a macro. If you have recorded a macro and are not pleased with the way it executes, you can record the macro again, using the same name. You will be asked if you want to overwrite (delete) the existing macro. You can also choose Tools ➤ Macro, select the macro from the macro list, and click the Delete button to delete the macro from the template. If you delete a macro that has a toolbar button, you also need to choose View ➤ Toolbars (or right-click on a toolbar and choose Toolbars) and remove the macro's button from the toolbar.

You can edit macros, copy macro modules from one workbook to another, add spots for user input or the insertion of specific information, and otherwise customize macros. Excel has extensive on-line help information on macros. When you have mastered the information in this session and want to learn more, choose Help ➤ Answer Wizard from the menu bar and enter **macros** to find help on macros.

What You Have Learned

In this session, you learned how to record simple macros. You know how to create global macros and view a macro in a Visual Basic module. You learned how to execute your macros from the Macro dialog box and how to assign a macro to the Tools menu or a toolbar. Finally, you have learned how to overwrite or delete a macro that you no longer need.

Focus Questions

1. What is a macro?

2. What is the difference between a workbook macro and a global macro?

3. Why would you want to create a global macro?

4. How do you make a macro available just to the workbook you are working on?

5. What are the four ways to access specific macros?

6. How do you delete a macro?

Reinforcement Exercises

Exercise 1   Record a global macro that checks the spelling in the active worksheet and then sends it to the printer. Name the macro SpellPrint, add it to the Standard toolbar, and test it on the *County Sales* worksheet. Reset the Standard toolbar to remove the button.

Exercise 2 Record a global macro that opens the Page Setup dialog box and:

- Changes the footer to (none);

- Uses a header with your name and the current date; and

- Sets all four margins at 1".

Name the macro StandardPageSetup. Execute the macro to see that it works the way you designed it.

Exercise 3 Create a personal toolbar using your name. Add the SpellPrint and StandardPageSetup macros to the toolbar.

Exercise 4 In *Wildlife Federation,* create individual macros to complete the tasks below. Store the macros in the *Wildlife Federation* workbook. Create your own macro names. When all macros are recorded, create a new toolbar named *[your last name] WF.* Add all the macros to the toolbar.

a) Create a macro to format a range of cells for currency, no decimal places.

b) Record a macro that creates a header that includes "All rights reserved, Wildlife Federation," the current date, and your name. The footer should include the sheet name.

c) Record a macro to change the paper orientation to landscape.

d) Create a macro to enter your name in bold in a selected cell.

PART V

Business Applications
in Excel

Using and Constructing Templates

TEMPLATES ARE WORKBOOK models that you use to create other workbooks. Templates let you quickly construct workbooks that are identical in format, giving your work a standardized look. Excel includes templates for many business and home office applications. At the end of this session you will be able to:

- Understand when you should use a template
- Use an existing template
- Create a template

Vocabulary

- CellTip
- lock
- template
- XLS
- XLT

SECTION 17.1: UNDERSTANDING TEMPLATES

In general, a template is a pattern used (and often reused) to guide the creation of a product. A template could be a pattern for a wooden rocking horse, a model for saw cuts required to fit a beam exactly to a joist, or a piece of cardboard showing the position of holes to be drilled to install a lock set. The template helps insure that the saw cuts and drilled holes are uniform: that they are the same each time.

An Excel template helps provide the same kind of uniformity for workbooks, worksheets, and charts. You can create templates for your personal use, but you might also create templates so that novice Excel users can enter information and calculate results without entering formulas. An Excel template can include text, numbers, formatting, formulas, and all the other Excel features you have learned in the previous 16 sessions. A template differs from a normal workbook in one important way: when you save a workbook that you created using a template, a copy is saved and the original template is not altered. This means that the template will be the same each time it is opened.

SECTION 17.2: USING A TEMPLATE

Excel includes predesigned templates that you can use or modify. To open a template, choose File ➤ New from the menu bar to open the New dialog box. (You can't simply click the New button on the Standard toolbar. The New button opens a new default file: an empty workbook.) Click the Spreadsheet Solutions tab to view the built-in Excel templates, shown in Figure 17.1.

Figure 17.1
The New
dialog box—
Spreadsheet
Solutions

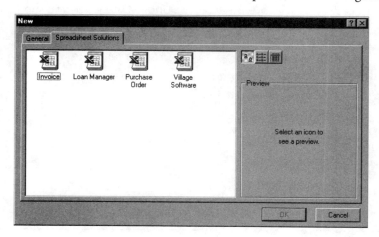

You can use the templates included with Excel to standardize and automate tasks you do frequently. Some templates are included in the Typical Excel installation; others you have to custom-install. (The latter can always be added later.) The Invoice, Loan Manager, and Purchase Order templates are part of the Typical installation. There are business templates and home or home-office templates. The Family Budgeter, for example, was designed to help track and manage household expenses; the Loan Manager was also created for home use.

Click once on any template icon to preview the template. To open an existing template, select the template in the Spreadsheet Solutions window; then click OK.

EXERCISE 17.1   **TO OPEN A TEMPLATE**

1. **Choose File ➢ New from the menu bar.**

2. **Click the Spreadsheet Solutions tab in the New dialog box.**

3. **Click once on a template's icon to preview the template.** Preview one or more templates.

4. **Double-click the icon or click the icon and then click the OK button to open the template.** Open the Loan Manager template.

■ Entering Data

The Loan Manager template, shown in Figure 17.2, is a typical template. There are three worksheets in the *Loan Manager* workbook template: *Loan Data*, *Loan Amortization Table*, and *Summary Graph*. (Hidden from view is the *Customize Your Loan Manager* worksheet; you'll work with that later in this session.) The *Loan Data* worksheet is activated when this template is opened.

Figure 17.2
The *Loan Manager*
workbook template

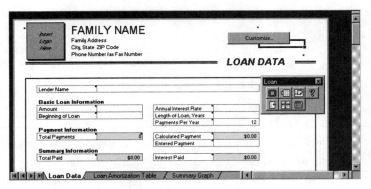

The predesigned templates include special toolbars. As you use each template, its toolbar is added to the list in the Toolbars dialog box. The Loan toolbar initially appears as a palette in the worksheet window. You can move the toolbar if you wish. To view the entire worksheet template, click the Size to Screen button on the Loan toolbar. Clicking the button again returns the worksheet to its original size.

Cells with a red dot include **CellTips** to explain the information you should enter in the cell. To view a CellTip, move the mouse pointer over the dot, as shown in Figure 17.3. You can click the Hide CellTips/Display CellTips button on the Loan toolbar to suppress or enable CellTip display.

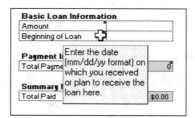

Figure 17.3
Viewing a CellTip

Each template includes sample data so you can examine completed worksheets before entering your data. To view the sample data, click the Display Example/Remove Example button on the template's Loan toolbar. To enter data in the template, click again to remove the example; then enter information in the template as you would in any worksheet. Activate the cell; then enter the information. The green shaded cells contain worksheet formulas; don't enter information in shaded cells.

EXERCISE 17.2	ENTERING THE LOAN DATA

In the *Loan Data* worksheet, enter the following information:

- Lender Name: Community Credit Union
- Amount: 12,000.00
- Beginning of Loan: 1/4/98
- Annual Interest Rate: 10.5
- Length of Loan, Years: 4

Once you've entered loan data, Excel will calculate the total number of payments, monthly (calculated) payment, total paid during the life of the loan, and total interest that will be paid, as shown in Figure 17.4.

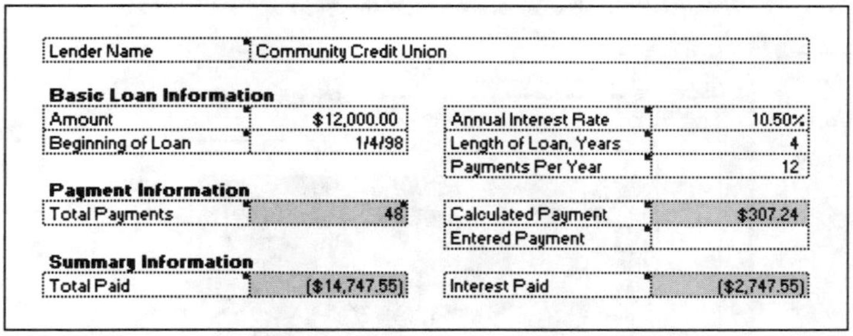

Lender Name	Community Credit Union		
Basic Loan Information			
Amount	$12,000.00	Annual Interest Rate	10.50%
Beginning of Loan	1/4/98	Length of Loan, Years	4
		Payments Per Year	12
Payment Information			
Total Payments	48	Calculated Payment	$307.24
		Entered Payment	
Summary Information			
Total Paid	($14,747.55)	Interest Paid	($2,747.55)

Figure 17.4 A loan calculation in the Loan template

Excel transferred the information you entered in *Loan Data* to *Loan Amortization Table* and *Summary Graph*. *Loan Amortization Table* is a month-by-month breakdown of the loan (see Figure 17.5). You can enter numbers in the Additional Principal column to see how additional payments, applied to principal, reduce the length of the loan. (Enter the additional payment as a negative number so it will be subtracted from the principal.) You can also see the effect of borrowing more (for example, with a revolving line of credit loan) by adding principal in the period when more money is borrowed. You would use the Refinance/Prepay button if you actually make an advance payment or the interest rate for the loan changes. This button isn't part of a toolbar. It's a type of button called a form button, and it is used to play a macro.

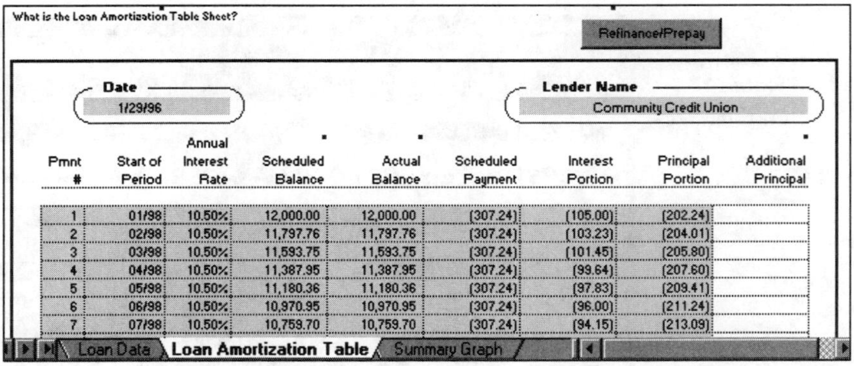

What is the Loan Amortization Table Sheet?

Refinance/Prepay

Date: 1/29/96

Lender Name: Community Credit Union

Pmnt #	Start of Period	Annual Interest Rate	Scheduled Balance	Actual Balance	Scheduled Payment	Interest Portion	Principal Portion	Additional Principal
1	01/98	10.50%	12,000.00	12,000.00	(307.24)	(105.00)	(202.24)	
2	02/98	10.50%	11,797.76	11,797.76	(307.24)	(103.23)	(204.01)	
3	03/98	10.50%	11,593.75	11,593.75	(307.24)	(101.45)	(205.80)	
4	04/98	10.50%	11,387.95	11,387.95	(307.24)	(99.64)	(207.60)	
5	05/98	10.50%	11,180.36	11,180.36	(307.24)	(97.83)	(209.41)	
6	06/98	10.50%	10,970.95	10,970.95	(307.24)	(96.00)	(211.24)	
7	07/98	10.50%	10,759.70	10,759.70	(307.24)	(94.15)	(213.09)	

Loan Data | Loan Amortization Table | Summary Graph

Figure 17.5 The *Loan Amortization Table* worksheet

The *Summary Graph* in Figure 17.6 shows the changing relationship between payments on interest and principal during the life of the loan. The default chart type for the template is 3-D Area, but you can click the Change Graph button and choose a different chart type from an AutoFormat Chart dialog box.

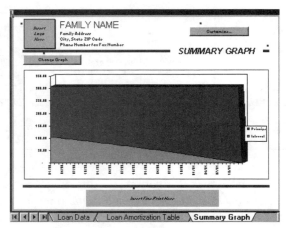

Figure 17.6
The *Summary Graph*
display

■ Customizing the Template

The top of all the worksheets in the template includes placeholders for generic title information: family name, address, a place for a logo or picture. To provide real information, click the Customize button on the "*Loan Data*" or "*Summary Graph*" worksheet to open *Customize Your Loan Manager*, another template worksheet that is normally hidden from view (see Figure 17.7).

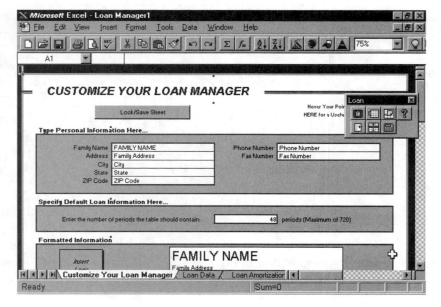

Figure 17.7
Customizing
a template

You can change the generic information for just this workbook, or change the template itself. **Locking** a template prevents users from accidentally changing the customized information in this workbook, but does not alter the template. You can always choose to customize again and unlock the template if you want to change it.

When you save the customization, you are modifying the template itself, so the customized information will appear each time you open the template. You shouldn't save changes to the template if you share your computer with other users. If, however, you are using Excel at home or in an office, it's more convenient to alter the template permanently by saving it. To lock or save template changes, click the Lock/Save button in the customization worksheet. A dialog box (see Figure 17.8) will open, allowing you to select between locking or locking and saving.

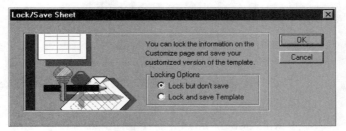

Figure 17.8
The Lock/Save
Sheet dialog box

EXERCISE 17.3   **CUSTOMIZING THE TEMPLATE**

1. Click the Customize button on the *Loan Data* or *Summary Graph* worksheet page.

2. Enter your personal information in the Personal Information section.

3. Click the Lock/Save Sheet button.

4. Choose Lock But Don't Save, then click OK.

5. Try to change the information in the Family Name field. Notice that Excel provides an error message.

6. Save the workbook on your disk as *Loan Manager*. Print the *Loan Data* and *Loan Amortization Table* worksheets. Close the *Loan Manager* workbook.

All of the templates provide complete systems for performing a specific real-world task in Excel. Some of the templates are linked to Excel database worksheets. When you use the Change Request, Expense Statement, Invoice, Purchase Order, Sales Quote, or Time Card templates, information entered in the workbook is automatically copied to a linked Excel database file. For example, when you use the Purchase Order template to create a Purchase Order, Excel adds a new record to a built-in Purchase Order database worksheet that is tied to the template.

SECTION 17.3: CREATING A TEMPLATE

You can create a template for workbooks you create frequently. For example, you might use Excel to complete a weekly payroll and put all the payroll worksheets for one month in a separate workbook. Rather than constructing a new workbook each month, you could create a monthly payroll workbook template. At the beginning of each month you could create a workbook using the template.

Your template will differ from a regular payroll workbook in three specific ways.

- The completed workbook will be saved as a template rather than a workbook.

- It will contain only the text, formulas and formatting that remain the same each month.

- The template will be saved in the Template folder on the computer's hard drive.

You can create a template from scratch or base it on an existing workbook. In earlier sessions, you created and formatted a payroll worksheet. You will use this worksheet as the foundation for a Payroll workbook template.

EXERCISE 17.4	COPYING THE PAYROLL WORKSHEET

1. Open the *Unicorn Software* workbook. Activate *July 6 Payroll*.

2. Select and copy the range of occupied cells.

3. Close *Unicorn Software*. When you are asked if you want to save the Large Clipboard (that contains the cells you just copied) choose Yes.

4. Click the New button on the Standard toolbar, or choose File ➤ New and select workbook to open a new workbook.

> **5.** Activate Sheet1. Click the Paste button to paste the clipboard in the new workbook.
>
> **6.** Adjust column widths as needed.

Next, you need to remove the text and numbers that will vary each week. Don't remove the formulas—although the results of the formula change, the formulas themselves remain the same. Unicorn Software has very little employee turnover, so you could leave the employee names in the template. If you were creating a template to be used with a different set of employees, or if employees changed frequently, you would also delete the employee names.

The *Payroll* worksheets have already been tested with data: the real numbers you used when the worksheets were created. When you create a template from scratch, you still need to enter (and then remove) values to test the template before saving it.

After you have finished deleting extra data, you will have one formatted template worksheet. There are 52 weeks in a year. No matter which day of the week is the payroll ending day, at least three months of the year (usually four) will have five payroll weeks. No month will have more than five payroll weeks. The workbook therefore needs to include five identical payroll worksheets, so you will need to copy *Payroll* to four other worksheets in the workbook.

EXERCISE 17.5 | **FORMATTING AND COPYING THE WORKSHEET**

1. If the *Unicorn Software* workbook contains fewer than five sheets, use Insert ➤ Worksheet to add worksheets.

2. Select the employees' hours and pay rates in Sheet1.

3. Choose Edit ➤ Clear ➤ Contents to clear the values but retain the formatting for the selected cells.

4. Select and copy the occupied range of the worksheet.

5. Click the Sheet2 sheet tab. Hold the Shift key and click the Sheet5 tab to select all four worksheets. Click the Paste button to paste the contents of the clipboard into all four worksheets.

6. Rename *Sheet1* to *Week1*. Rename the other four payroll sheets.

When you choose File ➤ New, Excel loads templates from the Templates folder. If you save your template on your floppy disk, you will not be able to use it as a template. Excel assigns the file extension **XLS** to regular workbooks. Templates are given an **XLT** file extension.

TIP

If you are familiar with Windows 95 file management (discussed in this book's Appendix), you can create a folder within the Templates folder to hold your personal templates. Apart from the General tab, tabs in the New Workbook dialog box represent folders in the Templates folder.

EXERCISE 17.6	TO SAVE A TEMPLATE

1. Click the Save button or choose File ➢ Save from the menu bar. (If the workbook has been saved previously, choose File ➢ Save As from the menu bar.)

2. In the Save As Type control, choose templates (*.xlt) from the drop-down list. The contents of the Save In control will change to the default templates folder.

3. Enter a name for the template in the File Name text box control. Name the template *[Your Last Name] Monthly Payroll*.

4. Click the Save button.

5. Close the *Monthly Payroll* workbook.

When you choose File ➢ New, the *Monthly Payroll* template will be included on the General page, as shown in Figure 17.9. Each time you create a workbook using the *Monthly Payroll* template, a new workbook is created. You can save each month's workbook with the month name: *Payroll—August 1998*. The template itself will not be altered when you create new workbooks.

TIP

To modify a template, you simply open the template, make the desired changes, and save the template.

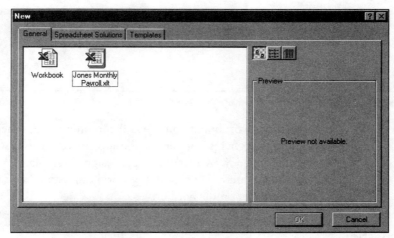

Figure 17.9
Monthly Payroll in
the New dialog box

EXERCISE 17.7   **USING THE TEMPLATE**

1. Choose File ➢ New from the menu bar. Select the *Monthly Payroll* template from the New dialog box.

2. Rename the sheet tabs August 7, August 14, August 21, and August 28.

3. Enter the information below on the appropriate sheets:

Name	Rate	HOURS FOR WEEK ENDING			
		7-Aug	14-Aug	21-Aug	28-Aug
Azimi	$8.75	0	44	24	32
Barzona	$9.00	32	32	32	28
Beckley	$8.00	50	0	32	32
Chiu	$10.00	14	22	22	28
Collins	$10.00	32	19	39	41
Jones	$9.50	44	46	28	0
Retzloff	$7.75	20	30	22	42

4. Choose File ➢ Page Setup. Change the paper orientation to landscape. Create or choose a header that includes your name. Include the sheet name in the footer.

5. Save the workbook as *August 98 Payroll*. Print the *August 21* worksheet. Close the workbook.

As you gain experience with Excel, you can add other features to templates, such as the buttons and toolbars used in the *Loan Manager* template. Use Excel's Help feature to find more information on template design and modification.

What You Have Learned

Templates are workbooks you use as the foundation of other workbooks. Using templates helps standardize the appearance of your worksheets and increases efficiency. Excel includes predesigned templates. You can create templates by constructing or modifying workbooks, and then saving them in the Templates folder on the hard drive.

Focus Questions

1. What is a template?

2. What are some advantages of using a template?

3. What is the difference between locking and saving customization changes?

4. What is the significance of shaded green cells in a template?

5. Where are templates stored?

6. What is the file extension for a template?

Reinforcement Exercises

Exercise 1   Use the *Invoice* template to create a new workbook. Customize *Invoice* as follows:

Wildlife Federation
4497 West Charles Plaza
Boston, MA 02108
phone: 617-742-0090
fax: 617-740-9999

Change the sales tax figure to 6%. Lock but do not save the changes. Activate the *Invoice* worksheet. Create an invoice for order number 10091 (shipped to you at your name and address) for 13 Iguana Long Sleeve T-shirts at 14.95 per shirt. Print the *Invoice* worksheet. Save the workbook on your disk as *Wildlife Invoices*.

Exercise 2   Create another workbook based on the *Loan Manager* template. Customize the workbook with your personal information. Lock, but do not save the customizing changes. Enter information for a three-year loan at 14% from a lending institution of your choice. Print the *Loan Analysis* and *Summary Graph* worksheets. Save the workbook on your disk as *[your name] Loan*.

Exercise 3   Modify *Peach Hill Theatre* to create a template workbook that contains 15 blank *Ticket Sales* forms (*Tix1, Tix2,* etc.) and the *Spring Prices* and *Summer Prices* worksheets. Save the template in the Templates folder as *[your last name]—Peach Hill Tix.* Close *Peach Hill Theatre*. Open *Peach Hill Tix* and test one of the ticket forms. Print the completed ticket form. Close the workbook without saving changes.

Consolidating and Outlining

CONSOLIDATION PROVIDES A **powerful** tool for worksheet summarization. Consolidation tables are used for month- and year-end reporting. Outlining lets you analyze portions of a worksheet, hiding or displaying data to provide another type of summary. At the end of this session you will be able to:

- Construct consolidation tables
- Create an AutoOutline
- Hide and display outline levels

▉ Vocabulary

- AutoOutline
- collapse
- consolidate
- consolidation table
- expand
- outline

SECTION 18.1: CREATING CONSOLIDATION TABLES

Pivot tables summarize relationally; they are used to relate the values in one column (typically in a database) to the values in another column. Consolidation tables summarize laterally: they are used to **consolidate**—to summarize data from one or more worksheets. Consolidation tables are often used to summarize budget information supplied by multiple departments or cost centers to prepare a final budget.

For example, each department of the PressWorks Company submits a budget that includes figures for income, expenses, and profit (or loss). Now it is time to figure out the total Company budget for 1999. Each department head has sent you an Excel workbook containing figures for 1999.

EXERCISE 18.1   **CREATING THE PRESSWORKS BUDGET WORKBOOKS**

1. Open a new workbook.

2. Activate Sheet1.

3. Enter the titles and row headings and formula shown below. Format column B for currency, no decimal places. Add any other formatting you desire.

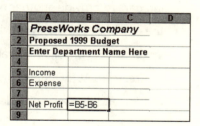

4. Copy A1:B8. Open a new workbook and paste the range into Sheet1. (If you use Edit ➤ Paste Special and then click OK, the worksheet formatting will also be copied.) Save the workbook as *PressWorks Printing.*

5. Open another new workbook. Paste the range in the workbook. Save the workbook as *Pressworks Binding.*

6. Open a fourth new workbook. Paste the copied range. Save the workbook as *PressWorks Marketing.*

7. In the *Printing, Binding,* and *Marketing* workbooks, enter the department name in cell A3 of Sheet1.

8. Enter the values shown here:

	Income	Expense
Printing	227,000	185,000
Binding	298,000	241,500
Marketing	14,250	41,000

9. Save the original workbook as *PressWorks 1999 Budget.* Save and close the three departmental workbooks.

TIP

The *PressWorks 1999 Budget* workbook could have been saved as a *PressWorks Budget* template after step 3 of Exercise 18.1.

Rather than reentering each department's figures in the *PressWorks 1999 Budget* workbook, you can create a consolidation table to add, average, or summarize all the departments' figures. Begin by selecting the cell in the upper-left corner of the consolidation table: the first cell you want to summarize. Then choose Data ➤ Consolidate to open the Consolidate dialog box, shown in Figure 18.1.

Figure 18.1

The Consolidate dialog box

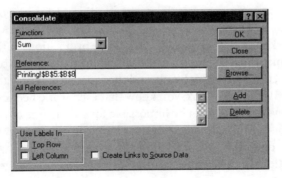

Select the consolidation method from the Function drop-down list. The methods include the standard summarization methods available in pivot tables and more advanced methods such as standard deviation. To create a total budget you would, of course, use Sum.

Activate the Reference control. Then enter the reference for the first range you wish to consolidate: the four-cell range in Sheet1 of the *Printing* workbook that includes the figures for income, expenses, and profit: *PressWorks Printing!B5:B8*. Click the Add button to add the range reference to the All References list.

TIP

The exclamation point (!) in the reference indicates that PressWorks Printing is the name of a workbook or worksheet. When the reference includes the name of a specific sheet within a workbook, the name of the workbook is placed in brackets: [PressWorks Printing]Sheet1!B5:B8.

Edit the contents of the Reference control by changing Printing to Binding. Editing is a little tricky; the cell pointer is active while the Reference control is selected. Use the mouse to move the text box insertion point; using the keyboard arrow keys moves the cell pointer in the active worksheet. Click the Add button to add the second reference to the list. Change Binding to Marketing and add the final departmental workbook to the list.

The All References list should now have three entries, cells B5:B8 in each of the three workbooks. If you make a mistake while entering ranges, you can select the incorrect range in the All References list and then click the Delete button to remove the reference from the list.

■ Consolidating by Position and Category

There are two ways to consolidate: by position, or by category. If you know that the relationship of the cells within the selected range will be identical in each workbook, you can safely consolidate by position. In the *PressWorks* workbooks, the relationship is the same. The first cell is income, the second is expenses, the third cell is blank, and the fourth cell is profit. Since you created the *PressWorks* workbook, you know that each worksheet is identical.

However, it would not be impossible for a user (one of the department heads, for example) to delete the blank row or add another row, changing the position of the cells in relationship to each other. Then, you could not use positional consolidation and would need to consolidate by category.

The Use Labels In control is very important; checking either box in this control instructs Excel to consolidate by category rather than position. When you consolidate by category, the range of cells to consolidate in each workbook needs to include a set of unique labels in either the top row or the left column. While the labels don't need to be in the same relative position in each workbook, they do need to be spelled the same way in each. You click the appropriate check box in the Use Labels In control to let Excel know the location of the unique labels.

EXERCISE 18.2	TO CREATE A CONSOLIDATION TABLE

1. **Select the cell that will be in the upper-left corner of the consolidation table.** Open the *PressWorks 1999 Budget* workbook. Select cell B5 in Sheet1.

2. Select Data ➤ Consolidate from the menu bar.

3. **Choose a Function from the drop-down list.** Leave the default setting, Sum.

4. **Click in the Reference control.**

5. **Select the first range of cells to be consolidated, then click the Add button.** Enter *PressWorks Printing!B5:B8*.

6. **Add all other ranges to be consolidated.** Change *Printing* to *Binding* in the Reference text box; click Add. Change *Binding* to *Marketing*. Click Add.

7. **If you are consolidating by category, click one or both check boxes in the Use Labels In control to specify label locations.** Since you are consolidating by position, leave the check boxes blank.

8. **If you want the contents of the consolidation table to reflect changes in the underlying data, click the Create Links to Source Data check box.** Do not create links.

9. **Click the OK button to close the dialog box and create the consolidation table.**

Excel summarizes the contents of the specified ranges of cells and creates the consolidation table, beginning at the cell you selected. The *PressWorks* consolidation table is shown in Figure 18.2.

Figure 18.2
The *PressWorks* consolidation table

PressWorks Company		
Proposed 1999 Budget		
Consolidated Budget		
Income	$	539,250
Expense	$	467,500
Net Profit	$	71,750

■ Linking Tables to Sources

Clicking the Create Links to Data Source check box constructs a dynamic link to the ranges included in the consolidation table. If values in the ranges change, the values in the consolidation table change. A linked consolidation table is a moving, changing table. An unlinked table is a snapshot—a picture of the underlying budgets at the time the consolidation table is created. You will want to consolidate using links during the budget creation process. When department heads make changes to their budgets, the consolidated budget will change each time it is opened. When the final budget has been produced, you should consolidate again without links to freeze the final budget so that future changes in the departmental worksheets don't change the consolidated budget.

When you create links to the source data, Excel outlines the completed consolidation table so you can view both the consolidated data and the underlying detail. If you create links and consolidate by category, Excel will include the name of each workbook in the outline.

EXERCISE 18.3	MODIFYING THE CONSOLIDATION TABLE

1. Select cells A5:B8 as the consolidation table area.

2. Choose Data ➢ Consolidate to open the Consolidate dialog box.

You need to delete the three existing references and create three new references that include the headings in column A. Rather than re-enter all three references, you will edit the existing references to create new ones, and then delete the original references.

3. Select the reference to *Printing*. Change B5 to A5; then click the Add button.

4. Delete the unedited reference that includes B5.

5. Repeat for the *Binding* and *Marketing* references.

6. Click Use Labels In Left Column and Create Links to enable both categorical consolidation and linking.

7. Click the OK button to close the dialog box and create the new consolidation table.

A gray bar has been added to the left edge of the worksheet. This is an outline bar. You will learn about outlining later in this session. This version of the consolidation table is linked to the three workbooks used in the consolidation. If you change the values in any of the three workbooks, the consolidation table will be automatically updated if it is open. If it is not open, the next time you open the *PressWorks 1999 Budget*, a dialog box (see Figure 18.3) will appear asking if you want to reestablish the links. Click the Yes button, and Excel will update the consolidation table.

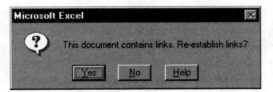

Figure 18.3
The dialog box for
reestablishing links

EXERCISE 18.4   **CHANGING UNDERLYING DATA**

1. Save and close *PressWorks 1999 Budget*.

2. Open *PressWorks Printing*.

3. Change the Income value to 303,000. Save the changes. Close *PressWorks Printing*.

4. Open *PressWorks 1999 Budget*. Click Yes to reestablish the links to the departmental workbooks. Note that the Income and Net Profit values in the consolidation table changed to reflect the additional projected income in the Printing department.

5. Save *PressWorks 1999 Budget*.

SECTION 18.2: USING EXCEL OUTLINES

The new table was automatically outlined, as shown in Figure 18.4. A plus button appears in the gray outline bar on the left side of the worksheet window.

■ Expanding and Collapsing an Outline

The plus button indicates that there is a lower level of detail associated with a heading. To view the detail, click the plus button. The lower level will be **expanded** (displayed). After adjusting the width of column B, the outlined consolidation table appears as shown in Figure 18.5.

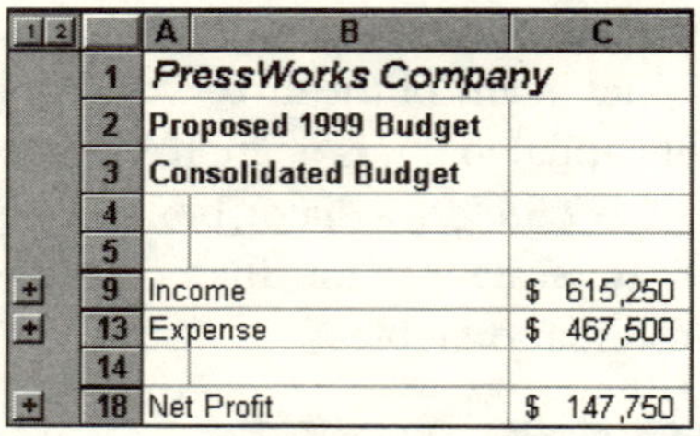

Figure 18.4
Outlined
consolidation
table

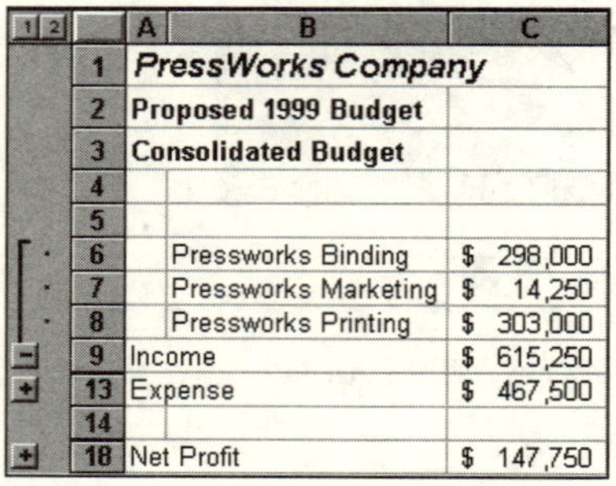

1 2		A	B	C
	1	*PressWorks Company*		
	2	**Proposed 1999 Budget**		
	3	**Consolidated Budget**		
	4			
	5			
	9	Income		$ 615,250
	13	Expense		$ 467,500
	14			
	18	Net Profit		$ 147,750

Figure 18.5
Expanding an
outline level
sheet

1 2		A	B	C
	1	*PressWorks Company*		
	2	**Proposed 1999 Budget**		
	3	**Consolidated Budget**		
	4			
	5			
	6		Pressworks Binding	$ 298,000
	7		Pressworks Marketing	$ 14,250
	8		Pressworks Printing	$ 303,000
	9	Income		$ 615,250
	13	Expense		$ 467,500
	14			
	18	Net Profit		$ 147,750

The plus sign has been replaced with a bracket terminating in a button with a minus sign. Click on the minus button to **collapse** (hide) the Income detail, returning the outline to the form shown in Figure 18.4.

The outline has only two levels of detail. The two buttons at the top of the gray outline bar allow you to expand or collapse all the levels of the outline at once. Click the button for the lowest level of outline you wish to display. To see just the summary information, click the 1 button. The 2 button expands all the outline levels. When you print an outlined worksheet, only the levels displayed are printed.

EXERCISE 18.5	EXPANDING AND COLLAPSING THE OUTLINE

1. Click the level 2 button to fully expand the outline. Print Preview the expanded outline.

2. Click the minus button to collapse the Net Profit detail. Print Preview the partially collapsed outline.

3. Click the level 1 button to collapse the entire outline. Preview the fully collapsed outline.

To turn the outline off and display the entire worksheet, choose Data ➢ Group and Outline ➢ Clear Outline from the menu bar. To turn the outline back on, select any cell in the consolidation table and choose Data ➢ Group and Outline ➢ AutoOutline.

EXERCISE 18.6 **TO TURN OUTLINING ON OR OFF**

1. **To turn off outlining, choose Data ➢ Group and Outline ➢ Clear Outline from the menu bar.**
2. **To turn outlining on, select any cell in the area to be outlined and choose Data ➢ Group and Outline ➢ AutoOutline.** Select any cell in the consolidation table before making the menu choices.
3. Save and close *PressWorks 1999 Budget*.

Outlines are not just used with consolidation tables. Outlining can be used for any worksheet that can be separated into logical components. Select any cell in the area of the worksheet to be outlined, and choose Data ➢ Group and Outline ➢ AutoOutline from the menu bar to have Excel outline the worksheet. Figure 18.6 shows a portion of the *Budget* worksheet from the *Personal Worksheets* workbook with outlining enabled.

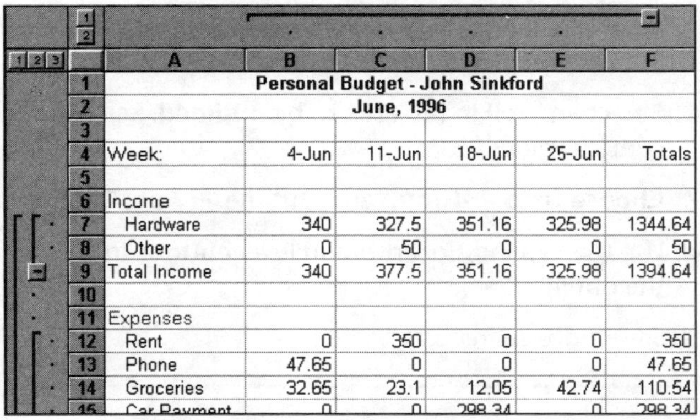

	A	B	C	D	E	F
1	Personal Budget - John Sinkford					
2	June, 1996					
3						
4	Week:	4-Jun	11-Jun	18-Jun	25-Jun	Totals
5						
6	Income					
7	Hardware	340	327.5	351.16	325.98	1344.64
8	Other	0	50	0	0	50
9	Total Income	340	377.5	351.16	325.98	1394.64
10						
11	Expenses					
12	Rent	0	350	0	0	350
13	Phone	47.65	0	0	0	47.65
14	Groceries	32.65	23.1	12.05	42.74	110.54
15	Car Payment	0	0	298.34	0	298.34

Figure 18.6
The *Personal Worksheets Budget* outline

Outlining is frequently used during budget preparation. It isn't unusual for an institutional budget to have hundreds or thousands of individual **line items:** accounts reflected in the budget. Some users need to access specific line items, but many do not. Leafing through a fifty-page budget to find departmental or functional totals can be very intimidating. Outlining lets you provide different users with different—and appropriate—levels of information.

The budget outline can be fully collapsed and printed (or charted and printed) as an "Executive Summary" for individuals who need to view major categories, but not specific details. All or part of the expanded outline can be used by people working with specific line items in the budget. Using an outline is easier and less prone to error than creating and updating a separate worksheet for users who only require summary information.

■ Determining Outline Levels

When Excel creates an AutoOutline, it analyzes the formulas in the worksheet to determine the outline levels. If a cell is **referred to** in a formula, it will be placed in the level below the cell that **contains** the formula. The *Personal Worksheets Budget* includes a Net Savings formula, which refers to the Total Income and Total Expense formulas. Net Savings will be assigned to level 1; Total Income and Total Expense will be assigned to level 2; and the cells that are included in Total Income and Total Expense will be assigned to level 3.

Two sets of outline controls appear in this worksheet. Since the worksheet also includes row totals, the columns have two levels: one for the total in column F and a second level that includes the weekly data in columns B through E.

EXERCISE 18.7	TO CREATE AN AUTOOUTLINE

1. **Open the worksheet you wish to outline.** Open *Traverse Tree Sales*. Activate the *Dec Cut* worksheet.

2. **Select any cell in the area to be outlined.** Select any of the cells that contain values.

3. **Choose Data ➢ Group and Outline ➢ AutoOutline**.

4. Use the Expand, Collapse, and level buttons to view different aspects of the outline.

5. Save *Traverse Tree Sales*.

Consolidating and outlining are often used together to summarize, view, and print restricted views of budget information. You can consolidate departmental budgets into a total budget, then collapse and print an overview of the total budget. Departmental budgets can be outlined so users can view line item details or summary totals.

What You Have Learned

Consolidation tables summarize information from different workbooks or worksheets in one worksheet. Tables can be created by position or by category. You can link the consolidation table to the source data so changes in the consolidated worksheets are reflected in the table. Consolidated tables that are created by category and linked are automatically outlined. You can create outlines for other worksheets by selecting choices from the Data menu.

Focus Questions

1. What does consolidation mean?

2. What are the two ways to consolidate?

3. Why would you link a consolidation table to source data?

4. What are some of the advantages of outlines?

5. How does Excel determine the levels of an outline?

Reinforcement Exercises

Exercise 1   Create a consolidated payroll report based on the *August 98 Payroll* workbook created in Session 17. The completed consolidation table for *Payroll* is shown in Figure 18.7.

Figure 18.7

The *Payroll* consolidation table

	A	B	C	D	E	F
1	Unicorn Software Payroll					
2	Week Ending					
3						
4	Name	Hours	Rate	Gross Pay	Taxes	Net Pay
5	Azimi	100	$ 35.00	$ 892.50	$ 169.58	$ 722.93
6	Barzona	124	$ 36.00	$ 1,116.00	$ 212.04	$ 903.96
7	Beckley	114	$ 32.00	$ 952.00	$ 180.88	$ 771.12
8	Chiu	86	$ 40.00	$ 860.00	$ 163.40	$ 696.60
9	Collins	131	$ 40.00	$ 1,315.00	$ 249.85	$ 1,065.15
10	Jones	118	$ 38.00	$ 1,168.50	$ 222.02	$ 946.49
11	Retzloff	114	$ 31.00	$ 891.25	$ 169.34	$ 721.91
12						
13	Totals	787		$ 7,195.25	$ 1,367.10	$ 5,828.15

All the payroll worksheets are already included in one workbook, so it makes sense to place the consolidation table in a blank worksheet in the *August 98 Payroll* workbook. Begin by copying and modifying one of the existing payroll worksheets to use for the consolidation table.

You can use either positional or categorical consolidation; the cell you select for the consolidation table depends on the consolidation method you select. Do not link the table to the data.

TIP

When the areas to be consolidated are in the current workbook, you can click sheet tabs and drag to select cells when entering References in the Consolidate dialog box. Or you can type the sheet name, an exclamation point, and the cell range as you would with references to other workbooks.

Name the consolidation table worksheet *Aug Total*. Print *Aug Total* and save *August 98 Payroll*.

Exercise 2   Open *Personal Worksheets*. Activate the *Budget* worksheet. AutoOutline *Budget*. Collapse all the row levels and print the worksheet. Save *Personal Worksheets*.

Exercise 3   a) Open *PressWorks Printing*. Copy Sheet1 and paste it into a new workbook. In cell A3, enter Warehouse. Enter these figures in the new workbook: Income: 0; Expense: 41,250. Save the new workbook as *PressWorks Warehouse*. Close *PressWorks Printing* and *PressWorks Warehouse*.

b) Open *PressWorks 1999 Budget*. In a blank worksheet, create an unlinked positional consolidation table that includes all four departments. Name the worksheet *Dept4*. Print *Dept4* and save *PressWorks 1999 Budget*.

Exercise 4   Complete Part (a) of Exercise 3 if you have not done so. Open *PressWorks 1999 Budget*. In a blank worksheet, create a linked categorical consolidation table that includes all four departmental workbooks. Name the worksheet *Dept4Link*. Fully expand the *Dept4Link* outline, and then print the worksheet. Save *PressWorks 1999 Budget*.

Using the "What-If" Tools

E XCEL'S WHAT-IF TOOLS are used with worksheet models to forecast possible solutions to business problems. This session focuses on using Excel to solve business problems when one or more variables are unknown. At the end of this session you will be able to:

- Explain how Excel is used for simple forecasting
- Create a model to represent business variables
- Use Goal Seek to solve for a single variable
- Use Solver in a single-variable model
- Use Solver to find optimal solutions by changing more than one variable

Vocabulary

- constraint
- fixed expense
- forecast
- Goal Seek
- iteration
- linear programming
- model
- optimal solution
- simulate
- Solver
- variable expense
- What-if
- wiffing

SECTION 19.1: FORECASTING AND MODELING

If you were going to fly across the continent for a week of business meetings, chances are you would at least think about checking the weather forecast to find out what type of clothing to pack. Even though you packed a raincoat, you wouldn't be too surprised if the rain turned to snow or even sunshine. And we all know that there is no point in filing a complaint about the weather. Regardless of the forecast, no one can personally alter the weather that actually "arrives." Following the forecast does, however, increase the possibility that you will be properly prepared.

Business **forecasts**—predictions of business factors like product demand, production costs, income, and expenses—are the "weather prediction" for a business unit's future. Like a weather forecast, the business forecast may be less than completely accurate. However, there is one important difference between a weather forecast and a business forecast. While you can't change the weather, managers can monitor the progress a business makes and alter business decisions so that actual performance is more closely related to the forecast.

Forecasts try to **simulate** or predict future behavior of variables like Gross Profit based on many types of information. A forecast may be based on:

■ Historical information like last year's earnings

■ Judgments or educated guesses by people in a position to help predict future performance: managers, clients, sales staff

■ Information about indicators like the prices charged by competitors, the local employment level, or the current interest rate

The more sources of information you consider, the more accurate your forecast will be. You might be more likely to trust a weather person who looked at a radar reading than one who simply looked out the window.

There are different ways to construct forecasts. In Excel, forecasting always involves creating a **model**: one or more worksheets that use formulas to show how different variables interrelate. You have used models in earlier sessions. The Loan Manager template used in Session 17 is a forecasting model. The worksheet includes the financial functions that detail the relationships between interest rate, principal, payment amount, and the number of payments. You can use the Loan Manager model to forecast the future of a loan. If you enter different values for principal or interest you can see how the payment amount or length of loan change.

You have also created simple models. The *Payroll* worksheets are models of the relationships between hours worked, pay rate, gross pay, taxes, and net pay. Inventory worksheets model the interactions of quantity, cost, and total cost. These are all known, well-defined sets of relationships, commonly understood and used in the business world.

Forecasting is always based on assumptions. Each model has specific, built-in assumptions, but there are some assumptions common to most models. One general assumption is that the future will be much like the present: the world's financial markets won't fall apart during the life of a loan, and you will need to make a loan payment this month, and every month in the future until the loan is paid off. There is also an assumption that a modeled forecast will not be perfect. There will always be some neglected piece of information that ends up being important (like the month that the payment is received late, resulting in a penalty).

Another assumption is that the distant future is more difficult to predict than the near future. (That's why it is difficult to get 50-year mortgages.) No one could have accurately predicted the last four years of stock market prices, or the increasing sales of PCs over the past decade. As the time period involved in a forecast increases, the accuracy of the forecast decreases, even if the model was essentially accurate when it was originally constructed.

Excel provides a number of good tools for numerical forecasting. You already know how to use many of these tools: the functions and formulas. For more advanced work, Excel includes specialized forecasting tools called What-if tools, used in **What-if analysis**. (Using What-if tools is sometimes called **wiffing**, short for "What-if"ing.)

There are several steps involved in building a model and using it to forecast performance:

1. Decide what you need to know from the model.

2. Make explicit assumptions.

3. Define and collect information for the model.

4. Create the model in Excel.

5. Use the model to forecast the future value of variables.

6. Compare real performance to the model and adjust the model (or change actual performance) as necessary.

The effort you spend on each step should be based on the importance of the information you intend to obtain from the model. You don't want to spend hours researching a decision to save two dollars. But you need to spend sufficient time when you are creating a model to support decision-making that involves hundreds of thousands of dollars.

Let's use a fictitious company, the WellBilt Manufacturing Corporation, to look at business modeling. WellBilt makes a variety of PC accessories. Its CD Division makes organizers for compact disks.

What You Need to Know

WellBilt needs to decide how many organizers the CD Division should make each month. You have been put in charge of collecting and modeling the information needed to decide how the CD Division can maximize monthly Gross Profit.

Model Assumptions

WellBilt assumes that they will still be able to market the CD organizers to large computer stores as they have in the past. More assumptions will be added as information is collected.

Collecting Information

You will need to collect information on the income generated by organizer sales and the expenses involved in manufacturing the CD organizers. Some of the expenses are **fixed expenses**: expenses that are the same amount no matter how many CD organizers are manufactured. Other expenses (like labor and materials) are **variable expenses.**

You talked to the Accounting department and found that the CD Division's fixed expenses are not expected to change from current monthly costs ($80,000 for building mortgage, maintenance, and salaries) in the next year. There are several pieces of variable cost information: hourly employees make $6.00; overtime hours are paid at time and a half. During a month, the current workforce can build 48,000 organizers without working overtime. Each CD organizer takes an hour to make and uses $1.25 in raw materials.

You also spoke with the Marketing department, which has already created an Excel statistical model to determine sales at various prices for the CD Organizer. They have determined that the formula Price=$20−(Quantity/5000) expresses the price needed to sell a particular quantity. In other words, the most anyone will spend for a CD organizer is $20. At a price of $19, Well-Bilt would be able to sell only 5000 units. For each additional 5000 units sold, WellBilt has to drop the price $1. This month, WellBilt manufactured and sold 45,000 units.

Creating the Model

You now have enough information to create an Excel model of the basic factors that influence production of CD organizers. (You also have some new assumptions: that the information from Accounting and Marketing is accurate, and that the model is good for the next year.)

The Accounting department information contains an IF statement: if production is less than or equal to 48,000 units, then the cost of labor is $6 per hour. Hours in excess of 48,000 cost $9 per hour—similar to the IF statement you created for *Payroll* in Session 15. Since this month's sales were 45,000, let's begin by modeling production of sales of 40,000, 45,000, and 50,000 units, as shown in Figure 19.1.

Figure 19.1
The CD Division model

	A	B	C	D
1	WellBilt Manufacturing			
2	CD ROM Disk Organizer Production			
3				
4	Income	High	Medium	Low
5	Units Produced & Sold	50,000	45,000	40,000
6	Unit Price	10.00	11.00	12.00
7	Total Income	500,000	495,000	480,000
8				
9	Expense			
10	Fixed Expense	80,000	80,000	80,000
11	Labor Expense	306,000	270,000	240,000
12	Material Expense	62,500	56,250	50,000
13	Total Expense	448,500	406,250	370,000
14				
15	Gross Profit	51,500	88,750	110,000

EXERCISE 19.1 | **CREATING THE CD DIVISION MODEL**

1. Open a new workbook.

2. Enter the titles in rows 1 and 2 of Figure 19.1.

3. Enter the row headings in column A and the column headings in row 4.

4. Enter the Units Produced & Sold figures in row 5.

5. In cell B6, enter the formula from the Marketing Department:
   =20-(B5/5000). Fill the formula to C6 and D6.

6. In B7, enter a formula to multiply Units Produced & Sold by Price.
   Fill the formula to C7 and D7.

7. In row 10, enter and fill the Fixed Expense information from the Accounting Department.

CONTINUES ON NEXT PAGE

> **8.** In B11, enter the IF formula to calculate the added expense of overtime production: =IF(B5<48000,B5*6,(48000*6)+(B5-48000)*9) and fill the formula to C11 and D11.
>
> **9.** Construct and fill the Material Expense formula in row 12: =1.25*B5.
>
> **10.** Enter and fill a formula for Total Expense in row 13.
>
> **11.** Enter and fill a formula for Gross Profit (Total Income − Total Expense) in row 15.
>
> **12.** Name the sheet *CD Div Model*. Save the workbook as *WellBilt*.
>
> **13.** Examine the formulas in the model. Compare them to the information from Marketing and Accounting to see how the model reflects the information provided.

The model indicates that lower levels of production produce higher levels of Gross Profit. Since your model includes the current level of production, you have a way to check the accuracy of the model. Is Gross Profit currently $88,750 a month? If it is not, you know that there is information missing from the model that you need to identify and include. If current Gross Profit is close to the figure in the model, you can have some confidence in the model's ability to predict Gross Profit at other levels of production. Remember, though, that the model has a limitation: it's only valid for the three production figures that you included. You can't draw conclusions about the Gross Profit at other quantities produced and sold without expanding the model.

SECTION 19.2: USING GOAL SEEK

You use the **Goal Seek** tool when you need to find a specific solution to a formula. Goal Seek is used to calculate backwards—to determine the values necessary to reach a specific goal. Once you have created a worksheet model, you can use Goal Seek to get a specific answer. For example, one of the WellBilt managers wants to know how many units must be manufactured and sold to result in Gross Profits of exactly $100,000 per month. You know the goal, and Goal Seek will help you find the answer.

Goal Seek changes the value of an underlying number (the Quantity Produced & Sold) until the value in the goal cell (Gross Profit) is equal to the goal ($100,000). Excel will begin by trying an upper and lower value for the Quantity Produced. If the goal falls between the initial values, Goal Seek then narrows the value in small increments until the Gross Profit value is within 0.01 of the goal. If the goal value is outside the initial range, Goal Seek will try larger values. Each attempt to meet the goal is called an **iteration**. The default settings (Tools ➤ Options ➤ Calculation) instruct Excel to try 100 iterations before giving up.

Choose Tools ➤ Goal Seek to open the Goal Seek dialog box, shown in Figure 19.2.

Figure 19.2
The Goal Seek
dialog box

You must enter references or values in all three controls of the Goal Seek dialog box:

Set Cell: the cell that will contain the goal result (Gross Profit cell)

To Value: the target value (100,000)

By Changing Cell: the cell that contains the value that will be incrementally changed to try to reach the goal in the Set Cell (Quantity Produced & Sold)

You can type in the Set Cell and Changing Cell references, or use the mouse to enter the references. The contents of the To Value control must be a value. After you have entered all three pieces of information, click the OK button and Goal Seek will begin testing different values in the Changing Cell.

There are two possible results of a Goal Seek operation: the goal can be reached within 100 iterations, or it cannot. If Goal Seek finds a value that results in the target value you specified, it will let you know in the dialog box shown in Figure 19.3.

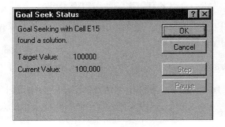

Figure 19.3
Goal Seek solved

The dialog box indicates both the goal value and Goal Seek's progress in matching the value. In this case, the match is exact. Goal Seek was able to find a value for Quantity Produced & Sold that resulted in a Gross Profit of exactly $100,000. Clicking the OK button replaces the figures in the Set and By Changing cells with the Goal Seek results. Clicking Cancel leaves the original figures in the two cells.

Some problems don't have a solution. Figure 19.4 shows the Goal Seek Status dialog box when a solution could not be found. The target value entered for Gross Profit was 250,000. Goal Seek has already tried 100 numbers. The last number tried is displayed as the Current Value—a very large negative number. Goal Seek has already tried both positive and negative numbers as large as the Current Value shown in the dialog box.

Even when Goal Seek can't find a solution, you know more than you did before: there is no solution. Given the current values for price, fixed expenses, and variable expenses, WellBilt cannot make $250,000 a month from the CD Division no matter how many CD organizers they manufacture. You can click Cancel to discard the value and close the dialog box.

Figure 19.4
Goal Seek:
no solution

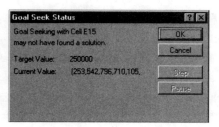

EXERCISE 19.2   **TO USE GOAL SEEK**

Open the *WellBilt CD Div Model*. Enter the label Goal in cell E4. Fill the values and formulas in column D to column E. The Units Produced & Sold and Fixed Expenses figures will change.

1. **Choose Tools ➢ Goal Seek from the menu bar.**

2. **Select a Set Cell (E15) where you want the goal value to appear. This cell must contain a formula.**

3. **Enter the goal value (100000) in the To Value control.**

4. **Enter the value to change (E5) in the By Changing Cell control.**

5. **Click OK to start Goal Seek.**

6. **To accept the solution, click OK in the Goal Seek Status dialog box to enter the Goal Seek solution in cell E5. To reject the solution, click Cancel.** Click OK to accept the solution.

Goal Seek found a solution for the goal value. If WellBilt manufactures exactly 42,646 units and sells them for $11.47 each, the Gross Profit for the CD Division will hit the $100,000 target. Goal Seek is a useful tool any time you know the value of the end result you are trying to achieve.

SECTION 19.3: USING THE SOLVER

The **Solver** is used to find the best or **optimal solution**. Optimization has many business applications. Solver can be used to find the least expensive solution to a problem, or a solution that maximizes income. Remember that our original assignment was to maximize Gross Profit. This is a job for Solver. Choose Tools ➢ Solver to open the Solver dialog box, shown in Figure 19.5.

Figure 19.5
The Solver
dialog box

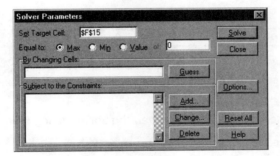

TIP

Solver is an add-in, and may not have been installed on your computer. Check Tools ➢ Add-Ins to make sure Solver is on the list of Excel add-ins installed on your system. If it is not, you can add it by running the Excel Setup program.

■ Solving for a Single Variable

Solver's Target Cell is the same as Goal Seek's Set Cell: the cell that the final result should appear in. You choose Max, Min, or Value in the Equal To control to indicate whether you are looking for the largest or smallest possible number, or a set value (as you did with Goal Seek). As in Goal Seek, the By Changing

Cells entry is the cell containing the value that Solver is to change to find the solution indicated. After you have made choices for these three controls, clicking the Solve button instructs Solver to find a solution. Like Goal Seek, Solver will try 100 iterations before reporting that it cannot find a solution. The results of a successful optimization are shown in Figure 19.6.

Figure 19.6
The Solver Results
dialog box

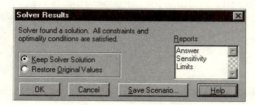

You can choose to place the Solver solution in the worksheet, or restore the original values.

CAUTION

If you choose Keep Solver Solution your worksheet, the original values will be deleted. You cannot undo this change.

EXERCISE 19.3 | **TO USE SOLVER**

Open *CD Div Model*. Enter the label Optimal in F4. Copy the values and formulas in column E to column F. Make sure the value for Fixed Expenses does not change.

1. Choose Tools ➣ Solver to open the Solver dialog box.

2. Set the Target Cell (F15).

3. Set an Equal To option. Choose Equal To Max.

4. Enter the cell to be changed in the By Changing Cells control. Choose cell F5.

5. Click Solve.

6. Click OK in the Solver Results dialog box to keep the Solver Solution or choose Restore Original Values and click OK to reject the solution. Keep the Solver Solution.

7. Save the workbook.

The CD Division's maximum Gross Profit ($123,203) occurs when 31,875 units are produced and sold for $13.63 apiece. The only way the CD Division can make a greater profit is to change one of the underlying variables. For example, the division could:

- Lower fixed expenses by finding a less expensive building

- Pay employees less (not a popular choice, and one that often backfires by resulting in lower overall production), or

- Boost marketing efforts so consumers will pay more for WellBilt CD organizers.

However, given the current relationships between the model variables, Solver has found the optimal solution.

Using Solver with Multiple Variables

Goal Seek can only be used to find a solution by changing one variable, but Solver can work with multiple variables at the same time. Solver also lets you provide specific **constraints**—limits for individual variables—to guide the optimization process. Our current What-if scenario has only one changing variable (Units Produced & Sold) and no constraints except those already included in the model's formulas. Many business problems are more complex: choosing between Choice A, Choice B, or a mix of the two. This type of problem requires a type of analysis called **linear programming** (also known as linear analysis)—finding the best intersection between two or more courses of action when changes in the variables would produce straight lines on a chart.

Thanks to your model, the CD Division is now making maximum profit. A work team in the CD Division suggests that the division expand its product line. Each of the division's six pressing machines can make Laser Disk Organizers as well as CD Organizers. Laser Disk Organizers sell for a higher price, but they also take longer to produce. Each CD Organizer produced and sold results in $3.87 profit for the division ($123,203/31,875). Marketing predicts that LD Organizers will make $5.00 per unit.

The CD Division needs to find out whether it would increase profit to spend part of their time making LD Organizers. (A machine can't do both at the same time.) WellBilt could simply try a new product mix for a couple of months, but if you construct an accurate model, Solver can help you determine the mix of products that will maximize profit. There are some specific constraints:

- It takes 3 pounds of material to make a CD Organizer. It only takes 2 pounds to make an LD Organizer.

■ The division has 50 pounds of pre-processed material available daily for each machine. Currently that material is used to make 16.67 CD Organizers daily.

■ One hour of machine time is required to make a CD Organizer. LD Organizers take 2 hours of machine time. (In a 24-hour day, a machine can turn out 24 CD Organizers, or 12 LD Organizers.)

We need to begin by creating a model that includes the relevant information for CD and LD Organizer production to help determine the best production mix. This model doesn't need a lot of formulas. A completed model for one machine with formulas displayed is shown in Figure 19.7.

Figure 19.7
The product
mix model

	A	B	C	D	E	F
1	WellBilt					
2	CD/LD Mix					
3						
4	Production Mix	Qty	Hours	Mat'l	Profit	Total Profit
5	Current					
6	CD Organizer	=D6/3	24	50	3.87	=B6*E6
7	Proposed					
8	CD Organizer	1	1	3	3.87	=B8*E8
9	LD Organizer	1	2	2	5	=B9*E9
10						
11					Max	=SUM(F8:F10)
12	Constraints					
13	Hours	=B8*C8+B9*C9				
14	Mat'l	=B8*D8+B9*D9				

Row 6 models the current production mix: 16.67 CD Organizers produced in each 24 hour period and sold at a profit of $3.87 each. Total Profit (column F) is Quantity multiplied by Profit.

The basic information on the production requirements for one CD organizer is in row 8. Each CD Organizer requires 1 hour of machine time and 3 pounds of material. Production information for LD Organizers is shown in Row 9.

The Max formula in F11 is the Total Profit for both CD and LD Organizers. Cells B13 and B14 total the hours of machine time and pounds of material used in the model. The total hours of machine time is the number of hours spent producing CD Organizers (CD Qty * CD Hours) plus the hours used to create LD Organizers (LD Qty * LD Hours). There are only 24 hours in a day, so this number will need to be less than or equal to 24. The number of hours in a day places a constraint on the optimal solution. The Solver dialog box allows you to open an Add Constraint dialog box and specify constraints, as shown in Figure 19.8.

Figure 19.8
Setting Solver
constraints

The amount of available material provides the other constraint. Another department processes the material, adding coloring and stabilizing agents. The department is operating at capacity, and the CD Division's share of the material is limited. There are only 50 pounds of available material that must be divided between the two products. The Mat'l constraint (CD Qty * CD Mat'l + LD Qty * LD Mat'l) cannot exceed 50.

EXERCISE 19.4   **CREATING THE PRODUCTION MIX MODEL**

1. Activate a blank worksheet in the *WellBilt* workbook.

2. Name the worksheet *Prod Mix*.

3. Create the worksheet shown in Figure 19.7.

4. Save the workbook.

You have created the model; now you can use Solver to determine the optimal product mix given the hours and material constraints.

EXERCISE 19.5   **SOLVING THE PRODUCTION MIX**

1. Choose Tools ➢ Solver from the menu bar to open the Solver dialog box.

2. Enter F11 (Max) as the Target Cell.

3. Leave the Max default setting for Equal To.

4. Set the By Changing Cells to B8:B9 (the quantities for the two products).

5. In the Subject to Constraints section, click the Add button.

6. Enter B13 (Hours) as the cell reference. Enter 24 as the constraint, then click the Add button. The constraint will be added and the dialog box cleared.

CONTINUES ON NEXT PAGE

7. Enter B14 (Mat'l) as the cell reference and 50 as the constraint, then click OK to add the constraint, close the Add Constraint dialog box and return to the Solver dialog box:

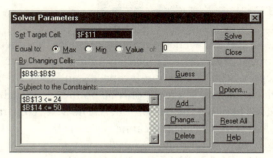

Note: If you Add the last constraint and then click OK, Excel thinks you are trying to add an empty constraint and a "Constraint must be a number, simple reference, or formula with a numeric value" dialog box will appear. If it does, click the OK button. You will return to the Add Constraints dialog box. Click the Cancel button to return to the Solver dialog box.

8. Click Solve.

9. In the Solver Results dialog box, click OK to Keep the Solver Solution.

10. Save *WellBilt*.

As you can see, the work team is correct. Producing 13 CD Organizers and 5.5 LD Organizers each day uses all 50 pounds of material and every available hour of machine time: the optimal solution. The increased efficiency also results in greater profits: $13.31 more per day per machine.

Although this session used examples from manufacturing, Excel's What-if tools are used in many types of businesses. Hospitals use Solver to determine optimal staffing. Banks use Goal Seek to calculate necessary reserves at changing interest levels. Fast food chains use Solver to minimize the amount of time customers must stand in line waiting to order a burger. Whenever you are trying to meet a goal or maximize efficiency or profit, Excel's What-if tools will provide information to support a decision-making process.

What You Have Learned

Excel models are worksheets whose formulas show the relationships between variables. Once you have created a model, you can use Goal Seek to adjust the value of one variable to reach a specific goal. Solver is used to find an optimal solution: the best combination of variables to produce the highest, lowest, or target value.

Focus Questions

1. What is a model?

2. What kinds of information might be included in a model?

3. Name three basic assumptions of forecasting.

4. What is the difference between a Goal Seek goal value and a Solver target value?

5. What is a constraint?

Reinforcement Exercises

Exercise 1   Open the *Unicorn Software* workbook. Activate the *June 22 Payroll* worksheet. Azimi wants to know how many hours she has to work for a Net Pay of $250.00. Use Goal Seek to find an answer to her question. Keep the Goal Seek solution. Print *June 22 Payroll*, then close the workbook without saving the changes.

Exercise 2   Open the *WellBilt* workbook; activate *CD Div Model*. Change the values in column E to answer the following questions:

a) What loss will be incurred if only 1,000 CD Organizers are produced?

b) What is the Gross Profit (or Loss) when exactly 48,000 units are produced?

Use Goal Seek in column E to answer the following questions:

c) How many units must be produced for a Gross Profit of $75,000?

d) How many units result in a Gross Profit of $105,000?

WellBilt's fixed expenses are going to change to $90,000 next month. Change the Fixed Expense value in column E and determine:

e) With the increase in fixed expenses, how many units will need to be produced for a Gross Profit of $100,000? What will be the selling price for each unit?

Close *WellBilt* without saving the changes.

Exercise 3   Open *WellBilt*. Activate the *CD Div Model*. Choose Edit ➤ Move or Copy Sheet. Click Create a Copy checkbox, then click OK to create *CD Div Model (2)*. Change the values and formulas in *CD Div Model (2)* to reflect the following information:

■ A new marketing initiative has increased the price consumers are willing to pay for CD organizers. The new top price is $22; the relationship between price and sales is:
=22−(Quantity/5000).

■ The CD Division work teams have increased productivity. They can now manufacture 50,000 units a month without working overtime.

TIP

You can easily change all the formulas. First select row 11. Choose Edit ➤ Replace. Enter 48000 in the Find What control; enter 50000 in the Replace With control, and click Replace All.

■ WellBilt found another supplier of materials for the CD organizers. The new supplier is more expensive. The average cost of materials for one organizer is now $1.40.

Save the *WellBilt* workbook, then use the appropriate tools to answer the following questions:

a) What is the Gross Profit when 50,000 units are produced?

b) What level of production is needed for a Gross Profit of $170,000?

c) What is the maximum possible Gross Profit?

Print the *CD Div Model (2)* worksheet. Save the workbook.

Exercise 4   Activate the *Prod Mix* worksheet. Access to a new supply of materials insures that there will be 60 pounds of material available daily for each machine. Use Solver to answer the following questions:

a) How many CD Organizers should be manufactured daily on one machine?

b) How many LD Organizers should be manufactured?

c) What will the new Max Profit be each day?

d) How many total pounds of material will be used daily?

Print and save the worksheet.

Importing, Exporting, and Linking

I N THIS FINAL SESSION, you will learn how to place files created in other applications in Excel worksheets. You will use clip art in worksheets and create embedded objects using other Windows applications. You will use pictures as data series objects in Excel charts. At the end of this session you will be able to:

- Insert clip art in a worksheet
- Format clip art
- Move and delete pictures
- Create and embed objects from other Windows applications
- Insert pictures as data series objects in charts

■ Vocabulary

- clip art
- drop shadow
- dynamic
- embed
- filters
- graphics
- import
- link
- object
- OLE

253

SECTION 20.1: USING GRAPHICS IN EXCEL

Charts are just one way to add visual interest to your work. You can add **graphics** (pictures) created in other programs to worksheets. You can even substitute graphics for the bars and columns in a chart! You can place graphics from a variety of sources in an Excel worksheet:

- Clip art images from the Microsoft Clipart gallery or any of the hundreds of clip art collections available on disk or CD

- Files created in graphic art packages like Windows Paint or CorelDRAW

- Pictures captured from paper using a scanner

- Drawings created with Excel drawing tools

- Picture objects you create using other Microsoft programs accessible from Excel, like Microsoft WordArt

You might think of graphics as being primarily used in desktop publishing to create interest or illustrate stories in newsletters or brochures. You add graphics to Excel worksheets for the same reasons: to engage the reader's eye or provide a broad illustration of the numbers used in a worksheet. It isn't unusual to add your company's logo to worksheets as a graphic.

Using Clip Art

Clip art is a generic term for graphics, which are often simple line drawings. The clip art that comes with Excel is kept in the Clipart folder. To place clip art in a worksheet, choose Insert ➤ Picture to open the Picture dialog box, shown in Figure 20.1.

TIP

The Microsoft clip art is stored in the Clipart folder in the Excel or MSOffice95 folder. This may be on your computer's hard drive, or on a network drive. Choose the Clipart folder from the Look In drop-down list.

Figure 20.1

The Picture
dialog box

Clip art files are listed in the Name scroll box. Select a file name and a preview of the actual illustration appears to the right of the scroll box. Take a moment and browse the available clip art. When you have selected an image, click the OK button to insert it in the Excel worksheet. The image appears beginning in the active cell, as shown in Figure 20.2. Cell entries under the clip art are covered, but not deleted. You can move the clip art later if you wish.

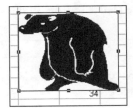

Figure 20.2

Inserting clip art

EXERCISE 20.1	TO INSERT CLIP ART

For this exercise, open a new worksheet and leave A1 selected.

1. **Select the cell where you want the upper-left corner of the clip art to appear.**

2. **Choose Insert ➤ Picture to open the Picture dialog box.**

3. **Scroll down the list of graphics available in the Name box.**

4. **View any of the available graphics by clicking a file name on the list.**

5. **Select the graphic that you want to insert and click OK.**

■ Sizing Pictures

Once the clip art is in place, clicking once on the image selects the image. As with charts, you know an image is selected if you see the small square "handles" on the sides and corners. Change the size or location of the clip art as you would size or move a chart. If you want the graphic to remain in proportion as you resize it, hold the Shift key while you drag one of the handles on any of the corners. The height and width of the graphic will move together so that it stays even.

TIP

If the graphic you are working with is too small or too big to work with easily, you may want to adjust the worksheet view by using the Zoom ratio drop-down on the Standard toolbar.

■ Copying, Pasting, and Deleting Clip Art

You copy or delete clip art just as you would a chart. Begin by selecting the picture. (You know it's selected because it has handles.) To copy, click the Copy button on the toolbar or choose Edit ➤ Copy. Once a picture has been copied to the clipboard you can paste it in another location using the toolbar or the Edit menu. To delete, click the Delete button on the keyboard.

EXERCISE 20.2 | **TO COPY AND SIZE PICTURE**

1. **Select the graphic that you want to size or crop.** Click on the graphic that you inserted in the first exercise.

2. **To resize the graphic, point to one of the handles and drag it with the two-headed sizing arrow.** Hold down Shift and drag the handle in the bottom-right corner to resize the graphic proportionally.

3. **To copy the graphic, make sure it is selected and then click the Copy button on the standard toolbar.**

4. **Select the cell where the copy of the graphic should be placed and then click the Paste button.**

TIP

If you include a graphic in a template, it will appear in each Excel workbook created using the template. This is the best way to include a personal or corporate logo in every copy of a specific workbook.

■ Formatting Pictures

Double-clicking a clip art graphic opens the Format Object dialog box, shown in Figure 20.3. Use the Patterns page to change the border or background (fill) of a picture. (You can only change the background on a picture that has a background. If there is no white space inside the picture, you can't fill it.)

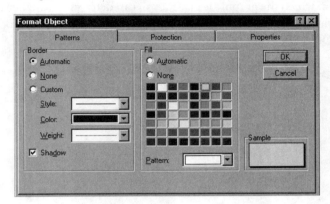

If the object already has a border (like the clip art object in Figure 20.2), you can choose None to turn the border off, or custom to change the color, style, or weight (thickness) of the border. Clicking the Shadow box places a **drop shadow** border around the image, as shown in Figure 20.4.

Figure 20.4

A formatted image

In Figure 20.4, the fill color (background color) and pattern have also been changed. Choose a color from the palette in the Fill section of the Patterns page. Patterns are selected from the drop-down list below the color palette. As you choose colors and patterns, the preview in the Sample box will change to reflect your choices.

EXERCISE 20.3	TO FORMAT CLIP ART

1. **Double-click the graphic you want to format.** Select the image you placed in Exercise 20.1

2. **Select the border settings you want to apply.**

3. **Choose a fill color and pattern, or leave the default, Automatic fill.**

4. **Click OK.**

■ Changing Clip Art Properties

The Properties page of the Format Object dialog box (see Figure 20.5) is used to set the relationship between a graphic and the cells on which the graphic is placed. If you never move the cells underneath a graphic, you don't have to worry about the graphic's position. If, however, you move or resize the cells on which the graphic is placed, you can determine whether the graphic should move or change size with the cells by choosing the options in the Object Positioning section of the Properties page.

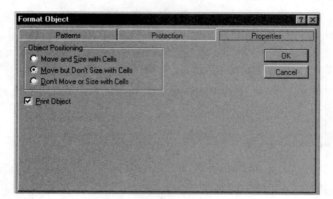

Figure 20.5
The Format Object
dialog box—
Properties page

Choosing Move and Size with Cells or Move But Don't Size with Cells from the Object Positioning options attaches or anchors the graphic to the underlying cells. The graphic is attached to the cells under its upper-left and lower-right corners. You can move either of these cells without affecting the graphic, but if you select and move a range that includes both cells, the graphic will move as well. When Move and Size with Cells is selected, changing the column width or row height of the cells under the graphic will change the size of the graphic.

Normally, you would choose either Move and Size with Cells (for a graphic that illustrates a particular group of cells) or Don't Move or Size with Cells (with a graphic that belongs in a particular spot in the worksheet regardless of the surrounding cells' contents). You won't often use Move But Don't Size with Cells.

By default, the Print Object setting is enabled. Since graphic objects take more time to print, you might choose to turn an object's Print property off if you want to quickly print a draft of a worksheet. You might also have an object that you want to appear on the screen, but not in printed copies of a worksheet—for example, a company logo that looks great in color, but not so great when printed in shades of gray.

SECTION 20.2: IMPORTING OTHER GRAPHICS

Graphic programs save images using different file formats. Each format uses a unique file extension. Excel includes **filters** that translate graphic images saved in a variety of formats into formats with which Excel can work. When you insert a graphic created in another application, Excel uses the filter to **import** the file. The clip art you used earlier in this session was imported: most clip art is saved in either a Windows Metafile or Bitmap format.

Filters are selected by the installer during the Excel or Microsoft Office installation process and can include:

Tagged Image File Format (TIF)

Windows Bitmaps/Windows Paint (BMP)

WordPerfect Graphics (WPG)

Macintosh PICT (PCT)

Windows Metafile (WMF)

JPEG File Interchange format (JPG)

Encapsulated Postscript (EPS)

Truevision Targa (TGA)

AutoCAD (DXF)

Computer Graphics Metafile (CGM)

PC Paintbrush (PCX)

Micrografix Draw and Designer (DRW)

CorelDRAW (CDR)

HP Graphics Language (HGL)

Compuserve (GIF)

Kodak Photo CD (PCD)

Filters for some of the file types listed above may not have been installed on your computer. The filters installed in a Typical installation are boldfaced.

If a graphic you want to use is saved in a file type you can import, you insert the graphic the same way you inserted clip art. If the graphic file isn't located in the Clipart folder, click the Look In drop-down list in the Picture dialog box and select the drive and folder where the file is located. (See *Appendix: Managing Excel Files in Windows 95* for help on locating files in drives and folders.)

An **object** is anything that can be created in another application and inserted in Excel. Video clips, documents created in Word, logos created in CorelDRAW, and audio clips recorded using the Windows 95 Sound Recorder are all objects. When you insert an object, you are using Windows' Object Linking and Embedding capabilities, referred to as **OLE** (pronounced "o-lay"). To insert an object, choose Insert ➤ Object from the menu bar to open the Object dialog box. (Here is another use for the Print Object setting: there's no point in printing the icon for an audio clip, since it can't be played in the printout.)

You can create a new object "from scratch," or place an object that already exists in a file on your hard drive or floppy disk. When you place an object from an existing file (see Figure 20.6), you can choose how it will be saved with the worksheet. The object can be linked or embedded. By default, Excel **embeds** the picture, saving it with the worksheet when the worksheet is saved.

The Object
dialog box

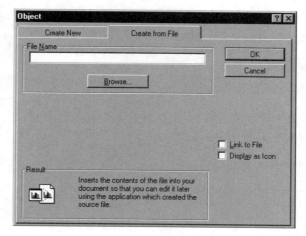

If the object is complex (a photograph or picture that uses many colors), the worksheet will take up a lot of space on disk. However, since the object is saved within the worksheet, it is there whenever you open the worksheet. Linking saves a reference to an object rather than the object itself. Linking uses less space, but ties your worksheet to the file that contains the object.

Linking Files

You can choose to have Excel save a **link** to the object instead of embedding the object. With a link, each time you open the worksheet, Excel goes to the object's location on a drive and loads the object into the worksheet. If the object isn't in the proper location, Excel will give you an error message and the worksheet will be opened without the object.

Despite the potential problems, linking is important. Linking definitely saves disk space. While clip art files are typically small because they are simple, it isn't unusual for a Encapsulated Postscript (EPS) or Tagged Image File Format (TIF) graphic to take up more than half of the space on a floppy disk. (Media clip files like sound and video may be larger than a floppy disk.) Linking is also **dynamic**, meaning that the current version of the linked object can be automatically loaded each time you open your worksheet. If the object changes, the change is reflected in all worksheets linked to the worksheet; this is not the case with the embedded object.

If you want to link a file, you must create the link when you create the object from the file. To instruct Excel to link rather than embed the picture file, check the Link to File check box in the Create from File page (see Figure 20.6) before choosing OK.

Embedding New Objects

Newly created objects become part of the worksheet and are always embedded in the worksheet. You can create a new object using other Windows applications accessible from your computer. If, for example, you want to add notes created in Word, record a sound clip, or open the Access calendar control in a worksheet, choose Insert ➢ Object and click the Create New tab of the Object dialog box, shown in Figure 20.7. The Microsoft WordPad program is part of the standard Windows 95 installation, so you'll use WordPad to create an object in Exercise 20.4.

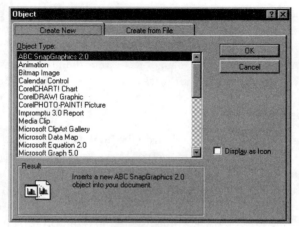

Figure 20.7
Creating a new
object

EXERCISE 20.4	**TO CREATE A NEW OBJECT**

1. **Open the worksheet in which you want to create a new object.**
   Continue to work in the practice worksheet used in Exercise 20.3.

2. **Choose Insert ➤ Object from the menu bar.**

3. **Click the Create New tab on the Object dialog box.**

4. **Select the application you want to use to create the new object.**
   Browse the applications you can use in the Object Type scroll box to
   create objects. Then, select *WordPad document*.

5. **Click OK.**

6. **Create the new object in the application window opened in the Excel
   worksheet.** Enter your name in the WordPad document.

7. **Click any worksheet cell to close the embedded application window
   and return to Excel.**

You now have a WordPad document included in an Excel worksheet.
If you want to edit the WordPad document, you simply double-click on the
embedded object to reopen the WordPad application within Excel. To delete
an object, select the object and press the Delete key on the keyboard.

OLE is a powerful tool. The more applications you install on a computer,
the more objects you can create within Excel. Excel worksheets are frequently

embedded in other applications like Word, either as existing files or by creating new objects embedded in Excel.

TIP

There is another way to link or embed objects that is particularly useful if you have other Office applications on your computer. If, for example, you want to embed or link part of a worksheet in a Word document, you can select and copy the worksheet in Excel, open the Word document, and choose Paste Special. The Paste Special dialog box includes options for linking.

SECTION 20.4: USING GRAPHICS AS CHART ELEMENTS

One of the most interesting uses of Excel graphics is as replacements for the standard bars and columns in charts. The chart in Figure 20.8 shows the increasing number of personal computers used at Traverse Tree Sales in the early 1990s. It's an interesting chart, but you can use graphics to make the chart even more representative of the data.

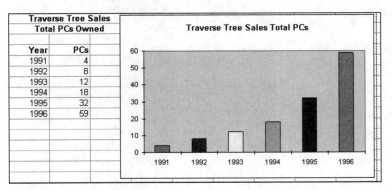

Figure 20.8

The *Traverse Tree Sales* PC Use chart

After opening the chart for editing, you can select the data series and choose Insert ➤ Picture. (Refer to Session 11 for help on selecting data series.) Change the Look In control to the Clipart folder (or choose another location for graphics you want to import) and choose a graphic to use in place of the standard bars. In Figure 20.9, the Hardware.bmp file has been inserted in place of the columns in the chart.

Figure 20.9

The modified
PC Use chart

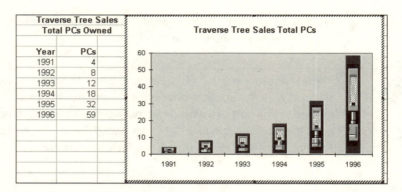

Traverse Tree Sales Total PCs Owned	
Year	PCs
1991	4
1992	8
1993	12
1994	18
1995	32
1996	59

Excel stretches the picture to fit each individual column. In this particular chart, the results of the stretch aren't visually pleasing. Someone using the chart could spend a bit of time figuring out what the picture is trying to represent. Double-clicking the data series opens the Patterns page of the Format Data Series dialog box, shown in Figure 20.10.

Figure 20.10

The Format Data
Series dialog box

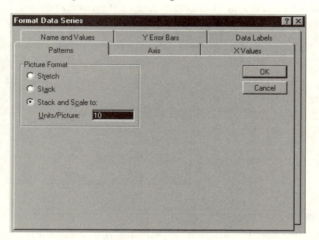

The default setting is Stretch. If you choose Stack, Excel will stack copies of the picture on top of each other until the resulting stack is the proper size. The Stack and Scale To option is used to make each picture represent a specific number. In Figure 20.10, each *Hardware* graphic will represent ten PCs. The stacked and scaled chart is shown in Figure 20.11.

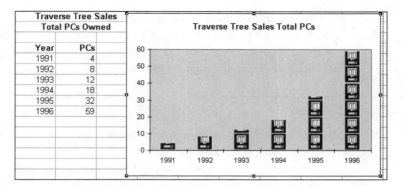

Traverse Tree Sales Total PCs Owned	
Year	PCs
1991	4
1992	8
1993	12
1994	18
1995	32
1996	59

Figure 20.11

The stacked
PC Use chart

TIP

You can only replace data series with graphics in two-dimensional charts. If you try to insert a picture in a 3-D chart, the picture is placed on top of the chart, not substituted for the data series elements.

EXERCISE 20.5 **USING GRAPHICS IN A DATA SERIES**

Open *Traverse Tree Sales*. In a blank worksheet create the worksheet and 2-D column chart shown in Figure 20.8.

1. **Double-click to activate the chart for editing. If the chart is a 3-D chart, choose Format ➤ Chart Type and change it to 2-D.**

2. **Select the data series.**

3. **Choose Insert ➤ Picture from the menu bar.**

4. **Select the graphic you want to insert.** Choose the *Hardware.bmp* file from the Clipart folder.

5. **Click OK.**

6. **To change the picture format, double-click on the picture in the data series to open the Patterns page of the Format Data Series dialog box.**

7. **Choose Stack or Stack and Scale. If you choose to scale, enter the number of units per picture.** Choose Stack and Scale to. Set the number of units to ten.

8. **Click OK.**

Not all graphics work well in charts. You should save a completed worksheet and chart before inserting pictures. Then, if the picture you insert doesn't improve the overall appearance of the chart, you can close the file without saving changes and return to the original chart.

What You Have Learned

In this session, you learned how to insert clip art into worksheets using the Picture dialog box. You now understand that there are various file formats for graphics, and you've seen how Excel can use filters to import graphics created in different formats. In addition, you now know how to link a graphic so that you save disk space and simplify changes to frequently used graphics. Finally, you know how to use graphics to represent a data series in a chart.

Focus Questions

1. List three examples of objects.

2. What is a graphic filter?

3. What is the difference between embedding and linking an object?

4. How does creating a new object differ from inserting an object that already exists?

5. What kinds of charts do not allow you to substitute graphics for chart elements?

Reinforcement Exercises

Exercise 1   Open a new workbook. In *Sheet1,* insert a clip art graphic using Insert ➤ Picture. Resize the graphic proportionally so it fills about half of the worksheet window. Copy the graphic using the Copy button on the toolbar and paste it into a second worksheet. Close the workbook without saving.

Exercise 2   Open the *Peach Hill Theatre* workbook. Insert a graphic that is a suitable logo in the *Ticket Sales* worksheet. Reformat the titles and other worksheet areas as required. A sample worksheet using the *Theatre* clip art file is shown in Figure 20.12. (HINT: Use Tools ➤ Options ➤ General to turn off gridlines.) Save and print the *Ticket Sales* worksheet before closing the workbook.

PEACH HILL THEATRE
TICKET ORDER FORM

Customer Name	**Margaret Marmot**
Customer Phone	**555-0000**
Number of Tickets	**5**
Section Code	**L**
Total Price	**$ 75.00**

Exercise 3   Open the *Unicorn Software* workbook. Choose a picture that would make a suitable logo for Unicorn Software. Include the logo in one of the *Payroll* worksheets. Make any formatting changes necessary. Print and save the worksheet.

Exercise 4   Open *Wildlife Federation*. Create a two-dimensional column chart to illustrate the number of *T-shirts* included in the inven-8tory. Save the workbook. Edit the chart using techniques you learned in Session 11; insert an animal graphic in place of the data series. Print the chart. Save the workbook.

PROJECT C: HOUSEHOLD OR OFFICE INVENTORY DATABASE

For this project, you will construct an inventory database for your home or office. A portion of a sample inventory is shown in Figure C.1.

GATHERING INFORMATION

Create a worksheet similar to the sample. You may choose to add columns for other information: place of purchase, owner, or any other field that would be useful to you. Print copies of the blank worksheet and use them while recording the information for your inventory. As you can see in Figure C.1, some types of items do not have serial numbers. You may not be able to reconstruct price and purchase date information for all the items in the inventory. Enter as much information as you can obtain.

CREATING THE DATABASE WORKSHEET

In the *Excel Projects* workbook (created in Project A), create an *Inventory* worksheet. Using a data form, enter the information you collected.

■ Sort and print the completed inventory twice: once by location, and again by item name.

■ Leave a blank row beneath the data, and total the cost of all items included in the inventory.

■ Turn on AutoFilter. Filter and print the information for one location only.

■ Save the completed *Inventory* workbook.

Store a printed copy of *Inventory* "off-site" (in a safety deposit box or another secure location) to provide backup information in case of an accident or loss.

WILSON HOUSEHOLD INVENTORY
April 12, 1998

Item	Location	Model #	Serial #	Price	Purchase Date
Packard Bell 108CD	Office	Pro 108CD	CD789902394	2,390.00	1/5/96
Desk	Office			375.00	1/7/96
Desk Chair	Office			126.14	1/7/96
HP DeskJet Printer	Office	DJ500	HP234-4456	227.65	3/12/95
Oak Bookcase	Office			65.00	1/7/96
Sharp CD Player	Den	6798-345	S439875	257.86	6/30/95
Magnavox TV	Den	3091-09876	J20009890	439.00	Dec-95
Sony Tape Deck	Den	HJ871-009	761098	124.72	Mar-96
Futon	Den			415.00	Spring 93
Recliner	Den	LZ234		651.34	Fall 94

Figure C.1

A sample inventory database

PROJECT D: ANALYZING SALES WITH PIVOT TABLES

This project uses the PivotTable tool to analyze sales and commissions for the Razorback Car and Truck Dealership. Razorback tracks individual sales of new vehicles and analyzes them on a weekly basis. A salesperson earns a 0.75% commission on the price of each sale. Begin by constructing the sales database for a week in January 1997, shown in Figure D.1, in the *Excel Projects* workbook. Leave a blank row below the database, and enter the label Total Sales and Commissions in column A. Total the Price and Comm columns. (Hint: the total for commissions is $2,633.55.) Save the workbook.

Analyzing Sales Information

Create a pivot table to answer the following questions:

1. What were the total sales for trucks?

2. What were the total sales for cars?

Razorback Car and Truck
Sales: Week of January 6, 1997

Date	Last Name	Type	Model	Sold by	Price	Comm
1/6/97	Daybrook	Truck	T-100	Amy	26,000	195.00
1/6/97	Johnson	Car	Ariva	Myha	19,600	147.00
1/6/97	Williams	Truck	T-100	Glen	28,500	213.75
1/6/97	Westman	Car	Del Mar	Glen	16,900	126.75
1/7/97	Marquis	Car	Ariva	Amy	20,000	150.00
1/7/97	Washington	Truck	T-100	Myha	28,500	213.75
1/7/97	Nguyen	Car	Corra	Amy	13,350	100.13
1/8/97	LaVine	Car	Corra	Myha	13,990	104.93
1/8/97	Morrell	Car	Del Mar	Amy	17,200	129.00
1/8/97	Juarez	Truck	T-50	Glen	22,000	165.00
1/8/97	Hritz	Truck	T-100	Myha	27,000	202.50
1/9/97	Compton	Car	Del Mar	Glen	15,900	119.25
1/9/97	Brawner	Car	Ariva	Myha	18,750	140.63
1/10/97	Morse	Truck	T-50	Glen	19,800	148.50
1/10/97	Reid	Truck	T-100	Amy	29,000	217.50
1/10/97	Minneman	Car	Corra	Glen	12,750	95.63
1/10/97	Smith	Car	Ariva	Myha	21,900	164.25

Figure D.1

A sample sales database

3. What was the grand total for sales?

4. What was the grand total for each salesperson?

Format the pivot table. Create a pie chart illustrating total sales for each salesperson. Print the pivot table and chart. Name the pivot table worksheet *Sales Pivot*.

Analyzing Commissions

Create a separate pivot table to answer the following questions:

1. What were the total commissions earned on sales of trucks?

2. What were the total commissions earned for cars?

3. What was the grand total for commissions?

4. What was the total commission for each salesperson?

5. Who earned the highest commission on trucks?

Format the pivot table. Create a two-series column or bar chart to show the commissions for each salesperson for cars and trucks. Name the worksheet *Comm Pivot*. Print the pivot table and chart and save the workbook.

PROJECT E: CONSOLIDATING AND OUTLINING

This project uses Excel consolidation tables to create a master supplies order list from departmental requests. Begin by constructing the *Departmental Order* worksheet shown in Figure E.1 in a blank workbook.

1. Format the Cost Each and Total Cost columns and the Totals row as currency.

2. Delete all extra sheets in the workbook. Save the workbook as *TriStar Order*.

3. Create copies of the workbook (using File ➣ Save As) for the *Programming*, *Research*, *Sales*, and *Production* departments.

4. Enter the order information for each department (see Figure E.2) in their individual workbooks. Save and close all workbooks.

Consolidating Departmental Worksheets

1. Create a consolidation table for the four departments in the *Tri-Star Order* workbook.

2. Use the outline to view the detail information for each item. Print the consolidation table with the outline fully expanded.

3. Collapse the outline. Use the consolidation table to create a chart illustrating total orders for supplies.

4. Print the consolidation table and the chart. Save *Tri-Star Orders*.

	A	B	C	D	E
1		Tri-Star Computing			
2		Supplies Order Form			
3		Department:			
4					
5					
6	Item		Quantity	Cost Each	Total Cost
7	HD Floppy Disks 10 pack			$ 5.40	
8	HD Floppy Disks 50 pack			$ 19.90	
9	DD Floppy Disks 50 pack			$ 17.23	
10	Pens - Black - 12 pack			$ 3.14	
11	Pens - Blue - 12 pack			$ 3.14	
12	Pens - Red - 12 pack			$ 3.14	
13	Sub 20 paper - ream			$ 4.76	
14	Sub 20 paper - case			$ 38.08	
15	Sub 60 paper - ream			$ 6.60	
16	Letterhead - ream			$ 21.39	
17					
18	Totals				

Figure E.1

The *Departmental Order* worksheet

Item	Prog	Res	Sales	Prod
HD Floppy Disks 10 pack	0	0	5	0
HD Floppy Disks 50 pack	5	12	0	50
DD Floppy Disks 50 pack	3	9	1	30
Pens - Black - 12 pack	5	5	15	3
Pens - Blue - 12 pack	5	7	4	0
Pens - Red - 12 pack	6	4	1	1
Sub 20 paper - ream	0	0	8	0
Sub 20 paper - case	5	4	0	2
Sub 60 paper - ream	1	1	0	2
Letterhead - ream	1	2	12	1

Figure E.2

Departmental information

Managing Excel Files in Windows 95

WHEN YOU HAVE ONE computer that you use regularly, you will probably want to save your workbook files on the hard drive to simplify and speed up access to your files. Knowing how files are organized on a hard drive is essential to locating workbooks easily. By learning how to work with Windows file management, you can work more efficiently and maintain better control of your work.

UNDERSTANDING FILE MANAGEMENT

Imagine that you have just purchased a new filing cabinet for your office. When you begin using it, you open the top drawer and begin stacking miscellaneous papers one on top of the other. When the first drawer is filled, you open the second drawer and do the same. Eventually the entire filing cabinet is filled with stuff. The only way to locate a particular document is to try to remember which drawer you put it in and start searching.

Throughout this book, you have been saving Excel workbooks on a floppy disk. (That's because in many schools and training centers, students aren't allowed to store their work on hard drives or network drives.) A floppy disk is just like one of the drawers of a filing cabinet. As you save more documents on a floppy, it becomes increasingly time-consuming to read through a long list of file names to identify individual workbooks. On a hard drive with a hundred or a thousand times the capacity of a floppy, it becomes even more complex. Your workbooks may become intermingled with those of other users. The documents that you create in other applications may be located in different places on the hard drive.

Windows 95 allows you to create folders and subfolders so that you can organize your documents, including workbooks, in a way that make sense to you. You can create folders for different projects (all the documents pertaining to XYZ Report), different types of documents (outgoing correspondence, personal, performance appraisals) or different people (all the documents for your boss). You can then open a specific folder and see only the documents related to that topic. The Windows Explorer is used to organize and manage documents.

USING THE WINDOWS 95 EXPLORER

To launch Explorer, click Start ➤ Programs ➤ Windows Explorer. The Explorer window has two sections or panes (see Figure A.1).

The icons shown in the left pane include the Desktop, the desktop icons—Recycle Bin, Network Neighborhood (if you have access to a network), and My Computer—the drives and hardware contained in My Computer, and all the folders that exist on the hard drive and any network connections. This is the basic structure of your computer system within Windows 95.

The computer is presented in an outline format similar to an organizational chart. The right pane shows the contents of the computer, drive, or folder selected in the left pane.

The Desktop appears at the top of the list on the left. Desktop features like My Computer (Windows' name for the computer you are currently using) are indented slightly to the right. Drives A and C are part of My Computer, so they are indented underneath My Computer.

■ Viewing the File Structure

A folder is a logical container to hold documents and programs. A Windows folder is the equivalent of a hanging file folder in a physical filing cabinet. A plus sign in front of a drive or a folder indicates that there are undisplayed levels of folders within the drive or folder. To view this second level, you can expand the folder by clicking on the plus sign.

The minus sign in front of a drive or folder means that you can click on it and collapse the level, removing the details about the folders at lower levels. As you move through the drives and folders, the Explorer window title bar changes to display the name of the last icon you selected in the left pane.

To see a list of the files (documents and programs) contained on a floppy, insert the floppy into the drive and click on 3½ Floppy. The files on the floppy will be listed in the right pane.

■ Getting Information on Properties of Files and Folders

Windows 95 maintains properties sheets, listing the characteristics and settings of pieces of hardware and software, files, and folders connected to or contained in your computer. Different icons are used to represent various types of hardware, software, documents, and folders. Folders have the file folder icon. Programs usually have a unique icon developed by the programmers. Documents use an icon similar to the icon used by the program used to create the document. To see the property sheet for a file, select the file and right-click to open a pop-up menu; then select Properties. The Properties sheet will have different tabs depending on the type of file you selected. Click the tabs (see Figure A.2) to see the file details.

Figure A.2

The properties sheet for a file

■ Using QuickView to Preview the Contents of a File

Properties sheets give you details about a file, but they don't show you the file's contents. QuickView allows you to see the text contained in a file without taking the time to open the program used to create the file.

To view an Excel workbook, select the workbook in the right pane and right-click to open the pop-up menu. Select QuickView. The viewer displays part of the first worksheet in the workbook. To view additional files, drag the file name into the QuickView window. When you find the workbook you are looking for, click the Open File for Editing button on the QuickView toolbar. Explorer will launch Excel and open the file you were viewing.

ORGANIZING YOUR DOCUMENTS

The first step in organizing documents is to create folders and subfolders to separate the documents into groups. Once you have folders, you can move and copy documents between folders and drives. You can also delete documents that you no longer need.

Creating Folders and Subfolders

It's best to choose names for your folders that are relatively short yet descriptive. If you are creating your first folder on the hard drive, you may want to create a main folder where all of your subfolders and documents will live. That way, no matter what application you are using, all of your documents can be saved to one main location. It's helpful to give your main folder a name that begins with the letter *A*. That way, it will always show up at the top of the alphabetized list of folders.

There are other file management methods. The main folder approach is one of many. Whatever method you choose should be well thought out in advance, and then used consistently.

EXERCISE A.1   **TO CREATE FOLDERS**

1. **Open the Windows 95 Explorer.**

2. **In the left pane, select the drive (and folder) where you want the new folder to appear.** Select your floppy drive.

3. **Choose File ➢ New ➢ Folder from the Explorer menu bar.**

4. **Type a name for the folder and press Enter.** Enter *Excel Projects*.

After you create your folder structure, you are ready to organize your documents.

COPYING, MOVING, AND DELETING FILES

There are two primary ways to move or copy files in Windows 95: cut/copy-and-paste and drag-and-drop. The file's original location is called the source. The new location for the file is called the destination.

■ **Using Cut/Copy-and-Paste to Move and Copy Files**

When you cut a file, the file is moved from its source to the Windows clipboard. You can then paste the file from the clipboard to its destination.

EXERCISE A.2	TO MOVE OR COPY A FILE USING CUT AND PASTE

1. Locate the file you want to move.

2. Point to the file icon and click once to select the file.

3. To move a file either choose Edit ➢ Cut from the Explorer menu or click the right mouse button and choose Cut from the pop-up menu. To copy a file, choose Copy.

4. Open the folder where you want to move or copy the file.

5. While pointing at the folder name or at the contents area on the right viewing pane, click the right mouse button and choose Paste to complete the cut/copy-and-paste operation.

6. If a file with the same name already exists in the destination, Windows will ask whether you want to replace the existing file with this one. Click Yes unless you change your mind about moving or copying the file. When you replace a file, the "incoming" file overwrites the one that already existed in that location. The old file is then gone. Be sure this is what you want before choosing Yes.

■ **Using Drag-and-Drop to Move and Copy Files**

You already know how to use drag-and-drop to move and copy text and numbers within Excel. The same techniques apply here to move and copy files. The only difference is whether you are moving or copying files within the same drive or between drives. Windows assumes that if you drag a folder or file from one location on a drive to another location on the same drive that you want to *move* the folder or file. But if you drag it from one drive to another drive (let's say, from the hard drive to a floppy), Windows assumes you want to *copy* the file.

Rather than trying to remember Windows' rules for moving and copying, you can override the default assumptions about drag and drop by using Ctrl and Shift. Hold down the Ctrl key and drag to *copy* a file.

When you drag the file from one place to another, you'll notice that a plus sign appears next to the pointer. When you copy a file, the original file stays intact and an exact copy is made at the new location. Hold the Shift key while dragging to *move* a file; a plus sign will not appear.

Dragging and dropping to an area you can't see on the current screen can be difficult until you are proficient with mousing and scrolling. As you gain more mouse experience, drag-and-drop operations become easier.

EXERCISE A.3 | **TO MOVE OR COPY A FILE USING DRAG-AND-DROP**

1. **Expand the folders in the left pane so that the destination folder is visible.**

2. **Locate the file you want to move or copy.**

3. **Point to the file icon and click once to select the file.**

4. **To move a file, hold down the left mouse button and the Shift key and then drag the file to its new location. To copy a file, hold down the Ctrl key instead of the Shift key.**

5. **If the file already exists in the destination, Windows will ask you if you want to replace the existing file with this one. Click Yes unless you change your mind about moving or copying the file.**

■ Selecting Multiple Files and Folders

There are many times when you may want to move or copy several files at once. If you want to move a folder and all of the folders and files it contains, select the folder and drag and drop it in the new destination. As always, using the Shift key ensures that the folder is moved, not copied

You can also select several files at once and move or copy them as a group to a new destination. To select several contiguous files, select the first file, move the pointer to the last file in the list that you want, and hold down the Shift key while selecting the last file. All of the files between the first and the last one will be selected, as shown in Figure A.3. You can then drag and drop just as you would for a single file.

Figure A.3
Selecting
multiple files

To select several files that are not adjacent to each other, select the first one, then hold down the Ctrl key while selecting each of the additional files.

■ Deleting Files and Folders

Just as you might clean out a filing cabinet every so often to keep it from getting too unruly, part of file management is deleting those files and folders that you no longer need. There are some basic rules, however, that you must follow to avoid destroying something that may be irreplaceable.

- Never move or delete a file if you don't know what it is. It might be a file that an application needs to run properly or it may belong to someone else who uses your computer.

- Make regular backups (second copies on a floppy or another drive) of important documents. If you delete something accidentally, you can use the backup copy.

- Open folders and check their contents before deleting them.

- If you're moving a file and Windows warns you that a file of the same name already exists in the destination, be sure to check the date/time; you probably don't want to overwrite a newer version of a file with an older version.

When you are ready to delete a file, select it and press the Delete key on the keyboard. You will be asked if you are sure you want to delete this file. Click OK to delete the file from a floppy disk. If the file is on a hard drive, click OK to move the file to the Windows Recycle Bin, a holding area for files to be deleted. If you change your mind, you can easily restore files from the Recycle Bin; however, files deleted from a floppy disk are not restorable since they are not moved to the Recycle Bin.

The files in the Recycle Bin take up space on the hard drive. You should empty the Recycle Bin periodically to free up space. (Explore the Recycle Bin, and choose Empty Recycle Bin from the File menu.) Emptying the Recycle Bin deletes all files in the Bin. To find out more about the Recycle Bin, consult Windows Help.

ACCESSING YOUR FOLDERS IN EXCEL

Once you have created folders and moved your workbooks into them, you will want to be able to access them easily in Excel. If you are the only person who uses the computer you are working on, you can even change the default directory so that your main folder opens whenever you want to open a file. If you share a computer with other users, it is important that you do not change the default directory.

■ Changing the Default Directory for Documents

By default, Excel saves documents to a folder called My Documents, which it creates during installation. To change this default directory to your main folder, choose Tools ➤ Options and click the General tab. In the Default File Location text box, enter the default location for Excel workbooks. For example, to save workbooks in a folder called My Excel Work on the computer's C hard drive, enter *C:\My Excel Work*. Then click OK to close the Options dialog box. If you are unfamiliar with the syntax for paths (such as C:\My Excel Work), you might want to get some advice from a knowledgeable colleague before changing this option.

■ To Locate Your Folders When Saving or Opening Workbooks

When you want to open a file that is located in one of your folders and your main folder is not set as the default directory, you have to direct Excel to your folder before you can open a document stored there. In the Open dialog box (File ➤ Open), click the Look In control. Use the Explorer-like list in the Look In box to locate your main folder. Double-click to open your main folder. The Name box will show a list of your folders and Excel workbooks. Open a workbook by double-clicking the workbook name.

Save a workbook to your main folder the same way. After choosing Save, select the drive to look in, and then locate your main folder. Double-click your main folder to open it. Enter the file name in the File Name control and click Save.

References

For more information about Windows 95 file management, use Windows Help or refer to *The Learning Guide to Windows 95*, Gini Courter, Alameda, CA: Sybex, 1995.

Glossary

3-D cell reference A formula reference to a cell or range in another worksheet.

absolute reference Used in a formula to refer to a specific cell, an absolute reference does not change when the cell containing the formula is copied or filled.

align To place text or numbers either to the left, center, or right relative to the boundaries of a cell or selection.

application window A Windows container that displays a program.

applications (apps) Programs that allow you to complete specific tasks such as creating budgets, lists, or letters.

arguments Parameters for a function, enclosed in parentheses.

array A special type of database in which one column or row contains unique values.

ascending order A to Z; 1 to 10.

AutoCalculate An Excel feature that displays a sum in the status bar when a range of cells is selected.

AutoComplete An Excel feature that completes a text entry if an identical entry has been made earlier in the same column.

AutoFill An Excel feature that allows you to copy a formula, weekday, or month name to other cells.

AutoFilter An Excel tool that displays drop-down arrows next to the field names in a database so you can set criteria for the records you want to display.

AutoFormat An Excel tool that allows you to choose from predesigned worksheet formats.

automatic calculation Excel's default calculation mode; all formulas are reevaluated after any cell is altered.

AutoOutline An Excel tool that automatically creates a hierarchical outline of the active worksheet or a selected area of the worksheet.

AutoSum A button on the Standard toolbar used to create totals.

AVERAGE A function used to produce the statistical mean for a selection.

bar chart A chart in which data points are represented by horizontal bars.

boldface A type style in which characters appear thicker than normal; used in Excel to make the contents of a cell more visible.

border A line above, below, to the left of, to the right of, or surrounding one or more cells.

calculated field A cell in a database that contains a formula.

cell The basic worksheet unit; an intersection of a row and a column.

cell address The column letter and row number that describe a cell's location.

cell pointer The shape of the mouse pointer within the worksheet: a large plus sign or "chubby cross."

CellTip A note that explains a cell's contents when you point the mouse at the red dot in the cell.

chart A graphical representation of numerical data.

chart area The area bounded by a chart's border, containing all the elements of the chart.

Chart Wizard A program that walks you through the process of creating a chart.

clip art Commercially available graphics and other images that can be imported into applications and then positioned, resized, and edited for use in various documents.

clipboard Part of the computer's memory reserved by Windows for cut, copy, and paste operations.

close To remove a window and its contents (application or document) from the desktop when you are finished working with it. Closing programs or files does not remove them from your disks or hard drive.

Collapse To reduce an outline or outline level so that all detail is hidden.

column A vertical unit within a worksheet, referenced by letter.

column chart A chart that uses vertical bars to represent data points.

column header The gray button at the top of a column, labeled with the column's letter.

column width The amount of space between the left and right boundaries of a column.

consolidate To summarize data from one or more worksheets.

consolidation table An Excel table created by summarizing information from multiple worksheets.

constraint A rigid, externally imposed boundary in an analysis, like the number of hours in a day.

context button The non-primary mouse button; for right-handed users, the right mouse button.

context menu A menu that pops open in response to clicking the right mouse button on a feature, tool, cell, or object.

copy To transfer a duplicate of selected cells to the clipboard for later use.

criteria Parameters that a user specifies to guide filtering or selecting records.

custom lists Lists maintained for AutoFill such as the names of days of the week and months of the year.

customize To change settings for a program or procedure to reflect user needs or preferences.

cut To move selected cells to the computer's memory for later use.

data Facts and figures to be entered in a worksheet.

data form A dialog box used to enter, edit, delete, or select records in an Excel database.

data points Numbers in a worksheet selected for representation in a chart.

data series A group of related data points.

database A worksheet that includes columnar fields and records contained in rows.

database management system (DBMS) Software, like Microsoft Access, that allows you to create and relate multiple sets of records.

default A predefined setting for hardware or an applications that the user can choose to accept or change.

delete To remove a cell, selection, column, or row from a worksheet; to clear the contents of a selected area.

descending order Z to A; 10 to 1.

desktop The control center for Windows 95.

dialog box A window that appears when a Windows-based program requires more information from the user to complete a task.

dpi Dots per inch, used to measure the resolution (clarity) of printed copy.

drag-and-drop A method for copying or moving cells.

drill down To move to additional levels of detail from a summary or consolidation.

drop shadow A graphic technique for borders and boxes that looks as if the box is casting a shadow.

dynamic Subject to change. Describes an object, field, or cell content that is linked to and changes in response to another object, field, or cell.

elements Parts of a chart that you can format individually.

embed To copy a file created in one application into a document created in a different application.

execute To run a program.

expand To change the view of an outline or outline level so that layers of detail are displayed.

explode In a pie chart, to pull one or more slices away from the center.

extension A three-letter designation following a period at the end of a filename, used to relate a file to the application used to create it.

field A category; a column in an Excel database.

field button A button that represents an individual database field in a pivot table layout.

field name The column heading in an Excel database worksheet; field names must be unique within a worksheet.

file name A unique name assigned by a user when a file is saved on disk.

fill handle The square box at the lower-right corner of a selection used to copy the contents of the selection to other contiguous cells.

filter a) In a database, to use criteria to display specific records; b) a program used to convert a file created in another application for use in the current application.

fixed expense In a business or household budget, an expense that is the same each month for a length of time: rent, a vehicle payment, or a lease contract.

font A complete set of characters in a specific typeface including design, weight, size, and style.

font color The color assigned to the characters in a cell; the default font color is black.

font size The height and width of characters, normally measured in points.

footer Text or fields appearing at the bottom of every page of a printed worksheet.

forecast To predict future values for one or more variables.

format To change the appearance of cells or worksheets.

Format Painter An Excel tool used to assign the formatting in the selected cell to other cells in a workbook.

function A small program that uses one or more arguments to perform a specific math or logical operation.

function name Excel's specific name that is used to call a function.

Function Wizard A program that helps you select a function and fill in arguments.

global macro A macro that is stored in the Personal Macros worksheet and thus available to all worksheets.

Goal Seek An Excel tool used to determine the values of underlying variables required to meet a specific target.

graphics Pictures or objects added to a worksheet.

gridlines Lines that show the boundaries of rows, columns, and cells on screen or in a printout.

hardware The physical parts of the computer, including the monitor, drives, microprocessor, printer, and other devices.

header Text or fields that appear at the top of every page of a printed worksheet.

HLOOKUP A lookup function that returns a value from a specified row index.

home cell Cell A1.

icons Small pictures that represent programs and files used in a graphical user interface.

IF A logical function that completes one of two possible actions based on the value of a logical test.

import To open or place a file created in one application in a different application.

insert To place a blank row or column in a worksheet and adjust the existing columns or rows.

italics A font enhancement that leans letters and numbers to the right.

iteration One attempt to solve a problem including one or more variables.

landscape A printing orientation with the long side of the paper at the top.

launch To start a program.

linear programming A sequential approach to problem solving that results in—or clearly excludes the possibility of—an optimal solution (also called linear analysis).

link To place an object or formula into a worksheet dynamically, so that any changes in the source will be reflected in the linked object/formula result.

list management A term for working with Excel database records.

lock To protect entries so they cannot be altered without first being unlocked.

logical function A function, like IF, that is used to instruct Excel to choose between actions.

logical operators Operators that return a value of true or false based on a comparison of two values or text strings: =, <>, <, >, >=, <=.

logical test The decision-making condition for a logical function.

lookup function A function that returns a value from an array.

lookup value The cell that contains a value used to select a row or column in a lookup function.

macro A user-created program that repeats a series of keystrokes, menu selections, or other actions to complete a frequently used task.

manual calculation A calculation method that recalculates worksheet formulas only when the user requests calculation or saves a worksheet.

margins The white space that surrounds the top, bottom, and sides of a printed worksheet.

maximize To make a window fill the entire screen.

maximum (MAX) A function used to find the largest value in a range of cells.

menu bar A bar containing lists of options available in a program or window.

microcomputer (PC) A powerful computer designed to fit on a desktop.

minimize To reduce an application or document window to the size of an icon, allowing it to continue running in the background while another program has priority.

minimum (MIN) A function used to find the smallest value in a range of cells.

mixed reference A formula reference that includes both relative and absolute cell references.

model A worksheet that uses formulas to create a representation of some segment of the real world.

module A unit of Visual Basic programming code; in Excel, macros are stored in Visual Basic modules.

mouse An input device that allows entry into the computer by pointing to objects on the screen and clicking on them.

move To reposition a range of cells from one location to another.

name A string assigned to one or more cells, used in place of a cell reference to refer to the cells.

name box The area at the left end of the formula bar that displays the active cell's address.

null set An empty set, the result of a filter or selection in which no records meet the criteria.

object Text, a graphic, or other artifact created in one application and placed in another.

OLE Object linking and embedding, a Windows feature for placing an object in an application other than the application it was created in.

open To retrieve a workbook from disk so it can be used.

operating system Software that manages computer resources such as memory, disk space, processor time, and peripherals; and thus allows application programs to run.

optimal solution The solution that most efficiently uses the resources contained in a model to achieve a minimum, maximum, or target value.

options A structured group of choices.

order of operations Mathematical rules that govern the sequence in which formulas are evaluated.

orientation The direction of print on a page: portrait or landscape.

outline To separate a worksheet into levels, each of which can be expanded or collapsed to show or hide different levels of detail.

page setup The combined settings that direct how a worksheet or chart will appear when printed.

paste To copy the contents of the clipboard beginning at the active cell.

pie chart A single-series chart used to show the relationship between points in the series.

PivotTable An Excel tool used to analyze the values in fields in a database or columns of worksheet data in relationship to other fields or columns.

placeholder A field for date, time, or other variable that is filled with the current value when a worksheet is opened.

play To run a macro.

plot area The area of a chart used for graphical representation of data.

point 1/72 of an inch; used to measure font size.

point method The technique of entering parts of a formula by clicking or selecting cells.

pop-up menu A menu that appears after the user clicks the right mouse button.

portrait A printing orientation with the short side of the paper at the top.

primary sort The field that a group of records will be sorted on.

print area The area(s) of a worksheet that will be printed; the default print area includes all occupied portions of a worksheet.

Print Preview An Excel feature used to view a worksheet's printed appearance prior to printing.

range One or more contiguous cells.

record a) Information for one unit or individual; one row in an Excel database; b) to have Excel save a group of actions as a macro.

relative reference Used in a formula to refer to a cell, a relative reference changes to reflect a copy or fill operation.

row A horizontal unit within a worksheet, referenced by number.

row header The gray button at the left end of a row labeled with the row's number.

save To copy a workbook from the computer's memory to a disk.

scaling Used to set the relationship between the worksheet's actual and printed sizes.

scroll bars The horizontal and vertical bars to the right and below a document window that allow you to move to parts of a workbook that are not currently displayed on-screen.

secondary sort A field used to order records that have the same value in the primary sort field.

select To choose one or more cells or objects in preparation for a specific action.

series chart A chart that can include more than one data series.

sheet tab A location on the bottom of a worksheet that contains the sheet's name; clicking the sheet tab activates the worksheet.

Shut Down An option located on the Start menu that closes all applications and prepares your computer to be turned off or restarted.

simulate To use a model to represent the results of changing variables.

size To reduce or enlarge a window or selected object.

software (programs) An application or operating system that provides specific instructions to the computer.

Solver An Excel add-in used to find optimal solutions to multivariable problems.

sort To place in ascending or descending order based on the value in a field.

Spelling An Office tool used to check for misspellings in a worksheet.

spreadsheet A program, like Excel, used to manipulate and analyze numerical information.

Start menu The menu that appears when you click on the Windows 95 Start button; it enables you to access Windows 95 features and applications.

status bar The bar at the bottom of a workbook window that gives you information about the current workbook; Excel also displays messages on the status bar.

subset A group of records within a database.

subtotal A total for a group of numbers within a larger list of numbers.

syntax The required and optional parts of a function.

Taskbar The Windows 95 desktop feature that contains the Start button and buttons for any current applications.

Template: A workbook pre-designed with all layout features, but lacking data, that can be opened and then renamed in order to produce frequently repeated designs.

tertiary sort The field used to order records that have the same values in the primary and secondary sort fields.

tick marks Interval marks on a chart axis.

toggle A button or menu selection that switches between one of two values each time it is selected.

tool tip The name of a toolbar button that appears when you point to the button.

toolbar A bar containing buttons that carry out specific functions such as saving, formatting, and printing.

trailing zero A zero to the right of the decimal point that is not followed by a non-zero digit.

TrueType font A type of font that appears on-screen exactly as it will appear when printed.

typeface A font's design.

undo To retract the last action taken.

variable expense In business, an expense that varies based on use, production, or some other business activity: labor expense, materials expense.

Visual Basic The programming language used with Microsoft Office applications.

VLOOKUP A lookup function which returns a value from a specified column index.

What-if Excel tools and add-ins used to provide support for decision making including Goal Seek, Solver, and the Scenario Manager.

wiffing Using What-if tools for decision-making support.

Windows 95 The newest version of Microsoft's graphical user interface designed to run on the newer, more powerful microcomputers.

workbook A document created in Excel.

workbook macro A macro saved in, and available only to, a single workbook.

workbook window A window, within the Excel application window, that contains a workbook.

worksheet A division of a workbook used for a set of numbers and labels; each Excel worksheet has 256 columns and 16,384 rows.

X-axis The label axis; the horizontal axis in most 2-D series charts.

XLS The file extension for an Excel workbook.

XLT The file extension for an Excel template.

Y-axis The value axis; the vertical axis in most 2-D series charts; the "depth" axis in 3-D charts.

Z-axis The value axis in 3-D series charts.

Index

TOP TWENTY EXCEL COMMANDS

To carry out any of these operations, either click the toolbar button or follow the menu path (the symbol points to your next choice). For some operations you'll make further choices once you reach the appropriate dialog box. For the Change Font operation, Excel provides no toolbar button.

1. Save a Workbook File ➤ Save

2. Open a Workbook File ➤ Open

3. Create New Workbook File ➤ New

4. Print Preview File ➤ Print Preview

5. Print Using Defaults File ➤ Print

6. Check Spelling Tools ➤ Spelling

7. Cut Selection Edit ➤ Cut

8. Copy Selection Edit ➤ Copy

9. Paste Clipboard Edit ➤ Paste

10. Undo Action Edit ➤ Undo...